Declaring His Genius

Declaring His Genius

OSCAR WILDE IN NORTH AMERICA

Roy Morris, Jr.

THE BELKNAP PRESS OF
HARVARD UNIVERSITY PRESS
Cambridge, Massachusetts
London, England
2013

Library of Congress Cataloging-in-Publication Data
Morris, Roy, Jr.
Declaring his genius : Oscar Wilde in North America / Roy Morris, Jr.
p.   cm.
Includes bibliographical references and index.
ISBN 978-0-674-06696-0 (alk. paper)
1. Wilde, Oscar, 1854–1900—Travel—United States.
2. Wilde, Oscar, 1854–1900—Travel—Canada. I. Title.
PR5823.M65 2013
828′.809—dc23   2012019340

To Robbie Bivin, Mamie Bivin, Brian Oakes, and Elizabeth Oakes, charter members of the Gulf Shores Alumni Association

Contents

America is not a country; it is a world.

—Oscar Wilde, 1882

Introduction

❧

"I HAVE NOTHING to declare except my genius," Oscar Wilde famously said—or is supposed to have said—to American customs agents when he arrived at the port of New York on the morning of January 3, 1882. No one actually heard him say it, but it sounded like something Wilde would have said, and by the time literary biographer Arthur Ransome quoted it first in his 1912 study of the author, the quip already had passed into legend. Like many of Wilde's best-known witticisms, real or imagined, it actually meant a great deal more than it said. The twenty-seven-year-old Wilde may well have been a genius—at self-promotion, if nothing else—but he would prove to have quite a bit more to declare during the course of his eleven-month-long speaking tour of the United States and Canada. And these declarations, made to an ever-changing audience of newspaper reporters, theatergoers, dinner guests, college students, art lovers, scene makers, politicians, millionaires, cowboys,

Indians, miners, train conductors, hotel clerks, and random passersby, would add immeasurably to the legend that Wilde was inventing for himself, almost as he went along. It is safe to say that after his 15,000-mile tour of North America, neither Wilde nor his host countries would ever be quite the same.[1]

Partly by intent, partly by instinct, Wilde pioneered the way in which modern celebrities are created, cultivated, and commodified. Long before Frank Sinatra, Elvis Presley, the Beatles, Bob Dylan, Andy Warhol, Marilyn Monroe, David Bowie, Madonna, or Lady Gaga, Oscar Wilde stamped himself on the collective consciousness of his age— and all before he wrote his first masterpiece. Indeed, it would be another eight years before he published his only novel, the brilliantly transgressive *Picture of Dorian Gray,* and even longer before he produced the series of devastatingly witty plays that culminated in his most enduring artistic achievement, *The Importance of Being Earnest,* in 1895. Nevertheless, during his time in North America he already carried himself like a master, striving at all times to embody his own advice: "One should either be a work of art, or wear a work of art." At his peak, he managed to accomplish both.[2]

Wilde's 1882 tour of North America was a complex media event, perhaps the most extensive of its time. Through the artful use of publicity, chiefly through interviews with local newspapers, Wilde functioned in essence as his own advance man, beating the drum for his upcoming lectures while carefully nurturing a more elevated image as the leading spokesman for the Aesthetic Movement, which he airily described as "the science of the beautiful." Behind him came a small but dedicated support staff of managers, handlers, publicity men—even a personal valet. In turn, these assistants were helped, not always intentionally, by the local artists, merchants, advertisers, and entrepreneurs of various stripes who hoped to capitalize on the outrageous visitor. To an extent that both surprised and gratified Wilde, he found that his fame, or at least his notoriety, preceded him to even the smallest, most remote hamlets and mining camps.[3]

During his extraordinarily crowded year in North America, Wilde seemingly went everywhere and saw everything, delivering 140 lectures in 260 days, from the Canadian Maritimes to the coast of California, from northernmost Maine to southernmost Texas. In the process, he helped to alter the way in which post–Civil War Americans, still reeling from the most destructive war in the nation's history, understood and accepted traditional concepts of masculinity. A vision of intentionally affected preciosity in satin knee breeches, black silk stockings, crushed-velvet coat, frilly lace collar, pale-green cravat, and patent-leather dancing slippers with silver bows on top, Wilde may have looked the part of the stereotypical fop, as caricatured in Gilbert and Sullivan's comic opera *Patience*. But appearances, as he quickly demonstrated, were deceiving. His firm handshake, boundless energy, unquenchable good humor, and unexpected ability to out-drink any and all challengers quickly won over his American hosts, who were naturally predisposed to appreciate rugged individualism in even its most exotic forms.

The affection ran both ways. As one modern scholar has noted: "Wilde found himself growing inordinately fond of Americans. A less likely love match could scarcely be imagined." Americans of all shapes and sizes took to the towering Irishman in the outlandish garb. Some, to be sure, came to his lectures to laugh, but many stayed to be entertained and even, on occasion, enlightened. However supercilious he sometimes seemed to listeners, it was never Wilde's intention to talk down to his audience. He "did not regard it at all as an aesthetic mission to a barbarous clime," he insisted to a Philadelphia journalist early in his trip, but rather as a casual conversation between friends. Inherently friendly himself, Wilde proved to be a good deal more adept at getting along with his colonial hosts than his waspish fellow countryman Charles Dickens had been a generation earlier. With a few notable exceptions, Wilde thoroughly enjoyed his encounters with the American public and its watchdogs in the daily press. He returned to England to tell his skeptical fellow-countrymen: "The American man may not be humorous, but he is certainly humane. He tries to be pleasant to every stranger who lands on his shores and makes every chance visitor feel that he is the favored guest of a great nation." Of course, being Wilde, he felt compelled to add: "We have really everything in common with America nowadays except, of course, language."[4]

Declaring His Genius: Oscar Wilde in North America chronicles that improbable collision of cultures during its subject's one-man British invasion, mounted eight full decades before his fellow Celts, the Beatles, conquered these same shores in 1964. It aims to be both expansive and reductive. Richard Ellmann's 1987 work remains the most comprehensive modern biography of Wilde, but like most cradle-to-grave biographies of a crowded and eventful life, it necessarily sweeps along, and Ellmann's account of Wilde's American tour, while touching on most of the high points, skimps a good deal on the broader social and historical context. By contrast, Lloyd Lewis and Henry Smith's 1936 doorstop of a book, *Oscar Wilde Discovers America,* though still useful as a starting point, is both ponderous and dated. Reading the book today is a little like being cornered by a garrulous old uncle at a wedding reception. There are a lot of stories, not all of them true, although most of them are entertaining. *Declaring His Genius* looks to split the difference between Ellmann's professorially brisk account and Lewis and Smith's sprawling, kitchen-sink approach. Everything in just proportion, as Wilde's beloved Greeks inherently understood.

Any account of Wilde's adventures in America must necessarily start with the numerous newspaper accounts of his visit, particularly the interviews he routinely gave along the way. Many of these interviews were collected and annotated by Matthew Hofer and Gary Scharnhorst in their 2010 volume, *Oscar Wilde in America: The Interviews* (University of Illinois Press). Anyone following Wilde's sinuously winding trail through the United States of 1882 owes the editors a large vote of thanks. Beyond the various newspaper accounts, a narrative of Wilde's American adventures also depends to a certain extent upon anecdote, word of mouth, and local legend. This is perhaps as it should be when dealing with Wilde, who after all became famous for being famous and whose fame was spread both by what he said and by what other people said about him. As much as possible, Wilde attempted to shape—or at least to stage-manage—the narrative of his tour, but he was not overly concerned with objective facts. As he would later write, "Truth is independent of facts always, inventing or selecting them at pleasure." The rest, to his eyes, was mere archaeology.[5]

Archaeologists, by definition, attempt to re-create the past by digging through its shards. *Declaring His Genius* sifts through the remains of Oscar Wilde's eventful eleven months in North America to piece together a coherent portrait of the artist as a young Aesthete at a pivotal time in his life. Like one of the figures on Keats's Grecian urn, it shows Wilde in suddenly arrested motion—literally a legend in the making. What it reveals about the creation of such legends is perhaps more relevant than ever in today's celebrity-drenched, tabloid-addicted culture. More than merely a verbal affair, Wilde's tour was also an extended visual event, with images of the poet saturating newspapers, magazines, advertising columns, sheet music, theater posters, billboards, storefronts—even trading cards. A particularly well-known and frequently pirated photograph of Wilde by New York tastemaker Napoleon Sarony went all the way to the U.S. Supreme Court and resulted in a landmark ruling on photographic copyrights.

In the end, with apologies to Lewis and Smith, Oscar Wilde may not have discovered America—a feat not even he claimed to have performed—but from a personal standpoint he accomplished something even more important: he discovered himself. The Oscar Wilde who left America in December 1882 was very different from the one who had arrived on her shores a year earlier. He was more assured, more experienced, more relaxed, and a good deal less artificial. To say the least, his horizons had been broadened. His friend Robert Sherard put it best: "America had taken the nonsense out of him." Wilde knew it himself. "The Oscar of the First Period is dead," he announced grandly upon his return to England, throwing away his knee breeches, cutting his long hair, and putting down his trademark sunflower. Thanks in large part to his time in America, he no longer needed such props to get attention. He was now on a first-name basis with the world.[6]

CHAPTER I

Too Too Utterly Utter

❧

On a wintry gray afternoon on the day after New Year's, 1882, a chilled boatload of newspaper reporters in a chartered launch thrashed across the waves in New York harbor toward the steamship *Arizona,* sitting at anchor off Staten Island. Night would be falling soon, but the journalists couldn't wait for the ship to clear quarantine the next morning. They were after answers to the burning questions: "Why have you come to America?" and "Do you really eat flowers for breakfast?"

The object of the reporters' quest was waiting serenely in the captain's quarters, utterly indifferent—or at least carefully feigning indifference—to the media storm about to engulf him. Oscar Wilde was used to such attention. By the time he arrived at the watery edge of America, he had already achieved a certain level of fame in England for his outlandish antics and deliberately provocative appearance. In late-Victorian-era London he was a walking, talking affront to polite society—all the more shocking since he came from a privileged background himself. The son of a prominent if eccentric Irish physician and an equally well-known and eccentric poet and political activist, Wilde had been raised in a hothouse atmosphere of artistic pretensions and personal license. His father, Sir William Wilde, had unapologetically fathered several illegitimate children before his marriage and, to his credit, continued to support them financially and professionally. One of them, Dr. Henry Wilson, eventually became director of the private hospital that Sir William had founded in Dublin. Meanwhile, Wilde's mother, Lady Jane Elgee Wilde, filled the household on Merrion Square in Dublin with a steady stream of artists, writers, actors, musicians, professors, and politicians, all of whom were expected to get up and perform for the other guests. Rumored to have had clandestine affairs herself, she was an outré presence in trailing scarves and jeweled turbans. "There is only one thing in the world worth living for," she said, "and that is sin."[1]

Despite their personal peccadilloes, Wilde's parents were both successful—even driven—individuals, traits their second son would eventually display himself. Sir William was one of the leading eye and ear specialists in Great Britain, authoring several comprehensive textbooks in his field of study. In 1863 he was appointed Surgeon Oculist to the Queen in Ireland, which meant that if Her Majesty visited the Emerald Isle again and got a sty or a coal cinder in her eye, he would be the one to remove it. She never made the return trip while he was alive, having gotten her nose out of joint over the refusal of the Irish people to place a statue to her dead husband, Prince Albert, in St. Stephen's Green, Dublin, and rename the park Albert Green. Perhaps it was for the best. There were rumors that Sir William, during a visit to Sweden, had operated on the king's eyes and, while the monarch was temporarily blinded, had made love to the queen. Apparently, there was nothing to the rumor, but Crown Prince Gustav, on a later visit to Dublin, joked that he was Oscar Wilde's half-brother. Wilde never bothered to deny it.

Lady Jane concentrated more on affairs of a political nature. She was an early and enthusiastic convert to the cause of Irish nationalism, contributing inflammatory poems and barricade-raising editorials to the *Nation* on such topics as the great potato famine and the mass exodus of Irish men and women to America. She adopted the pen name Speranza, meaning "Hope" in Italian, and began calling for armed rebellion against England, declaring that "the long pending war with England has actually commenced" and yearning for "a hundred thousand muskets glimmering brightly in the light of Heaven." On St. Patrick's Day, 1859, she attended the Lord Lieutenant's Ball in full patriotic rig: white silk skirts tied with white ribbons and bouquets of gold flowers and shamrocks. "Ah, this wild rebellious ambitious nature of mine," she wrote. "I wish I could satiate it with empires." Instead, she ruled over a somewhat smaller domain of talkers, arguers, disputers, and debaters, of whom she counted herself first among equals. "I express the soul of a great nation," she informed a fellow poet, adding that she was "the acknowledged voice in poetry of all the people of Ireland." Like her famous son, she knew how to make an entrance. "I soar above the miasmas of the commonplace," she cried. It is no accident that Oscar Wilde's plays are populated by witty, expressive, and formidable women. "All women become like their mothers," he would write. "That is their tragedy. No man does. That is his."[2]

Wilde's parents saw to it that he and his older brother, Willie, attended the best schools, starting with Portora Royal Academy in Enniskillen. (The Wildes' only daughter, Isola, the pet of the family, died of a fever when she was nine.) Portora styled itself "the Eton of Ireland" and specialized in sending boys to Trinity College in Dublin. Wilde soon outstripped his wastrel older brother academically, if not socially, winning prizes for poetry, Scripture, and Greek studies and moving on to Trinity on a full scholarship. From Trinity he passed effortlessly to Magdalen College at Oxford, where he studied under celebrated professors John Ruskin and Walter Pater and, almost as an afterthought, won the school's prestigious poetry award, the Newdigate Prize, for his Byronesque 1878 poem "Ravenna."

From the start of his undergraduate career, Wilde affected an airy indifference to formal education. Higher learning, he said, meant little to him, since "nothing that is worth knowing can be taught." He embarked instead on his own course of study at Oxford, which amounted chiefly to finding the best way to nurture his carefully cultivated image as an artist and make an immediate impression on all he met. He wore loud plaid suits, too-small bowler hats, and robin's egg-blue neckties, carried around dog-eared volumes of Dante's and Whitman's poetry, and began a lifelong habit of cigarette smoking. "I find it harder and harder every day to live up to my blue china," he sighed theatrically, decorating his undergraduate rooms with Japanese fans, silk screens, peacock feathers, and artfully draped curtains. Fresh-cut lilies perfumed the air. His china cabinet held a table-buckling array of exquisite pieces: two large blue china vases, two blue mugs, four soda-water tumblers, four plain tumblers, six port glasses, six gilt coffee cups and saucers, six Venetian bock glasses, two green Romanian claret decanters, one plain claret decanter, and six ruby champagne tumblers. Thus suitably equipped, Wilde hosted regular Sunday evening receptions, called "beauty parties," where tiptoeing servants in felt slippers proffered guests brimming bowls of gin-and-whisky punch, long pipes stuffed with choice tobacco, and cream-cheese-and-cucumber sandwiches. Wilde was called "Hoskie" by his classmates; his best friends were nicknamed "Bouncer" and "Kitten." Everything and everyone, he said in a phrase that soon swept the university and beyond, was "too too utterly utter" for words.[3]

Wilde embraced the social life at Magdalen (pronounced "Maudlin" in the English way), but haughtily avoided competitive athletics. Of Oxford's famously hearty oarsmen, he complained: "This is indeed a form of death, and entirely incompatible with any belief in the immortality of the soul." He failed to see the use, he said, of "going down backwards to Iffley every evening." Asked which sports he preferred, he replied: "I am afraid I play no outdoor games at all. Except dominoes. I have sometimes played dominoes outside French cafés." After breaking his arm in a pickup soccer game, he was moved to observe: "I never like to kick or be kicked. Football is all very well as a game for rough girls, but for delicate boys it is hardly suitable." If the later accounts of fellow students are to be believed, Wilde was not quite so delicate as he let on. At least two of his classmates passed along stories of the burly Wilde besting, or at least holding his own, in fisticuffs with bullying upperclassmen. All his life he seldom backed down from a fight, whether verbal or physical.[4]

Despite his professions of academic indifference, Wilde surprised everyone, including himself, by graduating from Oxford in 1878 with a rare double "first" in classics and modern literature. Like other matriculating seniors, then and later, he drifted a bit after graduation. He applied unsuccessfully for postgraduate scholarships in Greek and archaeology, failed to win a somewhat déclassé appointment as a school inspector, and hung around the fringes of college life, helping to costume and mount a performance, in the original Greek, of Aeschylus's *Agamemnon*. Finally, with the help of a small inheritance from his late father's estate, he moved down to London in early 1879 and immediately set out to conquer society, telling a school friend prophetically, "Somehow or other I'll be famous, and if not famous, I'll be notorious." In short order, he was both. Walking along the streets of the capital one day, he heard someone mutter, "There goes that bloody fool Oscar Wilde." "It is extraordinary how soon one gets known in London," he said happily.[5]

Wilde quickly became the public face of the Aesthetic Movement, a loosely organized, something-for-everyone grab bag of painters, writers, architects, and home decorators that was sweeping across England at the time. The Aesthetes were direct descendants of the Pre-Raphaelite Brotherhood, which under the leadership of poet-artist Dante Gabriel Rossetti and cofounders William Holman Hunt and John Everett Millais had emerged in the middle of the nineteenth century as England's first truly avant-garde movement. The Pre-Raphaelites, like the doomed Romantic poets they worshiped, championed individuality, nature, and freedom of expression, even as they signed their works with a communal "PRB." An early and enthusiastic supporter was Wilde's future Oxford professor John Ruskin, who gamely continued to support them after his own wife, Effie, left him and ran off with Millais. (Understandably, Ruskin drew the line at supporting Millais.) Wilde later praised the Pre-Raphaelites as young men who "had determined to revolutionize poetry and painting," even though "to do so was to lose, in England, all their rights as citizens. They had those things which the English public never forgives—youth, power and enthusiasm." He could have said much the same thing about himself.[6]

The Aesthetes, following a generation after the Pre-Raphaelites, also championed art for art's sake, stressing sensitivity, emotion, and what Wilde felicitously termed "the science of the beautiful." Somewhat more democratic than the art school–based Pre-Raphaelites, the Aesthetes featured a strong handmade component to their philosophy, encouraging English craftsmen to simplify their work in furniture, textiles, glass, and ceramics. The recent craze for Japanese fashions, memorialized in Gilbert and Sullivan's comic opera *The Mikado,* was incorporated into the movement. (The lily, an early trademark of Wilde's, was first imported from Japan in 1862.) The Aesthetes extended their reach to home decorating, a reflection of the newly empowered middle class and its desire to be both respectable and au courant. In this they followed the lead of author and artist William Morris, who tirelessly lobbied for a return to handcrafted furniture and furnishings in the face of shoddy industrialized products. Sounding very much like Oscar Wilde two decades later, Morris declared that "the true secret of happiness likes in taking a genuine interest in all the details of daily life." He practiced what he preached by personally designing and constructing, in 1860, a lavish new home in southeast London for himself and his family. Dubbed "Red House," it was built with red bricks dating back to the Tudor era and meticulously decorated from top to bottom with handmade carpets, stained-glass windows, intricately designed wallpaper, wall hangings, and painted ceilings. Painter Edward Burne-Jones, who

assisted Morris with the decorating, praised Red House as "the beauti-
fullest place on earth."[7]

The Great Exhibition in London in 1851, the first truly international
world's fair, had opened the eyes of the British public to a vast splendor
of home furnishings and interior designs. An astonishing six million
people, or one in every five English men, women, and children, attended the five-month-long exhibition. From giant machines to exotic
birds, from furniture to lighting to wallpaper to china patterns, the
crowds inside the Crystal Palace were overwhelmed by an embarrass-
ment of riches—14,000 exhibits in all. It remained for the more aesthetically adept to differentiate for the British public the properly beautiful from the merely popular. Wilde, with his strong undergraduate
interest in decorating and design, was more than willing to add his two
shillings' worth to the ongoing discussion. The long-standing, if usually
misquoted, joke that Wilde on his deathbed shuddered, "Either that
wallpaper goes or I do," was merely a comic exaggeration of the serious-
ness with which the Aesthetes approached the subject of interior decoration.

The Aesthetes were at war with the very concept of Victorian furnishings. The heavy-legged furniture, dark-paneled woodwork, and
over-stuffed rooms that constituted the typical upper-class home—and
were being assiduously copied by the nouveaux riches of the middle
class—offended Aesthetic sensibilities, which called for an altogether
lighter, airier touch. Wilde would later sum up the battle for English
homes in his essay "The Soul of Man under Socialism." The problem,
he wrote, was that "the public clung with really pathetic tenacity to what
I believe were the direct traditions of the Great Exhibition of international vulgarity, traditions that were so appalling that the houses in
which people lived were only fit for blind people to live in." The Aesthetes, he said, would have to civilize them. Not everyone was convinced
that such civilizing was necessary. Wilde's friend Vincent O'Sullivan observed: "[Wilde's] taste was not very sure, and it cannot be said that the
result of his crusade was good. The practical application of Wilde's aes-

thetic theories was Liberty gowns, and shoddy insecure furniture which soon became far uglier, as it was from the first far less comfortable than what it replaced. He forced solid British families to put out of doors the beautiful heavy Victorian furniture and curtains, so comfortable, so secure and to make their houses look like lawn tennis clubs on the Italian Riviera."[8]

From the start, Wilde's aesthetic sense mixed the teachings of his Oxford mentors Ruskin and Pater. Between them, Ruskin and Pater defined the opposite poles of English art criticism in the mid-nineteenth century. Ruskin, who was twenty years older, took the more rigidly moral approach to art, requiring that it address religious and social issues as well as purely artistic considerations. Pater, on the other hand, called for a more immediate and personal response to art, famously admonishing artists "to burn always with [a] hard, gem-like flame" and to evoke in their audience a similarly ecstatic response to their art. In the course of his own career, Wilde would fluctuate between the two poles, the formal and the personal. He praised Ruskin for combining "something of prophet, of priest, and of poet," while at the same time telling William Butler Yeats that Pater's groundbreaking *Studies in the History of the Renaissance* was "my golden book; I never travel anywhere without it . . . it is the very flower of decadence."[9]

Whatever his artistic and critical influences, Wilde was soon the Aesthetes' most visible proponent. As such, he became a frequent target for artist George Du Maurier of *Punch* magazine, who famously depicted Wilde as a flower-toting, world-weary dilettante with the ridiculous name of Jellaby Postlethwaite. Wilde played his part perfectly, dressing in crushed-velvet coat, satin knee breeches, black silk stockings, and pale green necktie, with a giant yellow-and-brown sunflower pinned to his lapel. He quickly became, in the words of one observer, "the most talked-about dandy since Beau Brummell." It was a role he was naturally prepared to play. "Individualism," he explained in his self-appointed role as Professor of Aesthetics, "is a disturbing and disintegrating force. Therein lies its immense value. For what it seeks to disturb is monotony of type, slavery of custom, tyranny of habit and the reduction of man to the level of a machine." He was nothing if not an individual. Even Queen Victoria herself took notice of Wilde's emergent celebrity, attending a performance of *Punch* editor Frank Burnand's comedy *The Colonel,* whose fake poet, Lambert Streyke, was clearly modeled on Wilde. It was, said Her Majesty, "a very clever play, written to quiz and ridicule the foolish aesthetic people who dress in such absurd manner, with loose garments, puffed sleeves, great hats, and carrying peacock's feathers, sunflowers and lilies." Everyone knew about whom she was speaking.[10]

Du Maurier was merciless, picturing Postlethwaite at "An Aesthetic Midday Meal" consisting entirely of a glass of water for his fresh-cut lily. "I have all I require," says the poet. In another sketch, a fainting Aesthete is revived by a St. Bernard dog in the Alps, where he has gone to look for the perfect flower after hearing that Postlethwaite had sat up all night contemplating a lily. "I have imitators," brags Postlethwaite upon hearing the news. "Milkington Sopley swore he never went to bed without an aloe blossom." In another famous drawing, Du Maurier depicted Postlethwaite outside a public bathhouse by the sea. Invited by an acquaintance to "take a dip in the briny," Postlethwaite wanly declines. "Thanks, no," he says. "I never bathe. I always see myself so dreadfully foreshortened in the water, you know." So valuable was Du Maurier's good-natured ribbing to the sudden spread of Wilde's fame that American expatriate artist James McNeill Whistler, a sharp-elbowed rival of both, once cornered the pair at an art exhibit and demanded to know, not entirely in jest, "Which one of you discovered the other?" In an irony of literature, Du Maurier would later write the best-selling novel *Trilby,* whose main character, Svengali, creates a famous opera singer out of a tone-deaf street urchin as an act of willful provocation. He would also outrage his erstwhile friend Whistler, who threatened to sue the author over Du Maurier's easily recognizable caricature of Whistler as a Bohemian idler in the book. In the end, Du Maurier revised the novel and partially appeased, though he did not formally apologize to, the supposed victim of his affront.[11]

How swiftly and comprehensively Wilde became the poster boy for the Aesthetic Movement was a tribute more to his precocious sense of self-publicity than to any artistic achievements of his own. In fact, he had none. "The poet is Wilde, / But his poetry's tame," *Punch* sniffed, drolly if accurately, when his first collection of verse was published. Wilde's growing prominence at this stage of his career was the result, instead, of a carefully cultivated public image, one that included paying homage to the leading actresses of the day. Sarah Bernhardt, Ellen Terry, and most especially Lillie Langtry came in for the full Wilde treatment of public adoration and private sycophancy, complete with bouquets of flowers thrown at their feet and sonnets of praise inscribed in their honor.[12]

Wilde was particularly smitten with Langtry, dubbed "the Jersey Lily" after her place of birth in the Channel Islands and a famous painting by John Everett Millais that showed her posing with the flower (actually a Guernsey lily). Wilde kept another painting of Langtry, by Edward Poynter, reverently displayed on an easel in his bachelor's quarters, which he shared with his old school friend Frank Miles. He described Langtry, perhaps generously, as "the loveliest woman in Europe" and called her beauty "a form of genius." If true, then photographs do not do full justice to Langtry, who displays in them a blunt nose, low forehead, cold eyes, prominent chin, and ruddy complexion. Tastes change. In her day, she was certainly considered beautiful, and besides Wilde and Whistler, she attracted such admirers as the Prince of Wales (the future King Edward VII), artist Edward Burne-Jones, sculptor Frederick Leighton, and writers as varied in gifts and temperament as William Butler Yeats and Max Beerbohm. Unlike her worshipers—the Prince of Wales excepted—Langtry was no intellectual, but she shared with Wilde a sense of the dramatic and an innate knowledge of how to make a vivid impression. At one fancy ball she wore a simple black Greek dress spangled with stars and crescents and strewed diamonds through her thick brown hair, calling herself the Queen of Night. She was less taken with Wilde's appearance, shuddering at his "coarse lips and greenish-hued teeth," but conceding that "the plainness of his face was redeemed by the splendour of his great, eager eyes." Moreover, "he had one of the most alluring voices that I have ever listened to, round and soft, and full of variety and expression."[13]

After camping out all night on Langtry's marble doorstep—or so he claimed, anyway—Wilde wrote a poem for her, "The New Helen," which he dedicated "To Helen, formerly of Troy, now of London." The work was included in the volume of mildly racy poems—_Punch_ judged the verses "Swinburne and water"—that Wilde published at his own expense in 1881. But his chief artistic creation, at the time, remained himself. "To get into the best society, nowadays, one has either to feed people, amuse people, or shock people," he observed. He lacked the funds to do the first, but he was more than prepared to do the others. With his sharp-tongued friend Whistler as his primary role model, Wilde crafted carefully prepared witticisms that he dropped into conversation with seeming spontaneity at London dinner parties. "I can resist everything but temptation," he would say, or "Nothing succeeds like excess," or "A little sincerity is a dangerous thing," or "I am not young enough to know everything." He looked upon his life at this point, said one Wilde scholar, "as a theater and adopted many of its roles—actor, press agent, scene designer, costume designer, ad-libber, and not least, audience." In a sense, he was the first true performance artist.[14]

The worldly Whistler, who was twenty years older than Wilde, was alternately amused and chagrined by his flamboyant apostle. Their relationship got off to a rocky start when Wilde, still an undergraduate, attended the opening of the privately funded Grosvenor Gallery in London in May 1877 and cheekily criticized Whistler's painting _Nocturne in Black and Gold: The Falling Rocket_ in the pages of _Dublin University Magazine_—his first prose publication. Whistler's painting, he wrote, "was worth looking at for about as long as one looks at a real rocket, that is, for somewhat less than a quarter of a minute." Wilde at the time was wearing a custom-made, bronze-colored suit tailored to look like a cello, with the instrument's hour-glass outline stitched on the back and giant quarter notes adorning the front pockets, a design he said had come to him in a dream. Whistler, who had a long memory, would return the favor several years later, famously sketching the then-overweight Wilde as a pig, complete with round belly and daintily curling tail.[15]

At least Whistler did not take Wilde to court over his criticism of the painting, as he did John Ruskin, who had snidely observed that "one had seen and heard much of Cockney impudence before now, but never expected to hear a coxcomb ask two hundred guineas for flinging a pot of paint in the public's face." Whistler sued Ruskin for libel, and a Westminster jury eventually found in the painter's favor, awarding him a symbolic farthing (about a quarter of a penny) in damages. Ever afterwards, Whistler wore the coin victoriously on his watch chain. Whistler and Wilde frequently jousted verbally, with neither man gaining the upper hand. Once, after the painter made a particularly pointed quip, Wilde exclaimed, "How I wish I had said that." Whistler instantly replied, "You will, Oscar, you will." Reacting to an imaginary conversation about art between the two, Wilde wired Whistler: "*Punch* too ridiculous—when we are together we talk about nothing except ourselves." Whistler replied: "Oscar, you forget—when you and I are together we never talk about anything but me." "It's true, Jimmy," Wilde responded, "that we were talking about you, but I was thinking of myself."[16]

Wilde became increasingly famous, although no one could quite say why. No less a personage than the Prince of Wales asked for an introduction, observing gracefully, "I do not know Mr. Wilde, and not to know Mr. Wilde is not to be known." Wilde went everywhere, attending gallery openings, plays (taking care to plant himself firmly at the front of the house, preferably in a box seat, for maximum exposure), dances, recitals, sporting events, and operas. He invariably signed guest books with a full-page autograph, adding enough ruffles and flourishes at the bottom of the page to prevent anyone else from signing beneath him. He saved his best efforts for dinner parties. "A man who can dominate a London dinner-table," he wrote, "can dominate the world." At one such party Wilde crossed swords with the celebrated librettist W. S. Gilbert, who grumbled: "I wish I could talk like you. I'd keep my mouth shut and claim it as a virtue." "Ah, that would be selfish," responded Wilde. "I could deny myself the pleasure of talking, but not to others the pleasure of listening."[17]

Seeking revenge, perhaps, or else knowing a readymade character when he saw one, Gilbert and his partner Arthur Sullivan composed the comic opera *Patience,* with its instantly recognizable parody of Wilde as the "fleshly poet" Reginald Bunthorne, a foppish young faker who "walked down Piccadilly with a poppy or a lily in his medieval hand." Lillie Langtry claimed later to be the inspiration for Bunthorne's flowery tribute, maintaining falsely that Wilde brought her a fresh flower each day from Covent Garden, while denying that it was all a pose. Since virtually everything Wilde did at the time—at least in public— was a pose, this was an unconvincing argument. Wilde himself would later downplay the gesture without disavowing it altogether, telling a New York reporter, "To have done it was nothing, but to make people think one had done it was a triumph."[18]

If Gilbert and Sullivan hoped to embarrass Wilde, they failed. He embraced the Bunthorne character wholeheartedly, attending a performance of the show in full costume and breezily acknowledging the cheers and gibes of fellow theatergoers with a wave and a bow. The only thing worse than being talked about, he said, was not being talked about. When the show opened in America in September 1881, its canny producer, Richard D'Oyly Carte, nicknamed "Oily" for his slippery business sense, saw an opportunity to gain additional publicity by bringing over the living, breathing embodiment of Reginald Bunthorne— Oscar Wilde. As D'Oyly Carte told a Philadelphia booking agent: "Not only would society be glad to hear the man and receive him socially, but the general public would be interested in hearing from him a true and

correct definition of this latest form of fashionable madness." Through
his intermediary, Colonel W. F. Morse, Carte offered to pay all of Wilde's
expenses and split the profits evenly with him from a twenty-city speaking tour. Habitually strapped for money, Wilde agreed. "Yes, if offer
good," he cabled Morse.[19]

Immediately sensing the possibilities for self-promotion, Wilde
prepared carefully for the tour. He read up on Charles Dickens's two
famous reading tours of America, attended lectures on the former colonies at the British Museum, and took private elocution lessons from his
American-born actor friend Hermann Vezin. "I want a natural style,
with a touch of affectation," Wilde told Vezin. "Well, and haven't you
got that, Oscar?" Vezin replied. He had his tailor make him a bottle-
green overcoat trimmed in otter fur, a round sealskin hat, and a complete stage outfit featuring all the visual flourishes of the reigning London Aesthete, down to a pair of patent-leather dancing slippers with
silver bows on top. If Americans expected to see the real-life Bunthorne,
Wilde intended to play the part to the hilt. The ever-caustic Whistler,
taking note of the new clothes, dashed off an open letter to Wilde in the
London World, pretending outrage at the poet's dress. "Oscar—How
dare you!" wrote Whistler. "What means this unseemly carnival in my
Chelsea? Restore these things to Nathan [a theatrical costume shop],
and never let me find you masquerading the streets in the combined
costumes of a degraded Kossuth and Mr. Mantalini!" (Hungarian revolutionary Lajos Kossuth had popularized a Polish peasant's cap similar
to Wilde's during his stay in England two decades earlier; Mr. Mantalini, a character in Dickens's *Nicholas Nickleby,* was known for his outlandish dressing gowns.)[20]

The gibe about revolutionaries must have hurt, since Wilde was
still dealing with the recent failure to cast and mount a London production of his first-written play, *Vera; or, The Nihilists.* In retrospect, one
would be hard put to imagine a less congenial subject for an Oscar
Wilde play than the turgid melodrama about anachronistic eighteenth-
century Russian revolutionaries. True, his Irish-born mother was an

outspoken nationalist who in her youth had called for a popular uprising to throw off the English yoke; and his father, too, had been a patriot, although more from a nature-loving point of view than a political one. But the Wildes, as Irish Protestants, were a long step away from the ever-smoldering rage at the heart of the Irish Catholic experience. And both Sir William and Lady Jane, as newly created members of the British peerage, had rather enjoyed their enhanced social position and were unlikely to have supported an up-from-the-bottom revolution.

Their son's decision to write his first play about Russian revolutionaries seems to have been based more on what was in the news than what was in his heart. He took both his plot and his title character from a well-publicized 1878 incident in which a young Russian woman named Vera Zasulich had attempted to assassinate the police chief of St. Petersburg for imprisoning her nihilist lover. The attempt failed, but the woman won widespread popular support for her bold romantic gesture. Wilde transferred the setting from late nineteenth-century St. Petersburg to late eighteenth-century Moscow, and the target from the police chief to the Czar of All the Russias, who is also coincidentally Vera's lover. Not overly concerned about historical details, Wilde has the nihilists—a philosophy unknown in the eighteenth century—travel by train and communicate by telegram, modern conveniences also unknown during the play's time frame. Perhaps the most unlikely aspect of *Vera* is the new czar's anachronistic conversion to democracy; he wants to be a friend to his people. Wilde may have been thinking of his own royal acquaintance, the Prince of Wales, who as the bon vivant heir to the unlovable Queen Victoria was hugely popular with the British public. When Vera kills herself rather than her noble boyfriend, exclaiming as she expires, "I have saved Russia!" she might have been speaking of the English royal family as well, since the Prince of Wales was married at the time to the sister of the new Russian czarina.

As poorly written as *Vera* was, it still might have made it to the West End stage, had history not inconveniently intruded. As it was, two very real political assassinations were on the minds of everyone at the time. In the spring of 1881, the vaguely reform-minded czar of Russia, Alexander II, had been blown to pieces by bomb-throwing anarchists in St. Petersburg. Four months later, American president James A. Garfield had been fatally shot in the back by a homegrown lunatic named Charles J. Guiteau while walking with secretary of state James G. Blaine through a Washington, D.C., train station. Garfield had lingered in agony for two and a half months while doctors fruitlessly probed for the assassin's bullet, before dying of blood poisoning largely induced by their non-sterile fumbling. The two tragedies had made the playgoing public—or at least the men who mounted the plays—loathe to support a new drama that centered on such literal or symbolic regicide. A scheduled copyright-registering performance of the play on December 17, 1881, at the Adelphi Theatre was abruptly canceled. Wilde's play, privately printed and bound in dark red leather with the title stamped in gold, would languish unproduced for the next two years. Given *Vera's* later disastrous one-week run in New York City in 1883, he would have been better off if it had remained unproduced.

One week after the cancellation of *Vera's* London début, Wilde set sail from Liverpool for the United States aboard the steamship *Arizona*, which plowed the northern Atlantic for the Guier Line. His departure was less heralded than most of his recent performances. "Nobody is sanguine about his success," wrote the London correspondent for the *New York Times*. "Nobody knows what he can do beyond writing poetry and posing as a leading figure in a limited circle." Whistler gave him a characteristic bit of tart advice: "If you get seasick, throw up Burne-Jones." In his baggage, along with his new stage costumes, Wilde had packed glowing letters of introduction from James Russell Lowell (the American ambassador to Great Britain) and Whistler's bête noire, Burne-Jones. Lowell, a poet himself, had reviewed Wilde's first book of poems favorably in the *Atlantic Monthly.* He wrote in Wilde's behalf to Oliver Wendell Holmes, the Boston Olympian and long-reigning "Autocrat of the Breakfast Table." Wilde, said Lowell, was "a clever and accomplished man [who] should no more need an introduction than a fine day."

Burne-Jones likewise advanced Wilde's cause to Harvard scholar Charles Eliot Norton: "The gentleman who brings this little note to you is my friend Mr. Oscar Wilde, who has much brightened this last of my declining years. He really loves the men and things you and I love." There is nothing to suggest that Burne-Jones was being ironic in his description.[21]

Wilde intended to spend the time aboard ship working on his upcoming lecture, variously entitled "The Beautiful," "The Artistic Character of the English Renaissance," and finally "The English Renaissance," but he kept putting it off to pose and preen for his 133 fellow passengers (he was no. 114 on the manifest). He began performing even before he set foot on American soil, letting it be known to others onboard ship that he was somewhat disappointed in the performance of the Atlantic Ocean. "I am not exactly pleased with the Atlantic," he supposedly told one shipmate. "It is not so majestic as I expected. The sea seems tame to me. The roaring ocean does not roar." The quote, as reported, made headlines throughout the English-speaking world: "Mr. Wilde Disappointed with Atlantic." (A letter appeared a few days later in the *Pall Mall Gazette*, stating, "I am disappointed in Mr. Wilde," signed "The Atlantic Ocean.") Wilde, who had experienced a cyclone during his crossing of the Mediterranean from Athens to Naples in 1877, longed openly for another transporting storm that "might sweep the bridge from off the ship." This was not exactly the sort of sentiment likely to be shared by queasy fellow-passengers during a late-December run across the notoriously fickle North Atlantic. Other passengers heard Wilde complain, "I care not for this tame, monotonous trip. It is too deucedly stupid, don't you know."[22]

The captain of the *Arizona*, a crusty, bearded, forty-year-old Scot named George Siddons Murray, conceived a similar dislike for his famous passenger. "I wish that I had lashed that man to the bowsprit on the windward side," he said later. Ironically, Murray came from a theatrical background himself. His parents and grandparents had run the Royal Theatre Company in Edinburgh for decades. His great-grandmother Sarah Siddons was the most famous Lady Macbeth of her day, enjoying a twenty-year association with David Garrick's Drury Lane Theater in London and making the acquaintance of such literary heavyweights as Samuel Johnson and Edmund Burke. Captain Murray himself became something of a celebrity in his own time, breaking the Atlantic crossing speed record at the helm of the S.S. *Alaska* (six days, eighteen hours, and thirty-seven minutes) and endorsing such products as Warner's Safe Rheumatic Cure and Honest Long Cut Tobacco. He attracted somewhat less favorable attention in 1891, when he lost the S.S. *Abyssinia* to a cotton fire off the coast of Newfoundland, although the ship's sinking seems not to have negatively impacted his career, which continued uninterrupted until his retirement in 1923.[23]

The December crossing was Murray's last as skipper of the *Arizona* before assuming command of the *Alaska,* and he probably wanted a quiet voyage and a good deal less commotion than Oscar Wilde inevitably brought along with him. In that desire he would be frustrated. While the *Arizona* rode at anchor off Staten Island on the afternoon of January 2, 1882, waiting to clear quarantine the next morning and dock across from the Battery on the Hudson River, Wilde emerged from Murray's cabin to meet the clamorous American press for the first time. A reporter for the *New York World* saw him strolling languidly on a gangway amidships. The media circus was about to begin.

The unnamed reporter, who had prepared himself by consulting Worchester's *Dictionary of the American Language* for a working definition of "aesthetics"—"the science of the sensations, or that which explains the cause of mental pain or pleasure, as derived from a contemplation of the works of art or nature"—put down a remarkably painstaking physical description of his quarry:

> Mr. Wilde is fully six feet three inches in height, straight as an arrow, and with broad shoulders and long arms, indicating considerable strength. His outer garment was a long ulster trimmed with two kinds of fur, which reached almost to his feet. He wore patent-leather

shoes, a smoking-cap or turban, and his shirt might be termed ultra-Byronic, or perhaps—décolleté. A sky-blue cravat of the sailor style hung well down upon the chest. His hair flowed over his shoulders in dark-brown waves, curling slightly upwards at the ends. His eyes were of a deep blue, but without that faraway expression that is popularly attributed to poets. In fact they seemed rather everyday and commonplace eyes. His teeth were large and regular. He is beardless, and his complexion is almost colorless. A peculiarity of Mr. Wilde's face is the exaggerated oval of the Italian face carried into the English type of countenance and tipped with a long sharp chin. It does not impress one as being a strong face."[24]

Other reporters clamored around, their pens "still wet with brine," as Wilde would remember picturesquely. In the now-familiar way of modern tabloid journalists, they peppered him with questions both pointed and pointless. First, why had he come to America? "I came from *Eng*-land because I *thought* America was the best *place* to see," Wilde replied in what sounded to American ears like peculiarly emphasized singsong. Could he define "Aestheticism"? "Well, Aestheticism is a search after the signs of the beautiful. It is the science through which men look after the correlation which exits in the arts. It is, to speak more exactly, the search after the secret of life." Other questions were less exalted. What time did he get up in the morning? Did he like his eggs fried on both sides or only one? What temperature of water did he prefer for his bath? How often did he trim his fingernails? If he was thrown off balance by any of the questions, Wilde did not betray any discomfort to the reporters. He responded to most of their questions politely and thoughtfully, occasionally interrupting himself with a surprisingly hearty laugh (the press had expected the humorously humorless Bunthorne), although he ignored a snarky inquiry about *Vera* and the copyright laws—always a touchy matter to authors on both sides of the Atlantic. Eventually, the reporters wandered off to question Wilde's shipmates, and he returned to his cabin to rest.[25]

The next morning, the reporters were back in force when the *Ari-*

zona docked and began discharging her passengers. Wilde, surrounded by admirers—or perhaps merely the usual swirling crowd of fellow travelers—was again wearing his beloved overcoat, which one perplexed journalist described as "a sort of bottle-green dressing gown." He seemed a little less agreeable in the morning light. Asked yet again what he meant by "Aestheticism," Wilde responded grumpily, "I have defined it about two hundred times since last night." He was here, he said, "to diffuse beauty—I say, porter, handle that box more carefully, will you?" Was the grain elevator on the New Jersey side of the harbor beautiful, someone asked. Wilde said he was too near-sighted to see it, but he "would examine it some other day and make a note." What was his last word on the subject of art? "Now, see here, don't you know I came here to lecture?" Wilde said with some asperity. "You come next Monday night to the hall and I'll answer these questions. I must get some breakfast now and see the town. Our voyage was so monotonous that I am glad to get on land and see some people. Goodbye." Opportunely, Colonel Morse arrived at that moment to shepherd Wilde away from the reporters and into a waiting carriage.[26]

Following Wilde's departure, an even more famous quote soon began making the rounds. When a customs officer asked him if he had anything to declare, Wilde had supposedly replied, "I have nothing to declare except my genius." Whether or not he actually said it—no one on the scene recorded it at the time—Wilde was canny enough to let it stand. It was, in fact, the perfect opening line for what would amount to a long-running one-man play written, produced, directed, and starring Oscar Wilde as a highly stylized version of himself. In due time it would be performed all across North America, from New York to San Francisco, from Boston to New Orleans to the raw boomtowns of the Wild West and the Canadian prairies. Thousands would come to look and listen—alternately amused, enlightened, perplexed, or enraged, but almost always entertained by the larger-than-life stranger who was now suddenly in their midst.[27]

CHAPTER 2

More Wonderful
Than Dickens

❧

$\mathcal{P}$URELY BY ACCIDENT, Oscar Wilde arrived in America at a particularly opportune moment for an English (or Irish) celebrity. The highly publicized marriage of New York socialite Jennie Jerome to Lord Randolph Churchill a few years earlier, which in time would give the world the remarkable Winston, had attracted widespread attention in the United States. And the heroes' welcome recently accorded to former President and Mrs. Ulysses S. Grant in London, where they were hosted by Queen Victoria, had led to a new round of Anglophilia—never far from the surface in supposedly democratic America. Indeed, English fashions had become so popular in the United States that one canny manufacturer of eyeglasses created a new fad by promising to give customers "a strong British stare." The time was right for a new English sensation to hit the shores, particularly one that promised to be as outrageous and entertaining as Oscar Wilde—Reginald Bunthorne in the flesh.[1]

The American public was long accustomed to being entertained by exotic curiosities. Showman P. T. Barnum had built a $4 million fortune around his New York–based "museum of curiosities," where he exhibited the "Feejee Mermaid"—a shaved monkey with a fishtail glued to its bottom—and assorted other oddities, including 907-pound John Jones, "the heaviest man alive"; Myrtle, a four-legged woman from Texas; Jo Jo the Dog-Faced Boy (appeal obvious); Fanny, the Ohio Big Foot Girl, whose size-30 shoes required three goatskins per pair; and Lizzie Sturgeon, an armless girl who played the piano with her toes. Those seeking more uplifting subjects could take advantage of the ongoing Lyceum Movement, which first took root in the 1820s and featured a broad-based series of lecturers catering to the insatiable hunger for knowledge of a self-educating public. Such spellbinding speakers as Henry Ward Beecher, William Lloyd Garrison, Susan B. Anthony, Julia Ward Howe, Frederick Douglass, Wendell Phillips, Anna Dickinson, and Victoria Woodhull mixed with an eclectic tribe of wandering divines, faith healers, spirit knockers, temperance lecturers, abstinence promoters, health food advocates, foreign traveloguists, and outright charlatans to entertain and enlighten audiences from New England to California. Wilde, in his turn, would perform many of the same services.

Less than two decades after a ruinous civil war that had killed more than 600,000 soldiers and civilians, Americans were boldly pushing ahead with their lives. It was the height of what the preeminent American author of his day, Mark Twain, indelibly dubbed the Gilded Age, a period of unrivaled growth and progress undergirded by economic rapaciousness and political corruption. Half a dozen years earlier, on the occasion of the United States' 100th birthday, the nation had engaged in a year-long orgy of celebration and self-congratulation whose focal point was the Centennial Exhibition in Philadelphia. The first world's fair held within the borders of the United States, the exhibition in its six months of existence had hosted a staggering 8.8 million visitors—roughly one-fifth the entire population at the time. Taking into account numerous repeat visitors, organizers estimated conservatively that one in fifteen Americans had trooped to Philadelphia to behold the wonders of the self-proclaimed "American Mecca."

These wonders were primarily mechanical. While paying homage to such quaint historical objects as George Washington's false teeth and Benjamin Franklin's hand press, the Centennial Exhibition had been carefully designed to highlight the nation's industrial vigor, at a time when such industry was still considered an unalloyed national blessing. The most popular sight at the fair was the gigantic Corliss steam engine, which simultaneously animated thirteen acres' worth of complex job-performing devices. No less a literary arbiter than novelist William Dean Howells, in his capacity as editor of the *Atlantic Monthly*, termed the Corliss engine "an athlete of steel and iron," and proclaimed the pullied, shafted, wheeled, and belted monstrosity the true voice of the country itself, since "it is in these things of iron and steel that the national genius most freely speaks." Oscar Wilde, who considered Howells one of the two best American writers of the age (Henry James was the other), would beg to differ with that formulation. He would later revise his opinion of the two novelists, judging their work to display "the realism of Paris filtered through the refining influence of Boston. Analysis not action is its aim; it has more psychology than passion, and it plays very cleverly upon one string, and this is the commonplace."[2]

Despite the glorification of mechanical objects and Progress with a capital *P*, Americans—particularly American women—still yearned for beauty in their personal lives. In the years following the Civil War, numerous women's magazines and special-interest newspapers sprang up, covering a wide range of topics, from how to be a good wife and mother to how to produce the perfect sweet-potato puff. Such publications as *Godey's Lady Book* and *Ladies Home Journal* carried columns entitled "To Girls" and "What Women Should Know," regularly filling their pages with detailed advice on how to select, attract, and ensnare a proper

husband while not appearing to do so. It required "intelligence, amia-
bility and beauty," said one editor—but no flirting. "It is not a woman's
place to seek a companion but her social duty to wait to be sought," the
editor, a man, advised. Even the obituary of a three-year-old girl took
pains to mention her precocious if unfulfilled domestic qualities: "At
that tender age, Cora had all the grace needed to be a loving wife."[3]

Once settled into her proper place and home, a woman could begin
decorating. That was where Oscar Wilde and the Aesthetes came in—to
advise, if not necessarily to consent. In the wake of London's Great Exhibition three decades earlier, there had been a blizzard of books published on the fertile subject of home decorating, from Charles Eastlake's
best-selling *Hints on Household Taste* in 1868 to a literal cottage industry
of publications by Mary Eliza Haweis, bearing such self-explanatory titles as *The Art of Beauty, The Art of Decoration, The Art of Housekeeping:
A Bridal Garland,* and *Beautiful Houses.* Women on both sides of the
Atlantic avidly sought help in keeping and decorating their houses, and
there was no shortage of volunteers, including Oscar Wilde, to assist
them. Haweis, the daughter of a painter, used some of the profits from
her self-help books to purchase Tudor House, the Chelsea home of
Wilde's hero Dante Gabriel Rossetti. Haweis retained many of the former owner's touches, including the blue-tiled fireplaces, pale-yellow
drawing room, paneled den, and subtly colored Persian rugs. She even
kept Rossetti's hand-painted "Pandora's Box" beside her on her writing
table while she dispensed her helpful hints.

Wilde consulted Haweis's work while preparing his own lecture,
"The House Beautiful," for delivery to American audiences. He hoped,
with a little gentle prodding, to help women on the other side of the
Atlantic open their eyes to beauty in all its forms and price ranges.
"Women have natural art instincts," he would tell them, "which men
usually acquire only after long special training and study; and it may be
the mission of the women of this country to revive decorative art into
honest, healthy life." Such art had always flourished most, he maintained, "when the position of women was highly honored, when women

occupied that place on the social scale which [they] ever ought to do." Wilde intended to give American women a helping hand, at least with regard to decorating. Otherwise, he stood a little in awe of his distaff American cousins, whom he would describe a few years later as "pretty whirlwinds in petticoats" who could "talk brilliantly upon any subject, provided that [they know] nothing about it." American women, at least the ones with the wherewithal and good taste to visit England and the Continent, were "bright, clever, and wonderfully cosmopolitan." They made excellent wives.[4]

American men, at the time of Wilde's visit, were not quite as carefree as American women—with good reason. Every city and town, in both the North and the South, featured its share of maimed and limping veterans, solemn reminders of the most destructive war in the nation's history. But the ongoing militarization of the American male had entered a quiescent phase, not to flare up again until the end of the century, when Teddy Roosevelt and the Rough Riders would come to epitomize the new sharp edge of American imperialism. For the time being, the recent internecine slaughter, if not its all-too-visible victims, had been set aside. Survivors on both sides of the Mason-Dixon Line had entered a period that modern historian Gerald F. Linderman has aptly termed "the Hibernation," a time in which the vast majority of ex-soldiers consciously or unconsciously sought to free themselves of war's hellish memories by studiously avoiding all talk of them. In the decade preceding Wilde's visit, the nation's most prestigious history publication, the *North American Review,* had published a grand total of one article on the Civil War; *Harper's,* the leading popular magazine, had published two. It would be another three years before *Century Magazine,* in late 1884, began running its well-received series of personal memoirs and recollections, "Battles and Leaders of the Civil War," inaugurating a new round of Civil War interest that has continued unabated to this day.

Part of the reason for Americans' determined silence on the war had to do with their characteristic urge to get on with their lives, particularly during an age in which there were vast new fortunes to be made and lost. But part, too, lay in the psychological consequences of the war, which had raised some troubling questions about masculine roles in a postwar society. In the United States more than in Wilde's England, Aestheticism—for men, at least—represented less an artistic movement than an approach to personal style and self-identity. For a fleeting moment, as measured on the continuum of national life, a not-inconsiderable number of American men began to reconsider their maleness. The old dominant role model—soldier—had gotten hundreds of thousands of them killed, wounded, or psychologically traumatized in a war that might well have been avoided. Perhaps it was time for a kinder, gentler approach.

Both by virtue of what he said and how he dressed, Wilde would serve as an avatar of the new, "Aesthetic" male. The young men who attended Wilde's lectures were not, for the most part, veterans of the war, but rather the sons, grandsons, brothers, and nephews of veterans. Postwar children themselves—the oldest wartime babies at the time of Wilde's visit were only twenty-one—many of the men in Wilde's audience were still college students. It stood to reason. Wilde himself was only a few years removed from university life; in some ways he was an eternal undergraduate. As an example of the new Aestheticism, the flamboyantly costumed visitor was a challenge to the traditional image of acceptable masculinity. As cultural historian Mary Warner Blanchard has observed: "A certain war-weariness induced some Americans to seek alternative modes of self-definition, as new formats—aesthetic style, for one—competed with older categories like the manly soldier in defining manhood." Wilde was nothing if not new.[5]

Some of the men in Wilde's audience quite likely were gay, as newspaper reports insinuated at the time. "Many aesthetic and pallid young men in dress suits and banged hair" (i.e., bangs) were to be seen lounging at the rear of the theater when Wilde spoke for the first time in New York, one observer wrote. "Banged hair" was a dead giveaway to readers, as was the suggestion that the men were being somehow furtive by loitering in the back of the room. Frequent allusions in the national press to Wilde's "effeminate" voice and mannerisms linked him to his purportedly gay audience. "The pallid and lank young man, Mr. Oscar Wilde, will find in the great metropolis . . . a school of gilded youths eager to embrace his peculiar tenets," the *Brooklyn Daily Eagle* observed. The *Washington Post* characterized Wilde's supporters as "young men painting their faces . . . with unmistakable rouge upon their cheeks." To be sure, the homosexual demimonde was quick to adopt Wilde as one of its own—perhaps quicker than he was ready to be adopted. Still, it was not as a proselytizer of outlaw sexuality that Wilde presented himself to the American public, but as a spokesman for art and beauty, in whatever exotic or commonplace forms they could be found in people's lives. The rest was not necessarily his business.[6]

Despite the fortunate timing of his tour, Wilde would find himself competing for press attention with two different media circuses, both of the distinctly Big Top variety. In the spring of 1882, just as Wilde was setting out across country, P. T. Barnum completed the controversial purchase of a twenty-one-year-old African elephant called Jumbo, a combination of the Swahili words *jambo,* or "hello," and *jumbe,* meaning "chief." Jumbo had been the prize attraction at the London Zoo for the past sixteen years, giving rides on his seven-ton back to thousands of zoo visitors, including such dignitaries as Winston Churchill, Theodore Roosevelt, and Barnum himself. Two years earlier, Barnum had merged his circus, modestly dubbed "the greatest show on earth," with James Anthony Bailey's London Circus. Always on the lookout for a new star attraction, the showman naturally thought of Jumbo. The impending sale, for $10,000, had galvanized the British public into a protest movement, with Queen Victoria, the Prince of Wales, John Ruskin, the Royal Society for the Prevention of Cruelty to Animals, and various members of the House of Commons going on record as opposing the transaction. Thousands of British children wrote imploring letters to their monarch asking her to intercede, but a London chancery court upheld the legality of the sale, and Jumbo sailed for New York aboard the steamship *As-*

syrian Monarch in late March 1882, during which voyage he was said to have imbibed, like countless other transatlantic voyagers before him, a truly elephantine quantity of whisky, beer, and champagne.

All the hubbub surrounding the elephant led to a Jumbo-size mania, which historian Lloyd Lewis elaborated as an insatiable demand for "Jumbo-bracelets, Jumbo-bangles, Jumbo-beefsteaks, Jumbo-cigars, Jumbo-earrings, Jumbo-soups, and Jumbo-kisses." A London woman was even alleged to have named her baby Jumbo, sex unspecified. What if anything Wilde thought about the controversy went unrecorded, although there were rumors, possibly floated by Barnum himself, that the showman had offered to pay Wilde two hundred pounds to ride, or at least lead, Jumbo down Broadway while holding a sunflower. The *New York Daily Saratogian,* reporting the rumor, noted a little ungenerously that "some innocent-minded people, thinking Oscar was the larger of the two, were said to be believing that Jumbo would ride Oscar."[7]

The second circus, considerably less light-hearted but equally ridiculous, centered on the trial of presidential assassin Charles J. Guiteau in Washington. The fifty-four-day trial was reaching its climax when Wilde arrived in New York; Guiteau would be convicted and sentenced to death on January 25. By then, the American public had been treated to a show trial that was good deal more show than trial. Guiteau was quite probably insane—he was certainly one of the oddest individuals ever to shoot a president. His stated reason for attacking Garfield, whom he had met briefly in the White House when he presented the bemused chief executive with a copy of a campaign speech Guiteau had written and a demand that he be appointed ambassador to France, involved the intramural squabbling between the "Stalwarts" and the "Half-Breeds," the conservative and slightly less conservative wings of the Republican Party. Guiteau professed to be a Stalwart, as was Garfield's vice president, Chester A. Arthur, who had now succeeded his slain predecessor in the Oval Office. "I am a Stalwart and Arthur is president," the gunman had exclaimed, a little prematurely, after shooting Garfield on July 2. Following the president's lingering death on September 19, Guiteau sent Arthur a list of personally acceptable diplomatic posts. Arthur, unsurprisingly, did not respond.

Guiteau, who was something of a jackleg lawyer himself, insisted on acting as his own defense counsel, thus proving incontestably the adage that whoever represents himself has a fool for a client. He loudly cursed the trial judge, the prosecutors, his own court-appointed attorneys, witnesses, and even the jury deciding his fate. Sometimes he couched his testimony in the form of epic poems and sought legal advice from random spectators in the courtroom. He insisted alternately that he was sane or that he was insane, depending on his mood, and dictated a personal ad in the *New York Herald* soliciting applicants for the post of Mrs. Charles J. Guiteau—"a nice Christian lady under thirty years of age." Guiteau also argued, not altogether wrongly, that "the doctors killed Garfield; I just shot him." Given the fact that the stricken president had died of blood poisoning caused by constant unsterilized probing of his otherwise nonfatal bullet wound, this was technically true, if rather beside the point. When the jury returned its verdict after a mere thirty minutes' deliberation, Guiteau informed them that they were "all low, consummate jackasses"—again, not something designed to win him sympathy in court. Guiteau remained unworried; he fully expected General William Tecumseh Sherman and the United States Army to break him out of jail in time for him, Guiteau, to run for president in 1884. That didn't seem likely, but a Philadelphia owner of refrigerated railcars did offer to take Guiteau's "beautifully frozen" body on a coast-to-coast tour after the assassin's execution and split the profits with Guiteau's heirs. Guiteau told the businessman to take it up with his lawyer.[8]

Wilde took no notice of the assassin's trial. He was never heard to refer to Guiteau during his time in America, feeling perhaps that it was not his place to comment. Instead, upon his arrival in New York, Wilde checked into the Grand Hotel on the corner of 31st Street and Broadway, in the heart of the theater district. His two-room suite overlooked the new iron-and-tin Wallack's Theatre; just down the street were Daly's

Theatre and the Academy of Music. Appropriately enough, Wilde's first excursion in the city was to the Union Square studio of famed fashion photographer Napoleon Sarony. The diminutive Sarony, about the same height as his imperial namesake, wore a six-inch-high oriental fez to make himself look taller. There was nothing he could do about his age (sixty-one), but the Canadian-born photographer had so much nervous energy and sheer joie de vivre that he seemed much younger. He favored heavily brocaded military uniforms, complete with self-awarded medals, jackboots, and sword. His second wife, Louise, called Louie, joined him each afternoon for a stroll through nearby Washington Square, sporting rented theatrical costumes that she wore once, then returned. Sarony had begun his professional life as an illustrator for Currier & Ives before opening his own photographic studio in 1866. The studio was as baroque as its owner: its main waiting room, on the fifth floor, was jam-packed with background props, including Egyptian mummies, suits of medieval armor from China and Japan, Russian sleighs, religious icons, jade and wooden Buddhas, and a stuffed, twenty-foot-long Nile crocodile suspended from the ceiling. *Galaxy* magazine correspondent Richard Grant White, visiting the studio a few years before Wilde, described a menacing array of "iron structures of torture, and a smell as of a drug and chemical warehouse on fire in the distance."[9]

Sarony estimated that he had photographed 200,000 people in his studio, including 30,000 who were "famous" and 1,000 who were "world renowned." It was unclear where Wilde fell on the spectrum, but included in the latter category were Sarony's fellow Lotos Club member Samuel Clemens and Wilde's actress-friend Sarah Bernhardt, to whom the photographer paid $1,500 for the privilege of photographing her on his "fainting couch," an expense he recouped many times over by licensing the sale of thousands of postcard prints of the actress. In action, Sarony was a very hands-off photographer. He took no photos himself, delegating the task to his assistants while he gazed distractedly out the window. Nor did he develop the finished products, bragging that he did not know anything about the developing process. Instead, he focused on artfully posing his subjects, a task he described as "a surrender of self on the part of the sitter." Paradoxically, Sarony wanted his quarry to feel unposed, observing that "once conscious, the sitter begins to pose, and falsely. The moment a person is told to 'look natural,' at that moment he will look what he feels—perfectly idiotic. Posing is for professional models only."[10]

Sarony was ready and waiting when Wilde breezed in, accompanied by Colonel Morse, and announced—one hopes ironically—that he was "the Lord of Language." Wanting Saxony's imprimatur, Morse waived the posing fee, and the master went to work posing Wilde. "A picturesque subject indeed," Sarony gushed. He knew his business. In the next few hours Sarony and his assistants made twenty-seven separate photographs of Wilde, starting with a full-on head shot and progressing through a series of sitting and standing positions. Wilde wore a variety of costumes, sporting his green fur-trimmed overcoat and purple velvet suit in some, and knee breeches and black silk stockings over patent-leather pumps in others. He was also captured in formal evening wear, a padded smoking jacket, and a flowing black cape and broad-brimmed hat that made him look a little like a benevolent vampire. With his shoulder-length hair, parted in the middle, he strongly resembled the cavalcade of British rock stars who would invade America eight decades later.[11]

Wilde, of course, was used to posing, and the Sarony photographs have come down through time as the best-loved and most familiar of all the hundreds of visual representations of the writer. Sarony printed and sold thousands of copies of the photos, but it was two he did not license that caused the most trouble. Two years after the session with Wilde, Sarony sued Burrow-Giles Lithographic Company for illegally copying a pair of Wilde photos, one sitting and one standing, to use in ads for Ehrich Brothers Department Store and R. C. Brown & Co., among others. The ad for Ehrichs', located at the corner of 8th Avenue and 24th Street, showed Wilde sitting on a sofa, holding a book in one hand and his head in the other. Ironically (Wilde is bare-headed in the shot) the ad pitched the store's "Trimmed Hat Department" and assured customers that "The English Renaissance is fitly represented" by its merchandise, which was said to cost "about half" what it would cost two blocks over, on 6th Avenue. Other Wilde images were used to pitch Straiton and Storm cigars ("Too Too") and Piercy's "Esthetic Ice Cream and Confections." The legal case, *Burrow-Giles Lithographic Co. v. Sarony*, went all the way to the United States Supreme Court, which ruled in Sarony's favor after accepting counsel arguments that the Wilde photos were works of "photographic fiction." It is to be doubted that the subject, a fiction writer himself, would have agreed, but he was not called to testify, although he would go on record later as disapproving of the whole business of high-gloss self-advertising of the sort Sarony specialized in making. "Fashion," wrote Wilde, "is a form of ugliness so intolerable that we have to alter it every six months." Considering Wilde's habitual emphasis on image and image-making, the court's decision to extend copyright protection to photographers was both fitting and ironic.[12]

With his New York début at Chickering Hall on January 9 looming ever closer, Wilde continued working desultorily on his lecture, "The English Renaissance," a wide-ranging survey of the public and private roles of artists in modern society, between various luncheons, dinners, and receptions held in his honor across the city. Somewhat to his surprise, Wilde found himself the newest prize for high society's best-connected hosts and hostesses. "I am torn in bits by Society," he wrote happily to his actor friend Norman Forbes-Robertson in London. "Immense receptions, wonderful dinners, crowds wait for my carriage. I wave a gloved hand and an ivory cane and they cheer. Rooms are hung with white lilies for me everywhere. I generally behave as I have always behaved—*dreadfully*."[13]

Dashing from one event to another in his carriage, Wilde, like most first-time visitors to New York, was struck by the sheer unceasing tumult of the city. "America is the noisiest country that ever existed," he said, conflating (like many New Yorkers) the city with the nation. He complained about being awakened each morning by steam whistles and horse-drawn cabs rather than by English nightingales, and joked that there were "no gorgeous ceremonies" to ennoble the streets. "I saw only two processions," he sighed. "One was the Fire Brigade preceded by the Police, the other was the Police preceded by the Fire Brigade." Still, he quickly felt at home in New York, where the highest circles of society were clamoring for his exotic presence. His coming-out party took place on the afternoon of January 5 at the 25th Street home of Mr. and Mrs. Augustus Hayes, Jr., and was attended by no less a personage than the mayor of New York, William Grace, and a heady froth of judges, ministers, corporation counsels, railroad barons, bishops, marquises, and even a Medal of Honor winner.[14]

Hayes, the author of a recent travel book, *New Colorado and the Santa Fe Trail,* had lived in China for several years, and had done up his home in Japanese fashion, with sliding paper partitions and umbrellas dividing the rooms. Wilde made his entrance quietly, wearing a black Prince Albert coat, knee breeches, silk stockings, kid gloves, and a dark-blue handkerchief in his breast pocket. He stood at ease, chatting smoothly with Mayor Grace and Brigadier General William Jackson Palmer, whom Wilde had met on the voyage over and who had won the Medal of Honor during the Civil War before becoming one of the West's leading railroad developers. The Hayes's décor put Wilde in mind of his friend Whistler's rooms in London, moving Wilde to assure the mayor that Whistler was the leading painter in England, "only it will take England three hundred years to find it out."[15]

Following the reception, Wilde accompanied his hosts and nine other guests to the nearby Standard Theatre, where *Patience* (inevitably) was being performed. The play had already begun when they sat down in their box seats, and Wilde waited with well-honed timing until the stage Bunthorne, embodied by J. H. Ryley, made his next appearance, tricked out as Wilde. "Caricature is one of the compliments that mediocrity pays to those who are not mediocre," Wilde observed, leaning forward over the box as the entire audience turned in their seats to gape at the real-life Bunthorne. The party went backstage afterwards to meet the cast, and a crowd of people gathered outside the theater to catch another glimpse of Wilde, but he escaped unseen through a side exit.[16]

Three days later Wilde attended a more literary reception at the East 38th Street home of New York journalists David and Jane Croly, better known by her pen name, "Jennie June." This time he was not the guest of honor; venerable New England novelist Louisa May Alcott was. The Crolys were well-known in journalistic circles. David Croly had been editor of the *New York World* and the author of a notorious, anonymously published pamphlet entitled *Miscegenation,* which came out at the height of the Civil War and attempted, unsuccessfully as it turned out, to discredit Abraham Lincoln and the abolitionist cause by linking it to the still-toxic idea of intermarriage between the races. Mrs. Croly— Jennie June—had been born in Leicestershire, England, before immigrating to America when she was twelve. Beginning as a staffer at her husband's newspaper, she had pioneered the concept of the women's column, launching "Gossip with and for Women" at the *World* and becoming the New York City correspondent for a number of out-of-town newspapers, including the *Washington Post.* She went on to become editor of *Demorest's, Godey's,* and *Home-Maker* magazines, routinely patrolling the city in search of scoops and advising her female readers that "girls are none the worse for being a little wild, a little startling to very proper norms, and much less likely, in that case, to spend their time gasping over sentimental novels, and imagining that every whiskered specimen they see is their hero."[17]

Wilde did not venture an opinion on the literary merits of *Little Women* or the romantic dreams of modern American girls. He spent most of his time at the Crolys' reception talking to Canadian-born actress Clara Morris, the reigning "It Girl" of the American stage, whom he hoped to entice into starring in the still-languishing *Vera.* Morris's current play, *The New Magdalen,* based on a Wilkie Collins story, had opened in New York three days earlier at the Union Square Theatre, with James O'Neill (father of the future playwright Eugene O'Neill) in a supporting role. After seeing her performance as Mercy Merrick, Wilde told a reporter: "Miss Morris is the greatest actress I ever saw, if it be fair to form an opinion of her from her rendition of this one role. We have no such powerfully intense actress in England. She is a great artist, in my sense of the word, because all she does, all she says, in the matter of the doing and of the saying constantly evoke the imagination to supplement it. That is what I mean by art. She is a veritable genius." Later, he would tell another reporter: "Clara Morris interested me enormously. Sarah Bernhardt told me there were two things in America worth seeing—one was Clara Morris's acting, and the other was some dreadful method of killing pigs in Chicago. She advised to go and see both. I went to see Miss Morris immediately upon my arrival in New York City, but the other I have deferred quite indefinitely."[18]

Wilde's instincts, as usual, were on target—Morris would have made a very good Vera. She was perhaps the world's first method actor, eschewing the crowd-pleasing artificiality of her fellow performers for a more naturalistic and emotional style of acting in which, she said, she attempted to "feel what my characters feel." When she failed to access a particular emotion, she would fall back on her own sense memories of a sad, deprived childhood in Cleveland, Ohio, where she had lived with her divorced mother just down the block from Eller's Theatre. "My God," said Sarah Bernhardt upon first seeing Morris perform. "This woman is not acting; she is suffering." The critic for the *New York Herald* agreed, terming her performance "terrible in its intensity . . . no school could give such a startling naturalness to insanity as it received from Miss Morris." Morris, whose dark, curly hair, oval face, and bright-blue eyes made her attractive without quite making her pretty, was a forerunner to modern tabloid-fodder actresses. She feuded with her fellow actors, argued constantly with producers over money, and regularly abused drugs, shooting up morphine in her dressing room between acts. In the end she lost her looks, her fortune, and finally her eyesight before being evicted from her New York home for failure to pay back taxes. But now, at the peak of her power, she agreed to read Wilde's play, but ultimately passed on it, confirming Wilde's privately stated impression to D'Oyly Carte that she was *"difficile"*—an impression with which any number of her thespian associates would have readily concurred.[19]

Wilde had more success in winning the support of another prominent New Yorker, Samuel "Uncle Sam" Ward, the brother of Julia Ward Howe of "Battle Hymn of the Republic" fame. At the time of Wilde's arrival, Sam Ward had just moved back to the city of his birth after a fabulous two-decade-long career as the most successful "social lobbyist" in Washington. The courtly Ward could trace his roots back to the Revolutionary War—one of his ancestors was the noted South Carolina guerrilla leader Francis "Swamp Fox" Marion—and to the highest echelons of New York society. He had married the granddaughter of John Jacob Astor, the richest man in America at the time, and after his wife died in childbirth, Ward had made and lost several fortunes. He had joined the Forty-Niners in the California gold rush, lived among the Paiute Indians, wandered through Central and South America, spied for the Union during the Civil War, and ultimately settled in the nation's capital, where he virtually pioneered the now-omnipresent profession of lobbyist. With a yearly operating budget of $12,000 for food alone, Ward pushed the interests of President Andrew Johnson's embattled administration, as well as those of a variety of private insurance firms, railroads, telegraph companies, and steamship lines. He was the willing mouthpiece for banking interests, miners, manufacturers, investors—anyone seeking to put his hand in the government till. In short order, Ward became known as both the King of the Lobby and the Prince of the Epicures.

Ward was renowned for putting on the best dinners in Washington. In his self-described role of "gastronomic pacificator," he hosted politicians on both sides of the aisle, whom he sought to bring together over the shared delights of fine wine and good meals. Ward himself never ate at his dinners; he fortified himself beforehand with a lamb chop and a single glass of wine. Nor did he encourage shop talk at the table. Instead, he and his guests held forth on the glories of Ward's sautéed chicken and the Sam Ward Cocktail, an apéritif invented by its name-sake and concocted of a hollowed-out lemon, yellow chartreuse liqueur, and shaved ice. A Democrat himself, despite his sub rosa pro-Union activities during the war, Ward managed to retain his popularity during the quarter-century of Republican domination of the White House. Even the Radical Republican senator from Massachusetts, Charles Sumner, was moved to confess: "I disagree with Sam Ward on almost every human topic, but when I have talked with him five minutes, I forget everything save that he is the most delightful company in the world." On one occasion, summoned before a congressional investigating committee and asked to explain himself, Ward suavely answered the charge that he had "wasted a great deal of money on good dinners." "I do not think money is ever wasted on a good dinner," he said. "If a man dines badly he forgets his prayers going to bed, but if he dines well he feels like a saint."[20]

Wilde gained entrée to Ward's sanctifying table through a letter of introduction from their mutual friend, poet-politician Richard Monckton Milnes, Lord Houghton. Milnes was a fixture of London society, one of those mediocre men who rise ineffably above the level of their actual achievement. He was a friend and champion of Lord Tennyson, Ralph Waldo Emerson, and the Decadent poet Algernon Charles Swinburne, with whom he shared a secret yen for flagellation, commemorated in one of the largest surviving collections of Victorian-era pornography, now housed at the London Museum of History. Milnes had met Ward when they were both young poets studying abroad, and Wilde, learning of their connection, had prevailed upon Milnes for a letter of introduction.

Ever obliging, Ward hosted a dinner for the new arrival at his flat at 84 Clinton Place, near Fordham University in the Bronx. As usual, Ward went all out, organizing his feast around a flowery theme. Lilies of the valley formed the table's centerpiece; two calla lilies tied with a red bow adorned Wilde's place of honor. Guests were given lily-of-the-valley boutonnières. Ward had written not one but two poems in Wilde's honor, along with a special song, "The Valley Lily," which he had another guest sing. (Wilde politely called for an encore.) The quality of the poems, if not the song, may be inferred from the quatrain: "Go it, Oscar! You are young / Owning a conviction, / To which you have wisely clung— / Beauty is no fiction!" In the spirit of the occasion, Wilde gave Ward a copy of his *Poems,* inscribed floridly: "L'art pour l'art, et mes poèmes pour mon oncle."[21]

Despite such triumphs, Wilde was not universally welcomed by New York literary society. Businessman-critic Edmund Clarence Stedman, stealing a moment from his money-making labors on Wall Street, was visibly angry. "This Philistine town is making a fool of itself over Oscar Wilde," he wrote to Thomas Bailey Aldrich, editor of the *Atlantic Monthly.* "So far as I know, the genuine writers, poets and journalists of this city have kept out of his way and are not over-pleased with the present revelation of the state of culture on Murray Hill and among our *soi-disant* intelligent and fashionable classes. He has brought hundreds of letters of introduction." One such letter was to Stedman himself, but the Jovian-bearded grandee refused to accept it, although Mrs. Stedman did attend (alone) the Crolys' reception for Wilde on January 8. Although Wilde probably was unaware of it, he was in good company in Stedman's disapproval; Walt Whitman was there, too. Conveniently forgetting the many hours he had spent drinking with Whitman and their fellow bohemians at Pfaff's beer cellar in Greenwich Village before the Civil War, Stedman had published a disapproving article on *Leaves of Grass* in *Scribner's* magazine a year earlier. In it, Stedman complained that Whitman was "too anatomical and malodorous." The ever-forgiving Whitman shrugged off Stedman's criticism, noting that it was "about as good as could be expected" from Stedman and joking that "You can't put a quart of water into a pint bottle. Stedman holds a good pint, but the pint is his limit."[22]

The time neared for Wilde's début at Chickering Hall on January 9. "If I am not a success on Monday, I shall be very wretched," he wrote to Betty Eberstadt Lewis, the wife of his London solicitor, two days before the show. Buckling down, he moved into a private home on 28th Street and completed his lecture, although he took the time to sit down for a joint interview with reporters from the *New York Tribune* and the *New York World,* meeting them in a brown velvet smoking jacket, brown trousers, red silk stockings, and olive-green cravat. Stepping somewhat on his own message, Wilde insisted: "You cannot teach anybody what is really beautiful. The true spirit of a painting or a poem cannot by any method be taught—it must be revealed." The Aesthetic Movement, at whose head he modestly placed himself, was aiming to unite writers and artists in an effort to connect directly with the public, in the face of what he termed "the absolute stupidity of the English people." By contrast, said Wilde, his initial reception in America had been "delightful. . . . Nothing could have been more cordial."[23]

Chickering Hall, at the corner of Fifth Avenue and 18th Street, was full to capacity for Wilde's maiden appearance, despite the fact that no one from the four hundred leading New York families was there. The Vanderbilts, Astors, Whitneys, Fishes, and Van Rensselaers were otherwise occupied with the annual Patriarchs' Ball at Delmonico's. That still left a sizable audience pool from which to draw, and a billboard reading "Standing Room Only" was posted in the lobby of the four-story hall, with tickets going for a dollar apiece. Private carriages disgorged a steady stream of well-dressed men and women, many wearing flowers on their coats and blouses. At exactly eight P.M., a furiously blushing Wilde walked onto the stage with his tour manager, Colonel Morse, who proceeded to deliver one of the shortest client introductions on record. "I have the honor to introduce to you Oscar Wilde, the English poet," he said, "who will lecture upon the 'English Renaissance.'" Morse exited, stage left, leaving Wilde alone at the podium. Hundreds of opera glasses were trained on the stage, and in the rear of the hall a long line of "aesthetic and pallid young men in dress suits and banged hair" looked on expectantly. Applause and laughter preceded Wilde's opening words.[24]

Wearing his complete Bunthorne outfit, sans sunflower, Wilde nodded to an unidentified woman in the audience, propped one foot on the base of the reading table, and began speaking in what a *New York Times* reporter described as "a voice that might have come from the tomb." (He was probably making an effort to sound serious and grown-up.) The English Renaissance, he said, had brought "a sort of new birth of the spirit of man . . . in its desire for a more gracious and comely way of life." Emphasizing the word "new," he said the movement was seeking "new subjects for poetry, new forms of art, new intellectual and imaginative enjoyments." It was a "passionate cult of pure beauty," devoted to form and sensitive in nature, centered on "great cosmical emotion and deep pantheism of science."[25]

There followed several paragraphs of rhetorical boilerplate, delivered in an improving vocal style that a trained observer, actress Helen Potter, described as "clear, easy, and not forced . . . the closing inflection of a sentence or period is ever upward." It was quickly apparent to everyone in the audience that Wilde, despite having studied Charles Dickens's earlier reading tours of America, was no Charles Dickens on the stage. Unlike the Great Boz, he was not a frustrated actor (or one with a celebrated actress mistress on the side). Nor, to be fair, was he performing scenes from a dramatic novel like *Oliver Twist* or *David Copperfield.* Instead, he sought to create a sense of communion with the audience by linking the American and French revolutions to the rather more peaceful revolution in art that he was spearheading in England. He apotheosized John Keats as the avatar of Wilde's immediate forebears, the Pre-Raphaelites, whom he sweepingly described as "a body of young men who had determined to revolutionize English painting and poetry." The Pre-Raphaelites, said Wilde, had endured the satirical jabs of a philistine society, but it served only to confirm "the perfect rightness of [their] work. . . . For to disagree with three fourths of the British public on all points is one of the first elements of sanity, one of the deepest consolations in all moments of spiritual doubt."[26]

Art, said Wilde, should remain aloof from the fleeting social problems of the day, since "to most of us the real life is the life we do not lead." The true artist should not admit anything "into the secure and sacred house of Beauty" that is disturbing or painful. Instead, art should be made purely for the sake of art. "It is not an increased moral sense, an increased moral supervision that your literature needs," Wilde continued. "Indeed, one should never talk of a moral or an immoral poem; poems are either well written or badly written, that is all. Any element of morals or implied reference to a standard of good and evil in art is often a sign of a certain incompleteness of vision, often a note of discord in the harmony of an imaginative creation, for all good work aims at a purely artistic effect."[27]

It was a long lecture—the *New York Times* found parts of it "monotonous"—and there were stretches of grim silence, interspersed with the usual coughs, whispers, and program-shuffling. Aware, perhaps, that he was losing some of his audience, a few of whom were actually nodding off, Wilde turned the attention back to himself—which was, after all, what most of them had come to see. "You have heard, I think, a few of you, of two flowers connected with the aesthetic movement in England, and said (I assure you, erroneously) to be the food of some aesthetic young men," he said with a smile. "Well, let me tell you the reason we love the lily and the sunflower, in spite of what Mr. Gilbert may tell you, is not for any vegetable fashion at all. It is because these two lovely flowers are in England the most perfect models of design, the most naturally adapted for decorative art." Having suavely brought the discussion back around to himself—or at least to the well-known Gilbert and Sullivan caricature of him—Wilde came to the end of his hour-long lecture. "We spend our days, each of us, looking for the secret of life," he said. "Well, the secret of life is in art."[28]

Wilde bowed once and left the stage to warm applause, "blushing like a schoolgirl," according to the *Times* reporter. He had survived his crucial first test. At a post-lecture reception hosted by Mrs. John Mack, an old friend of his mother, Wilde's entrance was greeted by an orchestra playing, apparently without intentional irony, "God Save the Queen." His Chickering Hall appearance took in more than $1,200, inducing the canny impresario, D'Oyly Carte, to compliment him a few days later as "a clever young man. I think I shall take him around the country." Other reviews were more mixed. George Alfred Townsend of the *Cincinnati Enquirer* praised "the stranger among us [as] a young apostle of beauty against a decaying age of trade and swap." But the *Nation* thought Wilde "can hardly succeed in this country. What he has to say is not new, and his extravagance is not extravagant enough to amuse the average American audience. His knee breeches and long hair are good as far as they go, but Bunthorne has really spoiled the public for Wilde." The *Chicago Tribune* called him "a twittering sparrow come to fill his maw with insects." And a less-than-flattering cartoon in the *New York Daily Graphic,* with the slug line "Aestheticism as Oscar Understands It," showed an epicene Wilde holding up a plate inscribed with a giant dollar sign. A verse below the cartoon urged readers:

> Conceive me if you can,
> A pallid and thin young man,
> A crotchety, crank'd young man,
> A greenery-yallery, chickering gallery,
> Dollar and a half young man.[29]

Wilde was unfazed by the negative reviews. "The hall had an audience larger and more wonderful than even Dickens had," Wilde wrote exultantly to Betty Lewis. "I was recalled and applauded and am now treated like the Royal Boy [the Prince of Wales]. I stand at the top of the reception rooms when I go out, and for two hours they defile past for introductions. I bow graciously and sometimes honour them with a royal observation, which appears next day in all the newspapers. When I go to the theatre the manager bows me in with lighted candles and the audience rise. Yesterday, I had to leave by a private door, the mob was so great." He had retained three secretaries, he joked, one to sign his autographs for him, one to handle all his dinner invitations, and one to send out requested locks of hair—the poor fellow, said Wilde, was rapidly going bald for his troubles.[30]

The trio of secretaries was imaginary, but the exuberance was real.

If D'Oyly Carte had thought he was sponsoring a walking, talking billboard for the American production of *Patience,* he would soon be dis-
abused of that notion. Oscar Wilde may have dressed as Reginald Bunthorne, but he was advertising something a good deal more complex
than that one-note comic opera character: he was advertising himself.
And now, thanks to half a decade of canny self-promotion (and D'Oyly
Carte's deep pockets), he had the entire United States in which to make
his sales pitch.

CHAPTER 3

Those Who Dawnce Don't Dine

❧

Wilde's opening night triumph at Chickering Hall, however provisional, gave him added confidence as he headed south to his second speaking engagement, at Philadelphia's Horticultural Hall, on January 17. Accompanied by Colonel Morse, the neophyte lecturer took a ferry across the Hudson River from Manhattan to Jersey City, where he would catch the southbound train for Philadelphia. A reporter for the *Philadelphia Press* waited at the ferry dock to join them for the train ride down. "There he is!" the reporter heard someone cry. "That's Oscar Wilde!"[1]

Wearing his now-familiar green overcoat, Wilde bustled off the ferry ahead of the crowd and climbed aboard the Philadelphia express, leaving his valet (as the reporter later wrote) "struggling hopelessly in the rear with a burden of baggage." This was the first public mention of Wilde's shadowy valet, an individual whose identity still remains a question mark today. Wilde had referred slightingly to him in a letter to Norman Forbes-Robertson as "my slave," airily declaring that "in a free country one cannot live without a slave—rather like a Christy minstrel, except that he knows no riddles." The only riddle is who he really was. Richard Ellmann, in his Pulitzer Prize–winning biography of Wilde, identifies the valet as "W. M. Traquair," apparently confusing him with St. Louis theatrical manager W. M. Traguier after misreading a passage in Lloyd Lewis and Henry Justin Smith's book *Oscar Wilde Discovers America,* which refers to Traguier just before mentioning Wilde's "liver-colored" valet, John. Lewis and Smith did not provide a last name for the servant. Such was the fate of black men in post–Civil War America: they were faceless as long as they were unoffending. Still unnamed, if no longer unnoticed, the gentleman in question would make another, more dramatic appearance later in Wilde's American journey.[2]

Wilde, Morse, and the industrious reporter took seats in the train's Pullman smoking car. After thumbing desultorily through a couple of his old mentor John Ruskin's books, *Fors Clavigera* and *The Poetry of Architecture,* Wilde looked out the train windows at the dreary marshes and underbrush along the way, which the reporter dismissed as "the horrors of a New Jersey landscape on a rainy day." Wilde complained that he was very tired, having been up late the night before at dinner with Mrs. Paran Stevens, née Marietta Reed, and at a reception hosted by Mrs. S. L. M. Barlow, whose husband was a prominent New York society lawyer. Running late, Wilde had missed breakfast. "I have been kept so busy answering letters," he complained. "Why, it is strange how people seem think I have nothing to do but answer letters."[3]

Despite, or perhaps because of, his boredom and hunger—a way-station sandwich helped a little—Wilde patiently answered the reporter's steady stream of questions. Yes, he said, American trains were very fast. Yes, they were very comfortable. No, they didn't have anything like them in England. But, said Wilde, he hated to "fly through the country at this rate. The only true way, you know, to see a country is to ride on horseback. I long to ride through New Mexico and Colorado and California. There are such beautiful flowers there, such quantities of lilies and, I am told, whole fields of sunflowers." Still, he supposed, "One cannot expect color in winter, when everything is so drear and brown. How dreadful those marshes on this side of New York. What a pity! And how unnecessary. They might plant them with something; so many beautiful things will grow in a marsh."[4]

On the subject of beautiful things, Wilde said the two classes of people he hoped to reach in America were "the handicraftsmen and the artists." As for the rather large segment of society in between, the idle poor and the idle rich, it was useless to try to teach them anything, he said. Still, "One of the most delightful things I find in America is meeting a people without prejudice—everywhere open to the truth. We have nothing like it in England." Wilde praised the beauty of American women, adding, "I have met many surpassingly beautiful young ladies since my arrival." He name-dropped Clara Morris, Sarah Bernhardt, and Lillie Langtry, but airily dismissed a question about his politics. "Oh, do you know, those matters are of no interest to me. I know only two terms—civilization and barbarism; and I am on the side of civilization."[5]

Revealing a canny insight into politics that immediately contradicted his supposed lack of interest, Wilde made a point that still rings true today, noting that "in our country there is seldom a piece of legislation that does not benefit one class more than another, and that perhaps makes the wretched party spirit more bitter." Again dropping names, he said that British prime minister William Gladstone—"the greatest prime minister England ever had"—had told him personally a short time before that the greatest danger from the United States was "the vast accumulation of capital. The personal control of capital, with the power it gives over labor and life, has only appeared in modern American life." Wilde exaggerated his acquaintance with Gladstone, whom he knew mainly from having bombarded the prime minister with unsolicited sonnets, but he was, if anything, understating the power and rapaciousness of America's robber barons. Their names alone were sufficient to make or break fortunes: John D. Rockefeller, J. Pierpont Morgan, Andrew Carnegie, William H. Vanderbilt, Henry C. Frick, Collis P. Huntington. "We have as yet nothing like it in England," Wilde would observe. "We call a man rich over there when he owns a share of Scotland, or a county or so." A few American titans, by themselves, were close to owning the entire country. At a time when the average worker brought home less than $900 a year, barely above the official poverty line of $560, the nation's richest man, John D. Rockefeller, was well on his way to becoming America's first billionaire, with annual profits of $81 million. (The spigot that turned Rockefeller's great wealth into an unstoppable torrent, Standard Oil Trust, was incorporated the same day that Oscar Wilde arrived in the United States.)[6]

As the Pullman train barreled south through New Jersey, the talk turned to literature, with the reporter wanting to know which American poets Wilde most admired. "I think that Walt Whitman and Emerson have given the world more than anyone else," Wilde replied. "I do so hope to meet Mr. Whitman. Perhaps he is not widely read in England, but England never appreciates a poet until he is dead." Wilde claimed that he and his good friends Rossetti, Swinburne, and William Morris sat around discussing Whitman's work. "There is something so Greek and sane about his poetry," said Wilde. "It is so universal, so comprehensive." Actually, Wilde had been an admirer of Whitman's long before he came down to London. His poet-mother had first read to him from *Leaves of Grass* when he was thirteen, and he and his undergraduate friends had carried around copies of that revolutionary masterpiece when they strolled through Oxford's various greenswards. Soon, he would get a chance to meet his hero in the flesh.[7]

As the train neared Philadelphia, Wilde again grew distracted and depressed by the scenery. Whitman and other poets, he said, had always been ahead of science, at least conceptually. Now he wondered, "Why does not science, instead of troubling itself about sunspots, which nobody ever saw, or, if they did, ought not to speak about—why does not science busy itself with drainage and sanitary engineering? Why does it not clean the streets and free the rivers from pollution? Why, in England there is scarcely a river at some point is not polluted; and the flowers are all withering on the banks!"[8]

A glimpse of Fairmount Park, where the 1876 World's Fair had been held, cheered up Wilde, and the final leg of the train ride over the elevated tracks into Philadelphia's Broad Street Station made him smile. Checking into the Aldine Hotel at four that afternoon, he grabbed a couple hours' rest before entertaining yet another reporter, this one from the *Philadelphia Inquirer.* Very quickly, he had learned the promotional value of the local press. Judging from the gushy article published in the newspaper the next day, Wilde had thoroughly charmed his new guest. Although few of his friends and none of his enemies considered him conventionally handsome or attractive—his idol Lillie Langtry termed him "large and colorless"—the presumably hardened Philadelphia reporter found Wilde's rather broad, flat face "thoroughly refined, and endowed with a liberal share of the beauty of expression. His head has something of the Gothic arched poetical outline, the nose is aquiline, the eyes bright blue, and clear and the mouth and chin are Hibernian, but of the highest Celtic type, and there is an air of refinement and gentle breeding pervading not only the face, but the entire man."[9]

Wilde quickly sought to demonstrate his good breeding. As he had done in his New York speech, he used the figure of John Keats to emblematize the lonely, suffering artist, making the questionable assertion that Keats "had the fellowship of no brother artists" during his short life. That would have come as news to Percy Shelley, Lord Byron, Leigh Hunt, and other leading Romantic poets, all of whom to one degree or another had mentored and befriended Keats; but the *Inquirer* reporter let it pass. "Our aim is to unite all artists in a brotherhood of art, and to draw closer together those who cultivate the beautiful," Wilde said. "This movement is designed in part to remove that isolation, to bring all artists, whether in painting, sculpture, music, or poetry, together, that they may aid each other in every way, and that each art may profit by the advance of its sister arts."[10]

Mindful of his location, Wilde stressed the democratic sentiments of the Aesthetes. "It is the most democratic impulse in the history of the world," he said modestly. "I don't know, of course, how it was in America, but we in England believe that the people, the artisan class have toiled long enough in unloved labor and amid unlovely, hard, repulsive surroundings. A man's work should be a joy to him." Sounding a little like Karl Marx, Wilde warned that "the toiling thousands of Great Britain are growing more and more dissatisfied every year with their dreary lives, filled only with incessant, unattractive toil. The problem of controlling them is only to be solved by making them happy in their labor, and brightening their lives with such material surroundings as it might be in power of art to bestow." Many Americans might have agreed with the first part of Wilde's formulation, if not his prescription for how to brighten their lives. Having endured a severe depression and a year-long series of bloody strikes a few years earlier, American workers were inured to long hours, low pay, and an unremitting state of class warfare between labor and capital. A few years later, in his long essay "The Soul of Man under Socialism," Wilde would call for an enlightened economic and political system that allowed men's innate individualism to flourish. Needless to say, the idea did not catch on in America.[11]

After the convivial opening, Wilde had a somewhat tetchy debate with the reporter over the comparative roles of artists and laborers, the reporter feeling the need to assure Wilde, a little tongue-in-cheek perhaps, that he "was not arguing but only seeking a clearer conception of the inner light. However happy it might make the loomhand to go into the fields and study the flowers for his patterns, or the stonecutter to imagine his groups of statuary, the tyranny of trade would prefer that the one should be in the stoneyard chipping at the marble for somebody else's designs, and the other hard at work in the factory keeping his loom in good running order." Wilde replied, a little weakly, that Aestheticism raised everyone "to a higher level," like that of the handicraftsmen in India, as though the specter of a Bombay basket weaver might somehow inspire a Philadelphia hod carrier to rush out and switch professions.[12]

Among Wilde's hosts in Philadelphia was publisher and editor Joseph M. Stoddart, who a few years later would bring out Wilde's only
novel, *The Picture of Dorian Gray*, in the pages of *Lippincott's Monthly
Magazine*. It was Stoddart who first recognized how potentially incendi-
ary Wilde's novel was, striking from the author's original typescript several graphic instances of implied homosexual content. Even so, Stoddart's editorial efforts did not sufficiently tame the novel to prevent it
from eliciting howls of outrage upon its publication in Great Britain.
Wilde would also prevail upon Stoddart to publish a collection of poetry by Wilde's old Oxford classmate (and fellow Newdigate Prize winner) Rennell Rodd, a good deed that, like many good deeds, did not go
unpunished. Rodd, well on his way to a career in the diplomatic service
that included a lengthy stint as British ambassador to Italy, took umbrage at Wilde's rather purple introduction to the book, *Rose Leaf and
Apple Leaf*. He was particularly nettled at the dedication that Wilde
made, in Rodd's name, to himself: "To Oscar Wilde, heart's brother . . ."
Rodd complained that the introduction made him seem like "a sort of
disciple" of Wilde's, and he eventually broke off their friendship. From
then on, Wilde considered Rodd a "true poet, and [a] false friend."[13]

Probably at Wilde's urging, Stoddart invited Walt Whitman to attend a reception in Wilde's honor on January 19. Whitman, a prematurely aged sixty-two, declined the invitation but sent along a calling
card announcing regally that "Walt Whitman will be in from 2 till 31/2
this afternoon, & will be most happy to see Mr. Wilde and Mr. Stoddart." At the time, Whitman was living with his brother George and
sister-in-law Lou in a three-story brick house at 431 Stevens Street, across
the Delaware River from Philadelphia in Camden, New Jersey. The
house, located on the corner of Stevens and West, was close enough to
the Camden and Amboy Railroad station to allow Whitman, who loved
spectacles, to watch as many as twenty trains a day unload and pick up
passengers. The ferry to Philadelphia was conveniently located a block
away, at the foot of Federal Street.[14]

Whitman had never entirely recovered from the serious paralytic stroke he had suffered in 1873 while working as a clerk in the Treasury Department in Washington, a job he had held for nearly a dozen years during and after the Civil War. The war years had "saved" Whitman—his word—by rescuing him from an idle bohemian existence in New York City and giving him a cause greater than himself to believe in. Going first to Washington to search for George, who had been wounded slightly at the Battle of Fredericksburg while serving with the 51st New York Regiment, Whitman had stayed to help "the boys," as he invariably called the young men serving in the Union Army. As a self-appointed visitor, Whitman had haunted the soldier hospitals in and around the nation's capital, making hundreds of visits and bringing the sick and wounded young soldiers the ineffable but not inconsiderable gift of his magnetic, consoling presence. His long white beard, wine-colored suit, and bulging knapsack of presents gave him a decided resemblance to Santa Claus, and he played the role to the hilt, bringing with him a sack full of humble but much appreciated gifts—candy, fruit, clothing, tobacco, books, magazines, pencils, and paper—to dispense to the convalescent and the dying. "Walt Whitman, Soldiers' Missionary," he styled himself proudly on the front of his wartime notebook.[15]

Whitman never forgot his soldier boys, but he increasingly worried that the nation as a whole, in its mad rush toward wealth and capital, had already forgotten them. "Future years will never know the seething hell and the black infernal background of the Secession War," he wrote in his 1875 reminiscence, *Memoranda During the War*. Like other thoughtful Americans, Whitman watched with a sort of wondering disgust the postwar scramble for money and power, "the almost maniacal appetite for wealth prevalent in the United States." Echoing Wilde's statement on the train ride down from New York, Whitman was even blunter and more despairing: "The depravity of the business classes of our country is not less than has been supposed, but infinitely greater," he wrote. "The official services of America, national, state, and municipal, are saturated in corruption, bribery, falsehood, maladministration. The best class we show, is but a mob of fashionably dress'd speculators and vulgarians." Even *Leaves of Grass,* the one-man pro-democracy movement that Whitman had been promulgating since its astonishing début in 1855, was now, in its latest edition, riddled with newfound angst: "Stifled, O days! O lands! In every public and private corruption! / Smother'd in thievery, impotence, shamelessness, mountain-high; / Brazen effrontery, scheming, rolling like ocean's waves around and upon you, O my days! My lands!"[16]

Fortunately, Wilde caught Whitman on one of his more upbeat days, taking the ferry across to Camden with Stoddart and arriving on Whitman's doorstep at precisely the appointed hour. Their advent was probably a good deal lower-key than Helen Gray Cone's witty parody in *Century* magazine a few months later, in which she has Whitman call out poetically: "Who may this be? / This young man clad unusually with loose locks, languorous glidingly toward me advancing, / Toward the ceiling of my chamber his orbic and expressive eye-balls unrolling?" Eye-rolling or not, Wilde made a gracious entrance. "I come as a poet to call upon a poet," he announced. "I have come to you as one with whom I have been acquainted almost from the cradle." The bit about reading him in the cradle must have stung, but Whitman was always happy to meet interesting, attractive young men. After making the introductions, Stoddart politely absented himself, and Wilde and Whitman spent the next two hours convivially sharing a bottle of Lou Whitman's home-made elderberry wine in the parlor downstairs before retiring to Whitman's third-floor study to talk of more elevated matters.[17]

With masts from the ships plying the Delaware River clearly visible through the window, Whitman's room seemed more like a seagoing captain's quarters than a poet's. There was a rough pine table on which Wilde noted pictures of Shakespeare and Dante, along with a small pitcher of water. Piles of newspapers—Whitman was an obsessive pack rat—filled every surface, so Wilde cleared off a stepstool to sit literally at Whitman's feet. Already they were on a first-name basis. "I will call you Oscar," the older man said, and Wilde placed his hand on Whitman's knee, replying, "I like that so much." How much of this was flirting and how much was simple wine-stoked bonhomie it is impossible to say, although it should be noted for the record that Wilde was not yet openly gay and Whitman, for all his groundbreaking frankness, never would be.[18]

The talk turned quickly to poets and poetry, with Wilde giving Whitman "many inside glimpses into the lives and doings of Swinburne, Dante Gabriel Rossetti, Morris, Tennyson and Browning." The fact that Wilde scarcely knew any of these other poets did not deter him from reassuring Whitman that the Aesthetes would go easy on them and not "shove the established idols aside." "We love him too much," Wilde said of Tennyson. That placated Whitman, who gave his qualified blessing to the movement. "I wish well to you, Oscar," he said, "and as to the Aesthetes, I can only say that you are young and ardent, and the field is wide, and if you want my advice, I say 'go ahead.'" He gave Wilde two complimentary photographs of himself, one for Wilde to keep, the other to pass along to Swinburne. Wilde would do so with all dispatch, earning him a fulsome thank-you note from Swinburne and a less gracious addendum from the whip-wielding poet to Wilde's newfound enemy Clarence Stedman, in which Swinburne described Wilde as "a harmless young nobody. I had no notion he was the sort of man to play the mountebank as he seems to be have been doing."[19]

Whitman, a former newspaper typesetter, told Wilde that he had always endeavored to make his verses "look all neat and pretty on the pages, like the epitaph on a square tombstone," which he demonstrated by sculpting the air for emphasis. Wilde was delighted by the gesture and later repeated it for others. When he ventured the starchy observation that he, Wilde, couldn't bear "to listen to anyone unless he attracts me by a charming style, or by beauty of theme," the older poet put him gently in his place. "Why, Oscar," said Whitman, "it always seems to me that the fellow who makes a dead set at beauty by itself is in a bad way. My idea is that beauty is a result, not an abstraction." Wilde quickly retreated. "Yes," he said, "I think so too."[20]

From there, the visit wound down. "Oscar, you must be thirsty,"

Whitman noted. "I'll make you some punch." If Wilde was expecting a fruity sort of English-afternoon concoction, he was surprised. Whitman came back with a glass of distinctly working-class American milk punch, a stoutish mixture of milk and whiskey. Wilde politely drank it at a gulp. Stoddart returned shortly to fetch Wilde back to Philadelphia. "Goodbye, Oscar," Whitman called from the front porch. "God bless you." Wilde promised to stop by again when he returned to Philadelphia in early May.[21]

On the carriage ride back to Wilde's hotel, Stoddart joked that the elderberry wine, at any rate, must have been hard to get down. "If it had been vinegar I should have drunk it all the same, for I have an admiration for that man which I can hardly express," Wilde said feelingly. "He is the grandest man I have ever seen, the simplest, most natural, and strongest character I have ever met in my life. I regard him as one of those wonderful, large, entire men who might have lived in any age and is not peculiar to any people." Whitman was somewhat less moved by the visit—he was after all the far greater poet—but he found Wilde "a great big, splendid boy, frank, outspoken, and manly. I don't see why such mocking things are written of him." Besides, as Whitman roguishly told another young acolyte, Henry Stafford, "Wilde had the good sense to take a great fancy to *me*."[22]

Wilde's Philadelphia lecture at Horticultural Hall did not go over as well as his visit to Whitman. If surroundings counted for anything, it should have been a rousing success. The hall, a holdover from the great Centennial Exhibition at Fairmount Park, featured rooms full of palm trees, cinnamon trees, yuccas trees, and gardenias. It was like being inside a hothouse nursery. But Philadelphia as a city was rather more conservative than New York, and many of the best people, although invited to attend, skipped Wilde's speech and an earlier reception at the home of Robert Stewart Davis, publisher of *Our Continent* magazine. Davis had sent out more than three hundred invitations, including one to the new president of the United States, Chester B. Arthur. The suave, cultured Arthur would have seemed like a natural to attend. A "spoilsman's spoilsman," as described in the press, Arthur owed his position first to New York senator Roscoe B. Conkling, who had forced James A. Garfield to put Arthur on the Republican ticket in 1880 as a compromise to conservative Stalwarts, and second to Charles J. Guiteau, who had shot Garfield, he said, in order to put a true Stalwart in the White House. One way or another, Arthur got the job. With the Guiteau trial nearing a climax, Arthur probably thought it his duty to remain in Washington for the verdict. Then, too, the president was already a notorious clothes horse and dandy—it was said that he changed clothes several times a day—and it would have only reinforced that image to be photographed standing next to an English poet in satin knee breeches. At any rate, the president stayed home at the White House.

For whatever reason, Wilde's gardenia-scented speech did not go over particularly well. Many of the city's swells were attending an opera that same evening at the more stylish Academy of Music, and the audience in the Horticultural Hall greeted Wilde with a giggle and a slight round of applause. It went downhill from there. As reported in the *Philadelphia Press,* "The audience listened at first with interest and then with sullen despair." When Wilde paused once to take a sip of water, the audience gave him an ironic round of applause, causing him to blush and momentarily lose his composure. The *Philadelphia Record*'s culture critic found Wilde's reception "most unenthusiastic." Wilde's face, said the critic, was "a blank from which the ponderous jaw was grinding out some dawdling chant." Unsurprisingly, Wilde pronounced himself dissatisfied with his reception in the City of Brotherly Love. "My hearers were so cold I several times thought of stopping and saying, 'You don't like this, and there is no use of my going on,'" he said. Afterwards, Wilde would describe Philadelphia as a city where the locals "judge a sculptor never by his statues but by the way he treats his wife; a painter by the amount of his income; and a poet by the color of his necktie." That it was the cradle of the Revolution did not help matters any with the British visitor.[23]

Things did not get any better for Wilde in Baltimore—in fact, they got demonstrably worse, compliments of a fellow D'Oyly Carte lecturer named Archibald Forbes. The peripatetic Forbes had made his reputation as a war correspondent, starting with the Franco-Prussian War of 1870–1871, when he had bet rightly on the Prussians to win the war and attached himself accordingly to Kaiser Wilhelm I's field headquarters. (Strange as it now seems, given the horrifying sweep of European military history in the next seventy-five years, most observers at the time thought that the French, under Napoleon III, would easily win the war.) The Scottish-born Forbes had washed out of the Royal Dragoons after five years of service; he found the other side of the cannon's mouth a good deal more congenial. During his first war, Forbes had demonstrated a knack for being in the right place at the right time. He had been standing around a French barn with Kaiser Wilhelm and Chancellor Otto von Bismarck when they received news of the great Prussian victory at Gravelotte, and a few weeks later he was the only English-speaking correspondent to personally witness Napoleon's surrender to Bismarck in a little weaver's cottage following the French debacle at Sedan. Thereafter, Forbes had switched locations, if not sides, sneaking into Paris to cover the rise of the Paris Commune and its swift decline, writing a remarkably graphic account of a communard's death at the hands of his reactionary fellow citizens. Forbes, being a true English gentleman, had tried to rescue the man from the ravening crowd, only to have the victim's brains splash cinematically onto his boots.

More splendid little wars had followed. Forbes got another worldwide scoop during the Russian-Turkish War of 1877, when he rode nonstop for three days and nights across the Russian steppes to personally deliver to Czar Alexander II the glad tidings of a Russian victory at Shipka Pass. The czar was so delighted with the news that he later bestowed on Forbes the Order of St. Stanislas, which found its place on Forbes's crowded chest alongside the Iron Cross, Second Class, for Noncombatants; the prestigious award Pour le Mérite, Civil Class; and the French Legion of Honor. Forbes had made another famous newsbearing ride two years later, during the nasty British war with the Zulus that brought the empire a horrific massacre of troops at Isandhlwana. Fortunately for Forbes, he was not there that day, or he would not have lived to write about it. After the ensuing Battle of Ulundi, he dashed through Zulu territory to bring news of the British victory there. The British commander, Lord Chelmsford, proving to be rather more of a stickler for military protocol than the continental Europeans, refused Forbes's application for a Victoria Cross, noting that Forbes had been also been carrying personal messages at the time. In Chelmsford's way of thinking, this made the correspondent more a mailman than a hero.

Wilde's trouble with the truculent Forbes began on the short train ride south from Philadelphia. Their mutual traveling secretary, Colonel Morse, had intended for Wilde to attend Forbes's lecture, "The Inner Life of a War Correspondent," in Baltimore, then make a joint appearance at a private reception hosted by local socialites Charles and Caroline Carroll at their elegant precolonial mansion, Doughoregan Manor. One can only imagine what Wilde would have made of Forbes's bloodthirsty talk, but the correspondent had already gone on record privately about his opinion of Wilde's appearance at Chickering Hall, writing to a female friend: "He wears knee breeches, but alas no lily. He can't lecture worth a cent, but he draws the crowds wonderfully and fools them all . . . which is quite clever." Wilde's crowd-drawing ability apparently moved Forbes to joke collegially on the train about the commercial potential of the Aesthetic Movement. This, in turn, provoked "a war of words" between the two, according to the Baltimore correspondent for the *New York Tribune,* who eagerly reported the incident the next day, adding that Wilde had refused to get off the train and continued on to Washington. Wilde blamed the mix-up on "the little wretched clerk or office boy" Morse had sent to meet him in Philadelphia, who, said Wilde, had instructed him to go straight through to Washington without stopping in Baltimore. Whatever the case, a mortified Mrs. Carroll was left with a lily- and sunflower-bedecked portico, a house full of well-dressed guests, and no Oscar Wilde.[24]

For the record, both Wilde and Forbes denied the tiff, but the old warrior was sufficiently provoked to insert a rare ad lib into his speech that night. Describing his 150-mile ride across Russia four years earlier, Forbes observed: "Now I wish it understood that I am a follower—a very humble follower—of the aesthetic ecstasy, but I did not look much like an art object then. I did not have my dogskin knee breeches with me nor my velvet coat, and my black silk stockings were full of holes. Neither was the wild, barren waste of Russia calculated to produce sunflowers and lilies."[25]

Once again, the newspapers were happy to prolong the feud, with the *Washington Post* quoting Wilde the next day as saying that he had never intended to go to Forbes's lecture in the first place, since "our views are wide apart. If it amuses him to caricature me in the manner which he did last night, well and good. It may serve a purpose, and judging from the fact, as stated, that his audience came to see me, it is answering one very good purpose. It is advertising Mr. Forbes at my expense." Since they were both horses from the same stable, so to speak, such reasoning did not endear Wilde to either his backer or his stablemate, who demanded that the poet retract his statement immediately. Writing to Forbes from his room at the Arlington Hotel in Washington, Wilde was unrepentant. "I feel bound to say quite frankly to you that I do not consider [your remarks] to be either in good taste or appropriate to your subject. I have something to say to the American people, something that I know will be the beginning of a great movement here, and all foolish ridicule does a great deal of harm to the cause of art and refinement and civilization here." Calling Forbes's remarks "poor fooling," Wilde advised him in the best Dutch-uncle style to omit them from his future lectures.[26]

Back and forth flew more letters. D'Oyly Carte was no help, having betaken himself to Jacksonville, Florida—as well he might—for his health. Colonel Morse, left squarely in the middle, made matters worse by asking for a $300 appearance fee for Wilde to lecture at Baltimore's exclusive Wednesday Club. Again, Wilde professed no knowledge of the arrangements, saying that he had never heard of the club in question.

With Forbes still making ominous noises about dealing with Wilde personally, the poet had the delayed inspiration to write to London solicitor George Lewis, who handled legal affairs for both parties, and ask him to tell Forbes in effect to cease and desist. Lewis complied immediately. "Like a good fellow don't attack Wilde," Lewis wired the growly war correspondent. "I ask this personal favour to me."[27]

That did the trick, at least publicly, and Forbes quit threatening to brain Wilde on sight. Behind the scenes, however, the old jingo continued to hold a grudge, repeating the false if entirely plausible rumor that P. T. Barnum had offered Wilde £200 to ride Jumbo the Elephant down Broadway with a sunflower and lily in either hand. Wilde, for his part, wrote a letter to the editor of the *Baltimore American,* again attributing the confusion to the phantom office boy and praying, without quite apologizing, that "I would not wish it to be thought that I could willingly be capable of any such unpardonable rudeness as your papers would seem seriously to charge me with." Privately, he groused to D'Oyly Carte that "another such fiasco as the Baltimore business and I think I would stop lecturing."[28]

Washington was no better, at least at first. Besides having to deal with nine reporters, eight telegrams, and eighteen letters, all without the help of Morse's useless young office assistant, Wilde complained (with some reason) about "the really brutal attacks" of the local newspapers. He had scarcely moved into the Arlington Hotel when he opened the *Washington Post* to a half-page drawing of him limp-wristedly holding a sunflower immediately below an identically posed missing link, "Mr. Wild of Borneo," holding a coconut. "How far is it from this to this?" the newspaper asked in a trailing headline between the drawings.

> We present in close juxtaposition this picture of Mr. Wilde of England and a citizen of Borneo, who, so far as we have any record of him, is also Wild, and judging from the resemblance in feature, pose and occupation, undoubtedly akin. If Mr. Darwin is right in his theory, has not the climax of evolution been reached and are we not heading down the hill toward the aboriginal starting point again? Certainly, a more inane object than Mr. Wilde, of England, has never

challenged our attention. Mr. Wild of Borneo doesn't lecture, however, and that much should be remembered to his credit.[29]

Ignoring two of the experienced showman's guiding tenets—that
any publicity is good publicity and that it is a mug's game to get into a
war of words with any newspaper, which, as Mark Twain once observed,
buys its ink by the barrel—Morse fired off an angry complaint, accusing
the *Post* of gratuitous malice, prejudice, bad judgment, and ill taste. Delighted with the reaction, the newspaper cavalierly denied "that we had
done Mr. Wilde an injustice by publishing his picture in conjunction
with that of his relative from Borneo," although it was possible "that we
may have done an injustice to the Borneo chap. *His* friends have not yet
been heard from." A subsequent *Post* review of Wilde's lecture at Lincoln Hall found—no surprise—that the appearance had been a failure.
Wilde's speech, said the reviewer, had been "severely commonplace and
kaleidoscopic," and the audience had been yawningly distracted before
"many arose and left." Not to be outdone, the *Washington Star* said
Wilde had exhibited "the attitude of an idle street boy watching a procession. . . . He has little or nothing worth saying." A few days later
Harper's Weekly ran a drawing of "The Aesthetic Monkey," showing an
ape in Wilde's familiar velvet suit, Byronic collar, and dapper cravat
moonily contemplating an enormous sunflower in a vase. A lily lay close
to hand, by his left elbow.[30]

Wilde, no neophyte when it came to the press, immediately sensed
that there had been a sudden and ominous shift in newspaper coverage.
The largely good-natured reporters who had braved the oily brine of
New York harbor to hail his arrival a few weeks earlier had been replaced
by editorial writers comparing him to aboriginal chimps and missing
links, and reviewers who encouraged the audience at his lectures to
laugh *at* him, rather than with him. "The whole tide of feeling is
turned," he fretted to D'Oyly Carte. "We must be very careful for the
future."[31]

It was good advice, but Wilde did not follow it. Instead, he delivered a stern tongue-lashing to a visiting reporter from the *New York Her-*

ald, saying that he had "heard much about the character of American journalism in England. If you expect English gentlemen to come to your country, especially gentlemen of letters and art, you must improve the character of your journalism." Wilde said that if he lived ten thousand years—and he modestly thought that his poems "may get me something like immortality"—he might get around to correcting some of the misstatements made about him personally and the Aesthetic Movement in general. He joked about catechizing a young Washington correspondent for various western newspapers—a fellow whom he judged to be about fifteen years old: "I asked him if he had been to school. He said he had left school some time since. I asked if he knew French. He said no. I advised him to learn French and counseled him a little as to what books to read. At last I gave him an orange and then sent him away. What he did with the orange I don't know; he seemed pleased to get it."[32]

Fortunately for Wilde, he did not have to depend on the local press to get noticed in the nation's capital. Thanks to that supreme political fixer Sam Ward, he gained easy access to the top level of Washington politics, at least on the Republican side, which until Grover Cleveland's upset victory in the presidential campaign two years hence was the only side that mattered, anyway. He was taken in hand by New Jersey congressman George Maxwell Robeson, who had been secretary of the navy under Ulysses S. Grant and who had managed the difficult feat, in Grant's administration, of not being indicted for fraud or other crimes. It wasn't exactly for lack of trying. Two separate congressional investigations had probed alleged kickbacks to Robeson from government contractors, including one highly suspicious and damningly specific payment of $320,000 from the firm of Alexander Cattell & Company, money which Robeson apparently used to purchase a seaside cottage at Long Branch, New Jersey, the same village where Grant kept a summer home. Robeson had survived the investigations without a scratch and now was serving as chairman of the Republican caucus, a ruddy-faced old gentleman with a drooping walrus mustache and side whiskers, like President Arthur.

Often described in the Washington press as looking like an English lord, Robeson took to the aristocratic Wilde immediately, squiring him about town in a carriage and pointing out the various touristy landmarks, invariably dotted with statues of the nation's military elite. "I think you have taken quite enough motives from war," Wilde advised. "You don't want any more bronze generals on horseback, I dare say. Suppose you try the motives that peace will give you now." And when he looked more closely at the statuary, the visitor expressed the wish that such sculpture might be done away with altogether. "To see the frock coat of the drawing-room done into bronze, or the double waistcoat perpetuated in marble," Wilde said, "adds a new horror to death."[33]

Mary Robeson, serving as her husband's second, led Wilde on a dizzying round of diplomatic visits, including a stop at the exclusive Bachelor's Club, where Wilde made his entrance "trying to make his eyes roll with poetic fervor," according to a woman reporter in attendance for the *Washington Star*. Once inside, Wilde met the scions of two legendary political families: secretary of war Robert Lincoln, the martyred president's eldest son, and Nellie Grant Sartoris, daughter of General and Mrs. Grant and the unhappily married (and later divorced) spouse of an English wastrel, spendthrift, and all-around abusive cad with the perfectly Wildean name of Algernon Sartoris. At the club, Wilde declined all invitations to dance, even with Mrs. Sartoris, noting in what the Americans heard as a broad British drawl: "I have dined, so I don't dawnce. Those who dawnce don't dine."[34]

At another star-studded reception hosted by Judge Edward G. Loring—the controversial jurist from Massachusetts who three decades earlier had occasioned a riot in his hometown of Boston by ordering an escaped slave named Anthony Burns returned to his Virginia owner—Wilde inadvertently made another enemy. Also in attendance that afternoon was another illustrious Londoner: the transplanted American writer Henry James, who was returning home for a brief visit after six years abroad. Robeson had recently taken the thirty-eight-year-old James to dinner with the president of the United States, who according to James had spent the entire dinner confusing him with his much-older uncle, the Reverend William James. The author, who had just published his sixth novel, *The Portrait of a Lady*, was already predisposed to dislike Wilde. A naturally shy, impeccably buttoned-down individual, James was a carefully closeted homosexual who found Wilde's outré personality, while not yet openly gay, altogether too flamboyant for comfort. The enormous yellow silk handkerchief and knee breeches Wilde wore to the reception didn't help matters any with James.

"'Hosscar' Wilde is a fatuous fool, a tenth-rate cad, and an unclean beast," James seethed to his troubled friend Clover Adams, the wife of author Henry Adams. Clover, the model for James's spirited and betrayed heroines Daisy Miller and Isabel Archer, was herself being betrayed that winter by her husband, who was carrying on an affair with their neighbor Lizzie Cameron, the much-younger wife of Pennsylvania senator David Cameron. Mrs. Adams put down Wilde's sexual preference as "undecided" and gratuitously termed him "a noodle," meaning apparently that he was impotent, or at any rate uninterested in sex. She resolutely refused to entertain him at her glittering salon on Lafayette Square, across from the White House, during his stay in Washington. Three years later, Clover, an amateur photographer, would kill herself by drinking potassium cyanide, a compound widely used as a developer in darkrooms. Her historian husband, usually so concerned with the past, quickly expunged all photographs, letters, and mentions of Clover from his personal papers, disappearing her as effectively as she had disappeared herself.[35]

No one paid any attention to Wilde at Judge Loring's reception, James maintained, though Loring's own daughter, Margaret, remembered it differently. Henry James, she told a friend, was "so boring," while Oscar Wilde was "so amusing"—another mark against Wilde in James's mental ledger book. But although Wilde would later famously say of James that he wrote fiction as though it were "a painful duty," at the time he had nothing but praise for the still-maturing novelist, telling a reporter that "no living Englishman can be compared to [William Dean] Howells and James as novelists." Howells, the acknowledged "dean of American letters," heard the quote and responded graciously that "Wilde would have invented literature if it had never existed." Wilde may not have known of Howells's compliment; he never responded. About that same time, however, a fellow wit, San Francisco journalist Ambrose Bierce, heard that Howells had called Bierce one of the three best writers in America. "I suppose Mr. Howells is the other two," said Bierce.[36]

Swallowing his dislike for Wilde, James called on the poet at the Arlington Hotel to thank him personally for his favorable reviews of *Washington Square* and *The Portrait of a Lady*. Things quickly went south. Seeking common ground, James talked of their adopted hometown, remarking mildly, "I am very nostalgic for London." "Really?" said Wilde. "You care for places? The world is my home." Something about James apparently brought out the worst in Wilde, who further offended his modest guest by ostentatiously name-dropping Charles Eliot Norton and Edward Burne-Jones, both of whom James knew far better than the parvenu Wilde knew them. James tried again. What were Wilde's immediate plans? "I don't know," said Wilde. "I never make plans, but go whither my feelings prompt." (In his 1888 novel, *The Tragic Muse,* James would get a measure of revenge, fictionalizing Wilde as the rootless aesthete Gabriel Nash, who is always pining to be somewhere else—"Where there's anything to feel I try to be there"—and exclaiming, "I rove, drift, float.")[37]

For the time being, the two writers, so different in temperament, style, and appearance, parted on polite if chilly terms. James would sponsor Wilde for membership in London's Savile Club a few years later (the effort failed), but he was always careful to note that the two were not really friends. Whatever slight friendship there may have been would not survive the catastrophic failure in 1895 of James's play *Guy Domville,* which had the dual ignominy of seeing the playwright hissed during his own curtain call and of being upstaged by Wilde's masterpiece, *The Importance of Being Earnest,* which replaced James's play during its London run at the St. James Theatre a few weeks later.

Wilde had more luck with a less-gifted but better-selling novelist,

Frances Hodgson Burnett, author of *The Little Princess, The Secret Garden,* and *Little Lord Fauntleroy,* which might almost have been a Wildean pseudonym. Attending a meeting of the Washington Literary Society at Burnett's fashionable home on I Street, NW, Wilde charmed the author by telling her that John Ruskin was big fan of hers and read everything she wrote. Yet another transplanted Briton, Burnett was a Lancashire lass who had immigrated to Tennessee as a teenager and married the lame but ambitious son of a Knoxville neighbor. She and her physician husband, Swan Burnett, had moved to Washington, where their home soon became a meeting place for social, literary, and political leaders in the nation's capital. Mrs. Burnett stole Wilde away from Mrs. Robeson and her other guests, waving them off with a dismissive, "I can see the rest of you at other times." Another Washington hostess, the wife of senator George H. Pendleton, made Wilde laugh out loud by responding to his lament that Americans had "no ruins, no natural curiosities, in this country." "Our ruins will come soon enough," Mrs. Pendleton said, "and we import our curiosities."[38]

Wilde could afford to be amused. Despite his somewhat poor critical reception in Philadelphia, Baltimore, and Washington, he had personally met and charmed some of the eastern seaboard's most important players, from Abraham Lincoln's son and Ulysses S. Grant's daughter to a motley cavalcade of politicians, lobbyists, scene setters, gate crashers, and taste makers. He had hoisted cups with Walt Whitman, traded barbs with Henry James, and survived a nasty war of words with the Prussians' favorite front-line correspondent, Archibald Forbes. And he had done so while standing up to a suddenly hostile press, taking its worst barbs with general grace and humor and putting the worst offenders deservedly in their places. It was good training for the next leg of Wilde's tour, which would bring him north to the true capital of the United States—at least in the minds of its patrician dwellers. He was going to Boston to beard the lions.

CHAPTER 4

What Would Thoreau Have Said to My Hat-Box!

❦

WILDE JOURNEYED to Boston via train by way of Albany, New York, where he lectured again on the English Renaissance to a sparse but receptive crowd at the Albany Music Hall. He then attended a reception at the Windsor Hotel, before returning to his room at the Delavan. Besieged by autograph hounds in the lobby, he sat down at a desk to sign the proffered slips of paper, joking, "I hope that I am obliging beautiful young ladies, for I make it a point to grant my autographs to no others." Soon, reporters were calling it "Wilde's policy," although he would actually sign anything for anyone—beautiful or not—unless they were too rude or overbearing in their demands.[1]

Already, Wilde had gone to some lengths to cultivate his female fans. Whether for show, out of simple good manners, or from a genuine interest in the opposite sex that would eventually give way to stronger same-sex attraction, Wilde in 1882 still displayed a fine eye for feminine beauty. He had been in love twice before with beautiful young women, not counting his histrionic public courting of Lillie Langtry in London. In 1877, back in Ireland, he had met blonde-haired, gray-eyed, seventeen-year-old Florence Balcombe, the dowryless daughter of a retired Crimean War lieutenant colonel who had named her in honor of that war's ministering angel, Florence Nightingale. Wilde had courted Florrie for two years while he was at Oxford, giving her a gold cross with his name on it. She had, he gushed to his friend Reginald (Kitten) Harding, "the most perfectly beautiful face I ever saw," notwithstanding the fact that she had "not a sixpence of money." Wilde's journalistic rival, George Du Maurier, agreed, later calling Florrie Balcombe one of the three most beautiful women he had ever seen.[2]

In the end, Florrie threw over Wilde for one of his old school friends, Bram Stoker, who was still several years away from writing his immortal ode to the undead, *Dracula.* When news of their engagement became public—Florrie hadn't bothered telling him herself—Wilde asked for his gold cross back, pointing out a little dryly that she could scarcely wear his name around her neck anymore. In January 1881, when Florrie made her stage début as a vestal virgin in Henry Irving's production of Lord Tennyson's drama *The Cup,* Wilde sent her a crown of flowers via actress Ellen Terry, asking Terry to give them to Florrie anonymously just before she went on stage. "I should like to think that she was wearing something of mine the first night she comes on the stage," said Wilde. "She thinks I never loved her, thinks I forget. My God how could I!" Years later, Florence Balcombe Stoker would become infamous in film circles for attempting to destroy all existing prints of W. F. Murnau's 1922 silent-film masterpiece, *Nosferatu,* after the director had failed to secure the necessary legal rights to the use of her late husband's novel. Happily for cinéastes, if not for Mrs. Stoker, a few stray prints survived her purging, and *Nosferatu,* like its source material, remains perennially undead.[3]

Wilde's second love was Violet Hunt, the willowy daughter of English landscape painter Alfred William Hunt and novelist Margaret Hunt, who was said to be the model for Tennyson's poem "Margaret." If one can judge by her photographs, Miss Hunt was even lovelier than Miss Balcombe—no small feat—and also younger, being just sixteen when Wilde met her in London in 1879. The precocious Violet was studying art at the Kensington Art School and already writing poetry and fiction. Ellen Terry, herself perhaps the most beautiful actress on the London stage, sportingly rated Violet as being "out of Botticelli by Burne-Jones." Wilde called her "the sweetest violet in England" and promised, "We will rule the world, you and I, you with your looks and I with my wits." Studying a map of Africa one day, he suggested on the spur of the moment that they run off together to the Dark Continent. "What, and get eaten by lions?" the more pragmatic Violet wondered. She, too, refused Wilde's marriage offer, finding him amusing but physically unattractive, "a slightly stuttering, slightly lisping, long-limbed boy." In the end, Violet Hunt married no one, although she lived for several years with English novelist Ford Maddox Ford, who had changed his last name from Hueffer to honor his uncle, Ford Maddox Brown. Like her mother, Violet became a novelist, and her long list of literary lovers, besides Ford Madox Ford, included H. G. Wells and Somerset Maugham.[4]

Florrie Balcombe and Violet Hunt were both in the distant past for Wilde when he arrived in Boston on the morning of Saturday, January 28, 1882, after an all-night train ride from Albany. He checked into the Vendome Hotel in the Back Bay section of the city and, as was becoming his custom, sat down immediately for an interview with a reporter, this one from the *Boston Herald.* The meeting took place in the parlor of his friend Dion Boucicault, who had an adjoining suite at the Vendome. Boucicault, whose full first name was Dionysius, knew the Wildes from his boyhood in Dublin, when he had been a frequent visitor to their home on Merrion Square. A popular playwright whose works included *The Corsican Brothers, The Vampire, The Relief of Lucknow,* and a successful remounting of Washington Irving's *Rip Van Winkle* with American actor Joseph Jefferson in the title role, Boucicault trod the boards himself, specializing in "pathetic" roles as forgotten men, hoboes, and other societal throwaways. He was married to the actress Agnes Robertson, the ward of British Shakespearean actor Charles Kean. Prefiguring by a decade Wilde's own ruinous scandal, Boucicault would outrage proper society three years later by eloping with a twenty-one-year-old actress named Josephine Thorndyke while on tour in Australia. The fact that his first marriage would not be annulled for another three years created bad feelings and bad publicity all around, and the courts attached Boucicault's hefty theatrical earnings as alimony payments to the quite publicly wronged Mrs. Boucicault.

Boucicault had been planning to direct Wilde's unproduced play, *Vera,* before it was canceled on the eve of its London début, and Wilde hoped to bring him back on board during his visit to America. The older, more experienced Boucicault fretted about Wilde's rough treatment in the press, telling one reporter hotly: "Have you met Mr. Wilde? No? Then of course you know very little about what sort of man he is. The press seems to lend itself to this heartless exhibition which may afford amusement to some, but will be fatal and ruinous to its object. Those who have known him as I have since he was a child at my knee know that beneath the fantastic envelope in which his managers are circulating him there is a noble, earnest, kind and lovable man." Now, on self-appointed guard duty, he sat in on Wilde's interview with the *Herald.*[5]

After some pleasantries about the weather and the countryside, Wilde expressed the desire "to see in New England many fine old houses like the 'Seven Gables.'" The reporter wanted to know what Wilde thought of Nathaniel Hawthorne, two decades after the author's death. "I admire Hawthorne greatly," said Wilde. "I think his *Scarlet Letter* has the grandest passion and is the greatest work of fiction ever written in the English tongue." Wilde had met the late novelist's son and literary executor, Julian, along with Julian's wife, Minnie, in London in 1879, but he was unable to get over to see them in Concord during his stay in Boston. He hoped to return to New England "in the time of flowers," but was unsure if he would be able to do so. "I never have any plans in seeing a country," said Wilde. "When it pleases me I stay, and go away when it ceases to please me."[6]

The talk turned to politics. Wilde mentioned that he had visited many political leaders in Washington, including former Speaker of the House James G. Blaine, who was laying the groundwork for his ultimately unsuccessful presidential bid in 1884. Wilde professed to being confused by the names of the American political parties, Republican and Democratic, which he deemed less precise than those of the Conservative and Liberal parties in England. Wilde wondered at the profusion of political classes in America. "They have one class here, the moneyed class," said Boucicault. Wilde repeated his earlier observation about the "enormous capitalists" in America, noting that "the moneyed interests are more solid in England, because the wealth is in the land, which has a fixed value." "Not in Ireland," Boucicault butted in. "That has a very unfixed value." The two agreed on the promise of American sculpture, which Wilde thought was the wave of the future for American artists, since "your clear, transparent atmosphere is best adapted to the grandest sculpturesque effects. In England, in our damp, dripping atmosphere, sculpture has a dreary look."[7]

In response to another question, Wilde said that he thought the most beautiful women in the world were to be found in London. "In England there is now a passionate love of physical beauty," he observed, perhaps with Lillie Langtry in mind, "so that if a woman there is very beautiful, she becomes, just on that account, as celebrated as a great poet or a great artist." He added smoothly that "here in America I find a vast amount of pretty women, and the greatest number I have ever seen together in my life thus far I have seen in Baltimore; it was at the Wednesday Club, where I was entertained last week." Boucicault ventured the opinion that there was a good deal of "fine Irish blood in the old Baltimore stock," which he said accounted for the large number of female beauties there. The interview concluded with Boucicault once again denouncing the press's treatment of Wilde, comparing it to the abuse poured on the Pre-Raphaelites twenty-five years earlier. Wilde, said Boucicault, had become "an object of ridicule, no slanders and malicious lies being too atrocious for certain people to invent." Wilde took a more expansive view, saying the attacks were harming not him, but rather the American public at large, since the true artist "goes his way and produces his work. An artist should not listen to, nor heed, ridicule and abuse."[8]

Utilizing a letter of introduction from Boston poet James Russell Lowell, the current American ambassador to Great Britain, Wilde got himself invited to lunch by Dr. Oliver Wendell Holmes at a meeting of the distinguished literary group the Saturday Club at the Parker House on Tremont Street. A nearby saloon featured a sunflower-bordered poster advertising an "aesthetic cocktail." The Saturday Club, founded in 1855, met every fourth Saturday of the month to discuss literature, art, and politics—not necessarily in that order. By the late winter of 1882, Boston had gradually lost its preeminent position in all three. Holmes and his fellow Brahmin rulers of Boston literary society—Ralph Waldo Emerson, Henry Wadsworth Longfellow, and John Greenleaf Whittier—were all old men. Nathaniel Hawthorne and Henry David Thoreau were long since dead; Lowell had traded literature for politics and moved to Europe. Even William Dean Howells, until recently the all-powerful editor of the *Atlantic Monthly,* was publishing his novels in New York City and pondering relocation to the Big Apple.

The New England Flowering, as it had been known, was curling into dust on the mantelpiece while a dominant new literary school, realism, was blossoming brightly in the garden outside. Howells, Henry James, and Howells's best friend, Samuel L. Clemens, writing as Mark Twain, were leading the way. Indeed, Twain had inadvertently signaled the passing of the New Englanders four years earlier, with his hilarious if poorly received speech at Whittier's seventieth birthday party at Boston's tony Brunswick Hotel on December 17, 1877. During his speech, which an embarrassed Howells considered nothing less than "a sort of demonic possession," Twain pretended to confuse the triply named "Augustans" (Longfellow, Emerson, and Holmes) with a trio of disreputable western gold prospectors. Twain had briefly been a prospector himself before finding gold in his fountain pen, and his rise, like that of Howells, reflected the advent of a more democratic and middle-class literature. The new school, said Howells, aimed for "nothing more and nothing less than the truthful treatment of material." Fiction should "cease to lie about life; let it portray men and women as they are, actuated by the motives and the passions in the measure we all know." Howells's own next novel, *A Modern Instance,* would be one of the first to deal frankly with the subject of divorce—scarcely one of the "more smiling aspects" of life that the author usually championed.[9]

Wilde, to his credit, seemed to sense the new direction in American literature, as evidenced by his praise of Whitman, Howells, and James. It was not the sort of literature he would produce himself—there was not a middle-class bone in Wilde's body—but it was inarguably new, and that was the pole star by which Wilde navigated. Still, he was eager to pay homage to the older Bostonians, even if a recent cartoon in the *New York Daily Graphic* depicted a starchy Beacon Hill matron turning up her nose at the sunflower-offering British visitor and sniffing: "No, Sir. Shoddy New York may receive you with open arms, but we have an Aestheticism of our own." Holmes and his fellows at the Saturday Club were more welcoming, if no less starchy, and Wilde made the acquaintance at lunch of clergymen James Freeman Clarke and Phillips Brooks, the latter of whom served briefly as Episcopal bishop of Massachusetts. It was, Wilde said with polite exaggeration, "a bright party of men at Dr. Holmes's."[10]

That same night, Wilde had supper with John Boyle O'Reilly, part owner of the *Boston Pilot,* who presented him at the two-year-old St. Botolph Club, named for the seventh-century abbot who had founded a monastery in the fens of East Anglia's Botolph Town, which had given its name (in corrupted form) to Boston. O'Reilly was a fabulous Irish patriot and adventurer. A founding member of the Irish Republican Brotherhood, or Fenians, he had been captured by the British as a young man and sentenced to twenty years' hard labor in western Australia.

Transported to the Antipodes aboard the notorious convict ship *Hougoumont,* which was making the final forced relocation of British convicts to Australia, O'Reilly escaped from captivity one year later via friendly American whaling ships and resettled in Boston, where he became editor and part owner of *The Pilot,* the unofficial mouthpiece of the Catholic Church in America. Said to be John F. Kennedy's favorite poet, O'Reilly would meet an inglorious death eight years after his evening with Wilde when he took an accidental overdose of his wife's chloral hydrate during a restless bout of insomnia.

For the present, O'Reilly led Wilde on another round of visits, including a performance of Aeschylus's *Oedipus Tyrannus* at the Globe Theatre, a performance that Wilde found lacking, since only one of the parts was performed in the original Greek. Afterwards, O'Reilly took his young charge to a meeting of the Papyrus Club at the home of Dr. James Read Chadwick, a colleague of Holmes on the faculty of Harvard Medical School. Among those Wilde saw at the Papyrus Club was a familiar face, Francis Marion Crawford, the wandering nephew of Sam Ward and Julia Ward Howe. Crawford, who had recently returned from a two-year sojourn in India, where he edited the *Indian Herald* in Allahabad, was living with his illustrious widowed aunt at her home in Boston while he resumed his study of Sanskrit at Harvard. When Crawford heard that Wilde wanted to meet Howe, he immediately extended an invitation in her behalf.

At some point in the evening, Wilde sat down for two more newspaper interviews at the Vendome. Boucicault was occupied with performing in a trilogy of his Gaelic-language plays at the Boston Museum, on Tremont Street, leaving Wilde on his own with the visiting reporters. The first, representing the *Boston Globe,* described "Oscar" on a first-name basis as having "large, mobile, and passably good-looking features, with full eyes that appear to languish but are really very shrewd and all-observing." Wilde made the improbable assertion that he didn't much read what was written about him in American newspapers, a claim that he immediately contradicted by denouncing the "scandalous treatment" he had received at the hands of "a Baltimore sheet, a rag of a news-paper." He added, "American papers are often a screed of falsehoods," a declaration that caused the *Globe* reporter to figuratively roll his eyes for his readers while Wilde fretted about what the reporter duly categorized as "the unfathomable frivolity and depravity of the American press." Through it all, wrote the reporter, Wilde's own eyes shone with an amused glint that "seemed to intimate that he very well understood the advantage of free advertising, and didn't so much care whether he was represented or misrepresented, as long as he was as far from a failure as at present." It was a sophisticated analysis of Wilde's pioneering ap-proach to publicity.[11]

If the *Globe* reporter was gently skeptical of Wilde's effects, the lit-erary editor of the *Boston Evening Traveler* was actively dismissive. Thirty-five-year-old Lilian Whiting, a descendant of Puritan zealot Cot-ton Mather and a poet herself, made it clear in an article reprinted in the *Chicago Inter-Ocean* on February 10 that she didn't think much of "the lily-laden lyrist." Wilde got off to a bad start by repeating "from some supremely poetical perception . . . tales of the atrocity of the American press." Whiting, whose father was a newspaper editor in Illi-nois, had grown up around newspapers and was notably unmoved by the complaints—she compared herself to Desdemona listening to Othello's paranoid rants. She did concede that Wilde "has been greatly misprinted, his individualities caricatured, his tastes exaggerated, his ap-pearance burlesqued. He is not great enough to merit so much atten-tion, and he is not necessarily an object of ridicule."[12]

What really set off Whiting was Wilde's "conceited" notion that he had anything to teach Americans such as Miss Whiting about art. "The American people need no missionary to proclaim to them the latest thought in England," Whiting grumped. "It is very probable that Mr. Wilde might learn rather than teach, while here." Like her Puritan ancestor, Whiting was also something of a mystic, though her own reli-gious revelations centered on the modish New Thought movement, a metaphysical approach to life and death which, in Whiting's view, rather blurred the border between the two. She was an indefatigable pilgrim to the other side, and the titles of her books reflect her New Age sort of philosophy: *Spiritual Significance: or, Death as an Event of Life; After Her Death: The Story of a Summer; The Life Radiant; The World Beautiful; The Golden Road; They Who Understand; The Joy That No Man Taketh from You;* and a volume of poems, *From Dreamland Sent,* that is exactly as bad as its title implies.[13]

On the last day of January, the morning of his scheduled speech at the Boston Music Hall, Wilde went to call on a decidedly better poet, Henry Wadsworth Longfellow, in a driving snowstorm. "I went to see Longfellow in a snow storm and returned in a hurricane, quite the right conditions for a visit to a poet," he remembered later. Longfellow, then seventy-four, had been quoted in the *Boston Evening Traveler* the day before as saying that "Mr. Wilde has written some good verses. He cannot be an ignorant man." Increasingly unwell—he would die two months later of peritonitis—Longfellow had resisted meeting Wilde, but Sam Ward's recommendation at length opened the door to the poet's Cambridge home, across the Charles River from Boston proper.[14]

Wilde's visit to Longfellow, unlike his pilgrimage to Camden to meet Walt Whitman, was more a courtesy call than an act of homage. Longfellow, Wilde said privately to freelance journalist Chris Healy, was "a great poet only for those who never read poetry." His Americanized transposition of English rhymes to frontier settings and homespun subjects such as Hiawatha, Evangeline, Miles Standish, village blacksmiths, and New England snowstorms was unlikely to delight the Oxford-trained ear of Wilde, but as usual the young visitor was courtly and deferential to his elders. What did Longfellow think of Robert Browning, Wilde wanted to know. "I like him well, what I can understand of him," said Longfellow. "Capital," said Wilde. "I must remember that to repeat." (You will, Oscar, you will, one hears James McNeil Whistler saying from across the Atlantic.) He roared with laughter at Longfellow's account of his meeting with Queen Victoria, years earlier, at Windsor Castle, during which Her Majesty evinced some familiarity with Longfellow's work. "Oh, I assure you, Mr. Longfellow, you are very well known," said the queen. "All my servants read you." Longfellow told Wilde he still lay in bed at night wondering if the royal remarks had been praise, or a subtle put-down. "It was the rebuke of Majesty to the vanity of the poet," Wilde explained later to fellow writer Vincent O'Sullivan.[15]

Wilde's own vanity was about to be challenged by a squadron of Harvard pranksters, but he would be ready for them. When he prepared to walk out on stage at the Boston Music Hall on January 31, the auditorium was full, notwithstanding a heavy snowstorm that interrupted carriage traffic. Julia Ward Howe was there, along with a large contingent of other women attendees. The two front rows, however, were strangely empty. Tipped off in advance—the newspapers had been full of warnings about the unruly behavior of Harvard undergraduates in the past—Wilde delayed his entrance backstage for fifteen minutes past the eight o'clock starting time. By then, the empty seats had been filled by a madcap procession of sixty Harvard men who marched down the center aisle in pairs, all carrying sunflowers and wearing Wildean costumes of knee breeches, black stockings, wide-spreading cravats, and shoulder-length wigs.

Julia Ward Howe was aghast to see her favorite grand-nephew, Winthrop Astor Chanler (Class of '86), at the forefront of the procession. "Wintie" Chanler was Sam Ward's grandson; his father was the late Democratic congressman John Astor Chanler. The younger Chanler was one of the eight famous "Astor Orphans" who had been left parentless before the age of fourteen by the early deaths, from pneumonia, of both their mother and father, within two months of each other. Each orphan had a legacy of $20,000 a year from the Astor estate, which Wintie used chiefly to finance a lifelong career as a fox hunter and country squire, broken up only by service in the Spanish-American War. One of his distant cousins married Theodore Roosevelt, and the president later stood as godfather to Wintie's son, future composer Theodore Ward Chanler, at a christening held in exclusive Newport, Rhode Island, in 1902.

Wilde let the college boys settle in, then walked onto the stage to amused applause. In place of his usual costume, he was wearing long trousers and a conservative coat—very much the grown-up in a crowd of adolescents. He opened his manuscript case and began to speak. "As a college man, I greet you," he said. "I am very glad to address an audience in Boston, the only city in America which has influenced thought in Europe, and which has given to Europe a new and great school of philosophy." He looked up and gave a practiced start as he appeared to notice the Harvard crowd for the first time. "I see about me certain signs of an Aesthetic Movement," Wilde said with a smile. "I see certain young men who are no doubt sincere, but I can assure them that they are no more than caricatures. As I look around me, I am impelled for the first time to breathe a fervent prayer, 'Save me from my disciples.' But rather let me, as Wordsworth says, 'turn from these bold, bad men.'"[16]

The bulk of Wilde's talk was given over to the same "English Renaissance" topics he had covered in New York and Philadelphia. The Harvard students attempted to reclaim the offensive by applauding lustily whenever Wilde paused for a drink of water, but they were hissed down by the rest of the crowd. Towards the end of the lecture, he again addressed the students directly. Describing the roadway he and his fellow Oxonians had built at the behest of John Ruskin, with the aim of teaching them the beauty of hard work, Wilde expressed the hope that "these charming young men might be inclined to follow our example; the work would be good for them, though I do not believe they could build so good a road. I beg to assure the students before me that there is more to the movement of aestheticism than knee breeches and sunflowers." Noting that he had visited Harvard earlier that afternoon and had been particularly impressed by the manly gymnasium there, he extended them a figurative olive branch, offering to present the college with a suitably Grecian statue evoking the unity of athletics and art. For that matter, said Wilde, he did not see why a prospective graduate couldn't receive a Harvard diploma for painting a picture or sculpting a beautiful statue as much as for completing a course in "that dreadful record of crime known as history." On this point, the students were won over entirely.[17]

It was a triumph for Wilde, done with grace, good humor, and a little sting. The newspaper of record, the *Boston Evening Transcript,* described it as such, noting that "Mr. Wilde achieved a real triumph, and it was by right of conquest, by force of being a gentleman, in the truest sense of the word." He had produced a "thorough-going chastening of the super-abounding spirits of the Harvard freshmen. Nothing could have been more gracious, more gentle and sweet, and yet more crushing, than the lecturer's whole demeanor to them." The *Transcript* compared him to such earlier British heroes as Wellington and Nelson— surely the only time that Wilde's name was ever mentioned in the same breath as the military victors at Waterloo and Trafalgar. Wilde could afford to be gracious in his own bloodless victory. "I could sympathize with them, because I thought to myself that when I was in my first year at Oxford I would have been apt to do the same," he told an interviewer a few days later. "But as they put their head in the lion's mouth, I thought they deserved a little bite."[18]

If Julia Ward Howe felt the need to atone for her grand-nephew's shenanigans, she would soon have the opportunity to do so. On February 4, the *Woman's Journal,* a magazine to which Howe regularly contributed, published a highly critical article on Wilde and the unoffending Walt Whitman by self-appointed moral arbiter Thomas Wentworth Higginson. The jowly, bewhiskered Higginson looked a fair amount like Wilde's recent Washington host, Massachusetts congressman George M. Robeson, with all the good humor taken out. (Higginson once had run for Congress himself, but had been defeated.) He was a man who took himself entirely seriously, and he was used to others taking him seriously as well. Since the early 1850s Higginson had been at the forefront of the nation's moral battles, beginning with the abolitionist movement to end slavery in the American South. He had been one of the leaders in the violent efforts to prevent the return of escaped slave Anthony Burns from Boston in May 1854, a confrontation initiated by the legal ruling of another of Wilde's Washington hosts, Judge Edward Loring. During the riot, Higginson had received a sword wound on the chin—which he thereafter kept clean-shaven to show off his personal badge of courage.

Fortunate to escape charges of inciting the riot, during which a federal marshal was killed, an unrepentant Higginson engaged in other illegal acts suborning violence, sending guns and money to the terrorist John Brown in Bleeding Kansas and participating as a member of the "Secret Six" in arming and encouraging Brown to lead a slave rebellion in Virginia. (Julia Ward Howe's husband, Samuel Gridley Howe, was another member of the group.) Higginson excused Brown's murderous rampages as mere disturbances of "the delicate balance of the zealot's mind," a description with which the half-dozen victims of the horrific massacre at Ossawatomie Creek might have quibbled, had they survived. After Brown's arrest at Harpers Ferry, Higginson sought to raise money for Brown's legal defense.

During the ensuing war that Brown's various outrages had hastened, Higginson served as colonel of an all-black Union regiment, the 1st South Carolina Volunteers, which saw light service in the comparatively sylvan regions of Hilton Head, South Carolina, and Jacksonville, Florida. Higginson was invalided out of the service for post-traumatic stress disorder after he nearly drowned during an ill-advised moonlight swim in the tidal waters off Hilton Head. In the meantime, he had begun a correspondence with a strange shut-in female poet from Amherst, Massachusetts, named Emily Dickinson, who had asked him to look over her poetry. He found the verses "spasmodic" and "uncontrolled," and advised her to hold off publishing them. Dickinson, he said somewhat unkindly, was "my partially cracked poetess."[19]

Whether Higginson was angered by Wilde's earlier visits with Judge

Loring and Walt Whitman, or merely by his lunch with Julia Ward Howe, it is impossible to say. But angry he was. He began his scathingly titled article, "Unmanly Manhood," by excoriating Wilde's racy poem "Charmides," which Wilde considered his best. In it, the title character, a young man, falls in love with a statue of the virginal goddess Athena and spends a delirious night caressing "her pale and argent body," working his way from her "breasts of polished ivory" down to her "grand cool flanks, the crescent thighs, the bossy hills of snow." Athena, as well she might, takes umbrage at the fondling and lures Charmides into drowning. His floating body is worshiped in turn by a water nymph, who dies of unrequited passion after failing to rouse him. In the end, Aphrodite intervenes and restores the dead lovers to life in the fields of Acheron, where "all his hoarded sweets were hers to kiss, / And all her maidenhead was his to slay." Higginson noted that Lord Byron had been banished from proper English society and George Moore had been "obliged to purify his poems for less offences against common decency than have been committed by Oscar Wilde."[20]

Higginson went on to lecture his friend and neighbor Julia Ward Howe about the proper role of women as

the guardians of public purity [and] the clergy of the public morals. Yet when a young man comes among us whose only distinction is that he has written a thin volume of very mediocre verse and that he makes himself something very like a buffoon for notoriety and money, women of high social position receive him at their homes and invite guests to meet him, in spite of the fact that if they were to read aloud to the company his poem of "Charmides" not a woman would remain the room until the end. We have perhaps rashly claimed that the influence of women has purified English literature. When the poems of Wilde and Whitman lie in ladies' boudoirs, I see no evidence of the improvement.[21]

That was too much for Howe, who had been intimately involved in the women's rights movement from its inception nearly four decades earlier. She fired back at Higginson with an open letter in the *Boston Transcript*. "As Colonel Higginson in *The Woman's Journal* took exception to the entertainment of Mr. Oscar Wilde in private homes, I as one of the entertainers alluded to, desire to say that I am very glad to have had the opportunity of receiving Mr. Wilde in my house. I also take exception to the right which Colonel Higginson arrogates to himself of saying in a public way who should and who should not be received in private houses." As for the linking of Wilde with Lord Byron—something Wilde would not have had a problem with—Howe noted piously:

> To cut off even an offensive member of society from its best influences and most humanizing resources is scarcely Christian in any sense. It must be remembered that if women are rightly "the guardians of the public purity," they are also the proper representatives of tender hope and divine compassion. Mr. Wilde is a young man in whom many excellent people have found much to like. Among his poems are some which judges as competent as Colonel Higginson consider to have much merit. He has come to our country thinking no doubt that he has something to teach us, but also, as I gather, quite willing to believe that he may learn something from his brief sojourn among us. I, for one, desire that the best homes may be open to him and that he may have the opportunity of seeing and conversing with our best people.[22]

Wilde had moved on from Boston before the Higginson-Howe controversy arose, but he wrote Howe a heartfelt thank-you note from the road. "Your letter is noble and beautiful," said Wilde. "I have only just seen it, and shall not forget ever the chivalrous and pure-minded woman who wrote it." In a follow-up letter he joked about traveling with an enormous trunk and a full-time valet and promised to visit Howe again at her Newport, Rhode Island, summer home. "But what would Thoreau have said to my hat-box!" he wondered. "Or Emerson to the size of my trunk. As long as I can enjoy talking nonsense to flowers and children I am not afraid of the depraved luxury of a hat-box." As for Higginson, Wilde dismissed his remarks as an example of "English Puritanism at its worst," produced by an "ignorant and itinerant libeler of New England." "Who, after all, that I should write of him, is this scribbling anonymuncule in grand old Massachusetts who scrawls and screams so glibly about what he cannot understand?" Wilde wondered aloud. "This apostle of inhospitality, who delights to defile, to desecrate, and to defame the gracious courtesies he is unworthy to enjoy?"[23]

By then, Wilde had run into more apostles of inhospitality. At New Haven, he had simply ignored the two hundred Yale students who attempted to imitate their Harvard counterparts by marching into the lecture hall wearing flame-red neckties and yellow sunflowers behind a similarly dressed manservant. But two nights later, at Brooklyn's Academy of Music, he had met a flinty reception from the standing-room-only crowd, including some prototypical Brooklyn rowdies who kept shouting, "'Urry hup, Hoscar!" and applauding ironically whenever he ventured to say something serious about art. Such responses, said Wilde from the stage, "were as ignorant as they are insolent." Vaudeville comedian Nat Goodwin, on stage nearby in the play *Hobbies,* caught a portion of Wilde's appearance between acts and hurried back to ad-lib an impersonation of the Englishman's haughtiness in his own show. Goodwin, a native of Boston, would have a long and successful career playing buffoons, although, like many comedians, what he really wanted to do was serious drama. Among the more dramatic roles he essayed were Shylock, Fagin, and Marc Antony, roles he somehow managed to shoehorn between his five marriages. His fifth wife, dancer-turned-actress Edna Goodrich, was the best friend of another one-time "Floradora Girl," Evelyn Nesbit, to whom she fatefully introduced New York architect Stanford White at the start of their notoriously ill-starred love affair.[24]

Wilde headed up the Hudson River Valley in swirling snowstorm, bound for Utica, Rochester, and Buffalo on successive days. His travel schedule throughout the tour was backbreaking, but Wilde soldiered on gamely, although he did write to Colonel Morse to suggest that Morse "arrange some more matinées; to lecture in the day does not tire me. I would sooner lecture five or six times a week, and travel, say three or four hours a day than lecture three times and travel ten hours." He also asked Morse to go to a good theatrical costumer and buy him two more coats to wear at such matinées. He specified that they "be beautiful; tight velvet doublet, with large flowered sleeves and little ruffs of cambric coming up from under collar." Wilde included a sketch of the ruffles and detailed instructions for two pairs of gray silk stockings "to suit grey mouse-coloured velvet," along with flowered sleeves "stamped with large pattern. They will excite a great sensation." To avoid becoming a walking advertisement for the costumer, Wilde specified that Morse not mention his name on the order. His measurements, for the record, were: waist, 38½ inches; pants, 30 inches to the top of the knee; sleeve, 32 inches; and neck, 17 inches.[25]

At Utica, Wilde was greeted with an article in the *Weekly Herald* inviting him to "descend from his pedestal of daffodils and come into contact with Oneida County snowbanks." A follow-up article by a female reporter compared Wilde to George Eliot in looks—unkind to both, in varying degrees—and also said Wilde resembled "a diluted Theodore Tilton." The latter reference was to the cuckolded husband of Elizabeth R. Tilton, whose notorious affair with their minister, Henry Ward Beecher, the brother of Harriet Beecher Stowe, had scandalized America seven years earlier. At the time, Beecher was the most famous preacher in the country, and his sermons at Brooklyn's Plymouth Congregational Church were attended by thousands, including the fledgling stage performer Mark Twain, who took notes on Beecher's charismatic stage presence for future reference. Beecher's showmanship, said Twain, combined "poetry, pathos, humor, satire and eloquent declamation," and turned the preacher into "a remarkably handsome man when he is in the full tide of sermonizing, and his face is lit up with animation." Mrs. Tilton apparently thought so, and their assignations made front-page news for months in the summer of 1875. Beecher escaped conviction by means of a hung jury and resumed his ministerial duties, and the wronged Theodore Tilton discovered a profitable new career—he had previously edited a religious newspaper for Beecher—as a traveling lecturer.[26]

Wilde left Utica after touring the Utica Household Art Rooms, which had sponsored his talk, and "alternately praising and criticizing" the displays he found there. In Rochester, on February 7, he ran into yet more trouble during his appearance at the Grand Opera House. Once again college students were behind the ruckus. Wiseacres at Baptist-run Rochester University had salted the local newspaper, the *Democrat and Chronicle,* with a bogus letter from Wilde accepting an invitation to attend an event called the Rochester Maennerchor Masquerade (the Maennerchor was a German singing and cultural society). An imposter, done up in full Wildean drag, had danced the night away with the "aesthetic maidens" in the Too Utterly Too Too Club before revealing his true identity. Wilde was understandably nettled when he sat down for the obligatory localized interview with a reporter from the *Democrat and Chronicle* prior to his eight o'clock lecture. In response to a question about his treatment in the press, the poet complained: "They have certainly treated me outrageously, but I am not the one who is injured. It is the public. By such ridiculous attacks the people are taught to mimic where they should reverence, to scoff at things to which they will not even listen." He warned that other eminent British artists and writers "would not think for a moment of venturing here in a public capacity. They know well enough the treatment they would receive, the questionable courtesy I have experienced."[27]

As if to prove his point, Wilde walked onto the Rochester stage and into a full-blown riot. About one hundred college boys were ready and waiting in the gallery, from which vantage point they immediately began what the *New York Herald* described the next day as "a running fire of hisses, groans, and hootings which compelled the lecturer to pause more than a dozen times when the hullabaloo became so noisy that the Aesthete's voice could not be heard." Wilde tried the old performer's

trick of folding his arms across his chest and staring silently at the offenders, but for once it failed to work. The students kept up their boo-
ing, and fifteen minutes into the speech a school janitor named Peter
Craig, done up in blackface, marched down the center aisle in a swallow-
tailed coat, one white kid glove, and a gigantic sunflower pinned to his
chest. The crowd erupted, some applauding, others hissing, and several
people walked out of the hall. A whip-wielding policeman attempted to
eject one of the more unruly students—how could he choose?—and a
general mêlée ensued, with more policemen rushing into the building
and turning off the gas lights. Wilde gamely finished his lecture in
"a tiresome monotone" and left the stage.[28]

The next day the *Rochester Union and Advertiser,* the city's Republican newspaper, trumpeted "Rochester's Deep Disgrace" and roasted the
university's presumably Democratic students for conduct "which would
be considered the height of boorishness at a country signing school or
spelling match." The *Daily News* in Chicago, where Wilde was headed
next, ventured the unsought opinion that the dust-up was actually
Wilde's fault, noting that "American audiences are usually kind and polite, and they had a right to interrupt a speaker if they chose, since they
had paid more for the space they occupied than had the lecturer. There
ought to be some mode of assuring this self-announced apostle of intellectual asininity and imbecility that he amounts to nothing." Next stop,
Chicago![29]

The Rochester contretemps attracted the attention of Wilde's fellow poet and costume-wearing showman Joaquin Miller, whom he had
met earlier in New York City. Miller had essentially reversed Wilde's
brand of performance art with his one-man Wild West Show in London
a decade earlier. A combination of Mark Twain, Bret Harte, and Arte-
mus Ward, minus their talent, Miller had re-created himself on stage as
a grizzled Indian-fighter and part-time sonneteer, the "Poet of the Sierras" and the "Byron of the Rockies." He was not entirely inauthentic,
although his claim that he had been born in a covered wagon while
crossing the Rockies was off by a good fourteen years. He had once been

wounded in the cheek and neck by a Modoc Indian's arrow, before switching sides and marrying a Modoc woman himself. He had also been a gold rusher, a Pony Express rider, a lawyer, a judge, a newspaper editor, and a convicted horse thief, as well as an inveterate womanizer whose lovers reportedly included American actress Adah Isaacs Menken, California poet Ina Coolbrith, an English baronet's daughter, an Italian countess, and a Cockney flower girl, as well as three more wives. One wonders when he found the time to write.

Miller had traveled to England in 1870, while Oscar Wilde was still a boarding student at Portora Royal School in Enniskillen, Ireland. By then he had changed his rather Germanic given name, Cincinnatus Heine Miller, to Joaquin in honor of the Mexican bandit Joaquin Murietta. He sported an enormous sombrero, white buckskin suits, cowboy boots, and spurs, and carried a bearskin over one shoulder while declaiming his "Songs of the Sierras" to rapt audiences of English swells. He was taken up by the Pre-Raphaelite Brothers, particularly Dante Gabriel Rossetti; and Wilde's future ideal of loveliness, Lillie Langtry, praised Miller for living "a life adventuresome." Once, at a banquet for fellow American expatriate Ambrose Bierce at London's exclusive Whitefriars Club, Miller arrived fashionably late, sporting a pair of dangling Bowie knives in case Algernon Charles Swinburne or some other dangerous desperado happened to menace the duchess of Kent. Desperate for attention, he plunged his hand into a fishbowl, pulled out a goldfish, and swallowed it whole, booming, "A wonderful appetizer!"[30]

When Miller read the news accounts of Wilde's Rochester misadventure at his home on West 33rd Street in New York, he was moved to write to him at once to commiserate. "My dear Oscar Wilde," he began, "I read with shame about the behavior of those ruffians at Rochester at your lecture there." He offered Wilde the hospitality of his father's Oregon ranch, "or should you decide to return here and not bear further abuse, come to my house-top and abide with me where you will be welcome and loved as a brother. And bear this in mind, my dear boy, the more you are abused the more welcome you will be. For I remember how kind your country was to me; and at your age I had not done one-tenth your work." Miller urged Wilde not to lose heart or come to dislike America, assuring him that "the real heart of this strong young world demands, and will have, fair play for all. . . . So go ahead, my brave youth, and say your say if you choose. My heart is with you; and so are the hearts of the best of America's millions." He closed, "Thine for the Beautiful and True."[31]

Wilde was traveling again when he received Miller's letter, but he immediately wrote back to thank him for his "chivalrous and courteous" letter.

> Believe me, I would as lief judge of the strength and splendour of sun and sea by the dust that dances in the beam and the bubble that breaks on the wave, as take the petty profitless vulgarity of one or two insignificant towns as any test or standard of the real spirit of a sane, strong and simple people, or allow it to affect my respect for the many noble men and women whom it has been my privilege in this great country to know. . . . I need not tell you that whenever you visit England you will be received with that courtesy with which it is our pleasure to welcome all Americans, and that honour with which it is our privilege to greet all poets.[32]

Wilde wrapped up the New York part of his tour with stops in Buffalo and Niagara Falls on February 8 and 9. Buffalo, on the frigid shores of Lake Erie, was in the midst of a civic housecleaning under the leadership of its new, walrus-like reform mayor, Grover Cleveland. The forty-four-year-old Cleveland, a lifelong Democrat, had been elected mayor in Republican-dominated Buffalo by the largest margin ever given to the city's chief executive. He began his duties by extending the working hours of municipal workers from their leisurely four P.M. quitting time and used his veto powers so frequently that he became known, not always disapprovingly, as Mayor Veto. In the course of wielding his powers, Cleveland vetoed a suspicious street-cleaning contract that went to the highest instead of lowest bidder, vetoed payments to city street sweepers for using their horses to provide delivery services while on city time, vetoed new sidewalk construction, vetoed the position of city morgue attendant—even vetoed the traditional Fourth of July donation to the venerable Civil War veterans' association, the Grand Army of the Republic. Common citizens loved him for his political courage, if not necessarily for his dour, perpetually disappointed personality. Cleveland would ride his popularity to the governor's mansion in Albany and, two years later, to the White House in Washington, having upset Oscar Wilde's erstwhile host, James G. Blaine, in a close election to become the first Democrat elected president since James Buchanan nearly thirty years earlier—the outright theft of the 1876 election from his fellow New York governor Samuel J. Tilden notwithstanding.

Showing the same industriousness as their mayor, Buffalo Aesthetes prepared an elaborate welcome for Wilde, redecorating the stage at the Academy of Music with a near-Byzantine sumptuousness. Persian carpets, Florentine velvets, Japanese lances, bronze plaques, gold hangings, ebony cabinets, and a marble pedestal bearing the bronzed bust of another famous and much put-upon traveler, Odysseus, stood before black lace-embroidered screens. The *Buffalo Courier* judged the preparations "rich in the extreme, if a little bizarre," and expressed doubt as to whether "Mr. Wilde has been more artistically environed at any time since he has commenced lecturing on this side of the Atlantic." Counterintuitively, perhaps, Wilde replaced his knee breeches and purple velvet coat with long gray trousers, fawn-colored after-dinner jacket, and similarly colored vest. This more austere look he accented with a rose-colored cravat and handkerchief. He kept his pointed patent-leather shoes, with their silver bows.[33]

Inspired by the industrious civic spirit of Buffalo and its crusading mayor, Wilde appended to his usual remarks on the "English Renaissance" another detailed account of his road-building days under John Ruskin as an Oxford undergraduate. One summer afternoon when he was nineteen, said Wilde, he had been walking along the High Street with a group of friends, "going to the river or tennis court or cricket field," when Ruskin ran into them on his way to the lecture hall. The professor told them "that it seemed to him to be wrong that all the best physique and strength of the young men of England should be spent aimlessly on the cricket ground or without any result at all, except that if one rowed well he got the pewter pot, and if one made a good score, a case-handled bat." He encouraged them to do some good, honest labor for a change. That was how the raised road from Lower Hinskey to Upper Hinskey got built, with Wilde joining other high-minded Oxonians in breaking rocks, clearing brush, draining swamps, and trundling overloaded wheelbarrows along a narrow plank. It had inspired him, Wilde concluded, to join the Aesthetic Movement a few years later. "I felt that if there was enough spirit among the young men to go out to such work as road-making for the sake of a noble ideal of life, I could from them create an artistic movement that might change, as it has changed, the face of England. Well, we have done something in England and we will do something more." It was not exactly the Gettysburg Address, but it seemed to go over well in Buffalo, and an expansive Wilde took time afterwards to praise the "refined and cultivated audience" for his warm reception.[34]

The next day it was on to Niagara Falls, where he checked into the Prospect House, which, as its name implied, overlooked the falls on the Canadian side of the border. Niagara Falls had been the destination of choice for middle-class American honeymooners since Aaron Burr's daughter, Theodosia, kicked off the craze in 1801. (Napoleon Bonaparte's brother Jerome followed Miss Burr into Niagara-sanctioned matrimony three years later.) Photography booths, souvenir shops, and the nineteenth-century equivalent of fast-food restaurants lined the walkways leading to the falls. "Every American bride is taken there," Wilde would tell his countrymen a few months later, "and the sight of the stupendous waterfall must be one of the earliest, if not the keenest, disappointments in American married life." Together with his business manager, J. S. Vale, whom Morse had hired to accompany Wilde after the scheduling debacle in Baltimore, the poet spent several hours touring the sights: American Falls, Bridal Veil Falls, Horseshoe Falls, the 1855 suspension bridge linking the two sides, Goat Island, the Ice Bridge, the Cave of the Winds, and Table Rock. Wilde grudgingly traded in his beloved green overcoat for the obligatory yellow rain slicker to wear while viewing the falls from below, but only after he had been assured that Sarah Bernhardt had also donned the hideous yellow oilskin during her own visit to Niagara.[35]

There were no daredevils that day attempting to go over the falls in a barrel or walk a tightrope wire across the gorge like Jean-François Gravelet ("the Great Blondin") had accomplished a few years earlier, but Wilde made the proper noises about the "impressive tableaux" he had encountered on his trek. His local guide, a man with the perfect tour-guide name of Jack Conboy, later told newsmen that he had "never before heard anyone take on so about a lot of ice." After lunch Wilde changed his tune, or at least appeared to do so to chauvinistic American readers. He was quoted in the *Buffalo Express* as saying that "when I first saw Niagara Falls I was disappointed in the outline. The design, it seemed to me, was wanting in grandeur and variety of line." Now he saw that the water was "full of changing loveliness" and that the "majestic splendor and strength of the physical forces of nature" were "far beyond what I had ever seen in Europe." He even quoted Leonardo da Vinci as saying that "the two most beautiful things in the world are a woman's smile and the motion of mighty water."[36]

Unfortunately—or fortunately, given the ensuing blizzard of additional publicity—only the first part of Wilde's nature critique made the newswires, and the quote "I was disappointed in the outline" of Niagara Falls, like his earlier comment about the insufficient majesty of the Atlantic Ocean, was ineradicably linked to his name. The *New York Tribune* grumbled that "it may now be recorded that as a show, Niagara takes precedence over the Atlantic Ocean." The newspaper noted that Lord Byron, in his day, had entertained an entirely different view of the matter, adding, "What the Falls thought of [Wilde] will probably never be known. The Falls, so far as we know, kept on falling." Whatever the case, Wilde once again had managed to top Mother Nature. He inscribed a properly sweeping benison in the visitors' album at Prospect House: "The roar of these waters is like the roar when the mighty wave democracy breaks on the shore where kings lie couched at ease." His own advance, if somewhat short of a mighty wave, continued to roll ever westward across the American frontier, undeterred by rowdy college students, carping editorialists, restless crowds, or jaded tour guides. As he defiantly told a reporter in Rochester: "I know that I am right, that I have a mission to perform. I am indestructible!" That, perhaps, remained to be seen.[37]

CHAPTER 5

No Well-Behaved River
Ought to Act This Way

❧

CHICAGO, CARL SANDBURG'S City of the Big Shoulders, was ready and waiting for Oscar Wilde when he arrived in town on the evening of February 10 after an all-day train ride from Niagara Falls. A poem in the *Chicago Daily News* announced the coming of "the simpering Oscar," who "comes with words sublimely dull, / In garb superbly silly, / To tell us of the beautiful, / The sunflower and the lily." Saying he had a brain "like April butter"—whatever that meant—the poem concluded with defiant frontier vigor: "We like to look at Western mules, / But not aesthetic asses."[1]

Of all the major cities in America, Wilde would have been hard put to find one less amenable to his message of non-purpose-driven art than Chicago. To be sure, New York, Philadelphia, Washington, and Boston were all capitalist metropolises as well, but these cities also had significant centers of culture dating back nearly two centuries. Chicago was

different. It was a comparative latecomer as a city, having been incorporated in 1837 (its first permanent settlement, Fort Dearborn, had been
burned to the ground by Potowatomi Indians during the War of 1812).
In fact, Chicago was now virtually brand-new, compliments of the Great
Chicago Fire of 1871, which had consumed seventy-three square miles of
downtown streets, 17,500 buildings, and upwards of three hundred citizens in one raging night of smoke and flames.

The fire had started about 8:30 on the evening of October 8, in a
barn at the rear of the Patrick O'Leary residence at 137 DeKalb Street,
on the West Side of the city. A one-legged drayman named Daniel
Sullivan, called "Peg Leg" for obvious reasons, saw the first arrows of
flame shooting from the O'Learys' barn and sounded the alarm. It was
already too late. The largely wood-framed city, which had been swelter-
ing through an unusually dry autumn, burned quickly. By midnight,
whole swaths of the city's South Side, including the notorious Irish slum
known as Conley's Patch, had been destroyed. Carried aloft on gale-like
gusts of sixty-mile-per-hour wind, flaming debris fell on the city's broad
shoulders like hot red snow, defeating all efforts by weary firefighters to
keep ahead of the blaze. Sheets of fire, described as making a sound like
the flapping of enormous ship sails, flew from building to building. One
frantic furniture store owner offered firemen a thousand dollars to save
his building. You might as well offer a million, he was told—nothing
could save it now.

In the wake of the fire, a long list of suspects was drawn up, beginning with Mrs. O'Leary herself, who, the *Chicago Times* later charged,
had started the fire in revenge for having been taken off the Cook
County welfare rolls. The newspaper, which listed the unfortunate
woman at twice her actual age—she was thirty-five—could produce no
tangible proof that she had even been on the public dole to begin with.
Other suspects included Mrs. O'Leary's cow (although which one of her
now-deceased five animals was the guilty party could not be ascertained); some roistering Irishmen said to have sneaked into the barn to

steal some milk; a trio of kids trying out their new bull terrier on the O'Learys' rats; an anonymous group of card players; and assorted other crackpots, revolutionaries, malcontents, and self-confessed arsonists. It was even suggested that the barn may have combusted spontaneously, which, given the enormous volume of foot traffic alleged to have passed through it on the night in question, was no less plausible than any of the other theories.

The upshot of the fire was a newly rebuilt city that civic leaders were always happy to show off to distinguished foreign visitors such as Oscar Wilde. In the darkness of his nighttime arrival, there was not much to see other than the towering shadows of grain elevators and the foul-smelling stockyards where Chicagoans went about the task of being "Hog Butcher of the Western World." Many of these butchers were immigrants—Irish, Polish, Italian, German, Greek, and Slovenian—but the men who controlled them and the city's other industrial workers were Anglo-Saxon Americans such as Philip Danforth Armour, who employed a veritable army of 20,000 workers at his meatpacking plant and liked to brag that his wage paying and his charitable food dispersals meant that he "gave more people food than any man living."[2]

Perhaps that was so, but Chicago had sprouted new, if not improved, slums since the Great Fire and had more than its share of the ever-hungry urban poor. When English reformer William Thomas Stead came to the city a decade later, he was moved by the sight of "the poor starving, derelicts" to wonder aloud, "What do you think Christ would do if He came to Chicago?" His answer, printed on the cover of his book-length exposé of the city, *If Christ Came to Chicago,* showed a militant Christ driving the moneychangers from the temple. The moneychangers all had the faces of prominent local businessmen, including Armour. Inside, Stead had helpfully printed a map of Chicago's red-light district, with the brothels circled in red and the saloons circled in black, alongside the names of the madams who ran the whorehouses. The book's entire 70,000-copy press run sold out in a day. Stead, a spiritualist in his later years, frequently predicted that he would die by drowning. He was as good as his word, going down with the *Titanic* in 1912, last seen serenely reading a book in the ship's First-Class library.[3]

Upon his arrival in Chicago, Wilde checked into the Grand Pacific Hotel, owned and operated by John Burroughs Drake. The Grand Pacific, located at the intersection of Clark, Lasalle, Quincy, and Jackson streets, was one of the so-called "Big Four" hotels constructed in the wake of the Chicago fire (the others were the Palmer House, the Sherman House, and the Tremont), whose strongest calling card was their assurance of being fireproof. The Grand Pacific had become the western headquarters of the Republican Party, and one year after Wilde's visit it was the site where moguls of the four great American railroads met and instituted Standard Time, as well as the country's four geographic time zones. The hotel was also famous for its sumptuous wild-game dinners and well-stocked wine cellar. Wilde partook freely of both, enjoying a room-service feast of brook trout, broiled quail, prairie-reared steak, sweets, and champagne. He "never thought such good wine could be obtained so far west," he said, but professed disappointment at the hotel's failure to stock his favorite brand of Turkish cigarettes.[4]

The hotel staff had arranged his suite in a picturesque tableau fit for an Indian pasha, with wolf and tiger skins thrown across a sofa set before a blazing fireplace. Wilde was reclining "in a very picturesque attitude," with his head lying on a gold silk shawl, when a reporter from the *Chicago Inter-Ocean* arrived for an interview. As always, Wilde paused a beat for effect, then sprang to his feet and shook hands with the reporter, a smile on his face and a cigar in his other hand. He wasted no time in flattering the host city, saying Chicago, like all the best American cities, had "a very high cosmopolitanism." The West in general, he said, struck him as "far more free of prejudice," meaning class warfare and social intolerance, than the eastern half of the country, which he found "pervaded by some folly of misinterpretation which they are already tired of in England." In response to the invariable question of why he had come to Such-and-Such City in the first place, Wilde replied that he was there to encourage the creation of beautiful works of art and "to make art not a luxury for the rich but, as it should be, the most splendid of all the chords through which the spirit of any nation manifests its power." Mindful of where he was, he added, "Life without industry is barren, and industry without art is barbarism." He disputed the reporter's contention that modern civilization was the greatest. "The greatest civilization of the world existed ages ago, and existed without steam engines," said Wilde. "Of what use is it to a man to travel sixty miles an hour? Is he any better for it? A fool can buy a railway ticket and travel sixty miles an hour. Is he any less a fool?" The reporter wisely left it at that.[5]

Wilde's Chicago lecture was not scheduled until Monday, February 13, and he spent the weekend touring the phoenix-city that had risen from the ashes on the shores of Lake Michigan. He saw the city's first cable car, on State Street, where it had made its maiden run two weeks before. He wordlessly toured the Chicago Art Institute; saw the hideous Interstate Industrial Exposition Building where the city hosted political conventions, orchestra concerts, trade shows, National Guard musters, and taffy pulls; and crossed the antique, hand-cranked drawbridge over the Chicago River to view the 154-foot-tall water tower on the North Side that was the city's pride and joy, having been the only public building to survive the Great Fire a decade earlier.

Wilde attended the usual round of dinners and receptions at the mansions of local art connoisseurs and millionaires, where he met, among others, department store magnate Marshall Field, who had coined the immortal marketing phrase "The customer is always right," and Mrs. John A. Logan, whose husband was an Illinois senator, former Union general, and personal friend of Abraham Lincoln. At one luncheon he reportedly advised that a lady "should wear a lily; she may wear a rose; but never, oh, never, a sunflower," which caused one embarrassed young débutante in attendance to surreptitiously slide her sunflower corsage onto the floor at her feet. There was a rumor that Wilde had met heavyweight boxing champion John L. Sullivan, who was in

town on a triumphant return to the North after knocking out Irish chal-
lenger Paddy Ryan in the ninth round of their bout a few days earlier in
Mississippi. As piquant as it is to imagine Oscar Wilde and John L. Sullivan trading bons mots over beer mugs in a Chicago tavern, the meeting never took place. Wilde was merely asked for his reaction to the
recent boxing match—"Even that has its artistic side," he said—and
Sullivan was persuaded, in a separate interview, to offer an opinion on
the Atlantic Ocean. He thought it was fine.[6]

Wilde's visit to Chicago attracted the usual mix of partly amused,
partly contemptuous publicity, with local newspapers carrying illustrated advertisements for men's clothing. One ad, featuring an awk-
wardly posing Wilde in full Bunthornian finery, touted the new spring
suits at Willoughby, Hill & Co., economically priced between ten and
twenty dollars. "Wild Oscar, or Balaam the Ass-thete" presumably en-
dorsed the new line, although it is doubtful that he was being quoted
directly in the store's tag line: "Don't buy nothing without 1st seeing our
new goods and low prices." He might, or might not, have been amused
by the ad's subhead: "Pants Down Again." A second ad, for A. J. Nut-
ting & Co. on Madison Street, even more improbably offered "Hoss-
Car Wilde" suits, described as "the Very Latest 'To [*sic*] Utter' Styles for
Railroad Men." A very butch-looking conductor sported a short jacket,
long pants, and a jaunty billed cap. Newspaper editorials wondered
aloud whether Wilde's Hibernian influence would carry over to "Neighbor Rafferty's" henhouse and if he could assist "Pat's wife" in selecting
the proper set of five-dollar decorated china.[7]

Hand-painted china was one of the topics addressed in Wilde's
newly written lecture, "The Decorative Arts," which he presented at
Chicago's Central Music Hall on February 13 to a gratifyingly large
crowd of 2,500 people. After only a month, he had already grown tired
of hearing himself talk about the new English Renaissance, and he
turned to the more practical applications of beauty in American homes
and schools. He began uncharacteristically with a joke about his supposed meeting with John L. Sullivan. He did not wish to reprove "the

wicked and imaginative editor" who had written the piece, he said, since he understood that "the conscience of an editor is purely decorative" anyway. As for the rest of American society, "If life is noble and beautiful, art will be noble and beautiful." It was more a technical than an artistic question, said Wilde, dependent on the development of homegrown handicraftsmen who were capable of seeing "the beautiful things of Nature" about them. Like many talents, learned or innate, this started in school, and Wilde recommended to the canny, hardheaded citizens of Chicago that they educate their children "not in that calendar of infamy, European history," but instead in art workshops that might prepare them for "a new history of the world, with a promise of the brotherhood of man, of peace rather than war, of praise of God's handicraftsmanship, of new imagination and new beauty."[8]

This was unobjectionable, if somewhat inconsistent, since Wilde seemed to be calling for the teaching of arts and crafts, on one hand, while also fobbing it off on God's good grace. He continued with the celestial theme, localizing it a bit by noting that the outpouring of humanitarian aid to Chicago in the wake of the Great Fire had been "as noble and beautiful as the work of any troops of angels." No one in the audience would have disagreed with that, but then Wilde made a serious misstep. Describing his visit to the waterworks by the lake, he noted, "I was shocked, when I came out of that place, to see the tower— a castellated monstrosity with pepper-boxes stuck all over it. I was amazed that any people could so abuse Gothic art, and make a structure look, not like a water-tower, but like the tower of a medieval castle."[9]

It was rather like criticizing the Statue of Liberty for lack of proper proportion—something that may have occurred to Wilde as well, had the statue been placed in New York Harbor at the time of his arrival. The crowd murmured angrily, and Wilde hastened to stress that he was merely talking about the appropriate use of materials in art, noting that Japanese artists could suggest an entire scene on a plate with only "a little spray of leaves and a little bird in flight." Meanwhile, he had seen young art students in Philadelphia painting elaborate scenes of moonlight and sunsets on dinner china. "They might paint sunsets if they liked and moonlight if they dared," he said, "but let them not do it on dinner plates. The use to which an object is to be put should be a guide to the subject. Such sunsets as these, if beautiful enough, should be handsomely framed and hung on walls. Soup should not be eaten from them. One doesn't want to eat one's clams off a harrowing sunset." As with literary realism, although he did not make the comparison, artists should look around them for subject matter, to the docks and playing fields, or "the reaper with his sickle." But above all, "no machine-made ornaments should be tolerated. They are all bad, worthless, ugly. People should not mistake the means of civilization for the end." Instead, American workmen ought to be able to work in "the bright and novel surrounds that you can yourself create. Stately and simple architecture for your city, bright and simple dress for your men and women, and streets clean enough for them to walk across without being soiled—those are the conditions of a real artistic movement."[10]

Wilde was convinced, he said, that the best art flourished in republics, not in monarchies or tyrannies. "We do not want the rich to possess more beautiful things, but the poor to create more beautiful things," he urged, "for every man is poor who cannot create." True creators should seek out "all that is noble in men and women, the stately in your lakes and mountains, the beautiful in your flowers and in your life. We want to see you possess nothing in your house that has not given delight to its maker, and does not give delight to its user; we want to see you create an art made by the hands of the people, for all art to come must be democratic, coming to all alike and hovering about, low and high, in unconscious existence."[11]

Despite his democracy-stressing peroration, many in the crowd were still angry at Wilde when they left the theater. One man cried, "I didn't expect to learn anything, and I haven't!" Newspapers the next day were filled with chauvinistic outrage. "He fails to note the degree in ·which it [the water tower] responds to the fundamental conception of art—economy and fitness," said the *Chicago Daily News,* adding that such basic notions had managed to produce "comfortable houses, and warm and easy toilets." Reporters descended on Wilde to seek clarification of his water tower comments. He wouldn't back down. "Why build it like a castle where one expects to see knights peering out?" he wondered, turning the questions back on the reporters. "Why don't you young men take your newspapers out of the hands of the old fogies and try to revolutionize the world?" he demanded. "Your newspapers are comic without being amusing." Perhaps, the *Duluth Tribune* observed dryly, Wilde had erred in his Chicago subject matter. "Oscar," reported the *Tribune,* "spoke of the 'beautiful in art,' and the 'joy in art,' and it was all Greek to the men and women who listened to him. Had he spoken of the 'beautiful in grain' or the 'joy in pork' he would have been understood and appreciated. . . . The Apostle of the Utter evidently has not learned how to suit himself to his audience."[12]

There was at least one true artist in Chicago, a young sculptor named John Donoghue, a "pure Celt" who had won Wilde's affections by bringing to his hotel a bas-relief of a pensive young girl intended to illustrate Wilde's elegy "Requiescat," written for his dead sister, Isola. Wilde returned the favor by visiting Donoghue's spartan studio in downtown Chicago, where the starving artist had been forced to beg leftover clay from nearby construction workers for his molds. Wilde recommended Donoghue to Charles Eliot Norton in Boston as the very man to do the statue of scholar-athletes that Wilde wanted to donate to Harvard. Thanks almost entirely to Wilde's backing, Donohue was able to secure other commissions and, ultimately, to move to Paris to live. After Wilde's marriage to Constance Lloyd in 1884, the honeymooning couple received a courtesy call from Donoghue at their Paris hotel, and they later purchased from him a bas-relief depicting, said Constance, "a nude figure full profile of a boy playing a harp, perfectly simple and quite exquisite in line and expression." In 1892 the sculptor created an enormous work, *The Spirit Brooding over the Abyss,* intended for display at his hometown's upcoming Columbian Exposition in Chicago. Since the sculpture was too large to be shipped in one piece, Donoghue had it sawed into pieces and shipped back to America, where, due to a scheduling mix-up, it lay unclaimed at the Brooklyn docks. Eventually, bemused dockworkers simply dumped the pieces into the harbor. Donoghue never got over the shock. A few years later he put a bullet through his temple, his suicide announced in the *New York Times* immediately below that of a White Plains man "driven temporarily insane by the heat."[13]

Wilde left Chicago on February 14, to the mutual relief of all involved. "Go, Mr. Wilde, and may the sunflower wither at your gaze," the *Daily News* bade farewell. His next stop, Fort Wayne, Indiana, was slightly more welcoming. As its name implied, Fort Wayne was a former military post, the site of various clashes involving English forces, their Indian allies, and the Americans during the Revolution and the War of 1812. It owed its name to Continental general "Mad Anthony" Wayne, who had routed Chief Little Turtle and the Miami Confederacy at the Battle of Fallen Timbers in 1794 and established an armed outpost at the confluence of the St. Joseph, St. Mary's, and Maumee rivers. Wilde arrived in town at 9:15 on the night of the fifteenth, after an express ride from Chicago. Tired and hungry, he checked into the Aveline House. Like any good advance man, his business agent, J. S. Vale, ignored the talent's needs in preference to those of the local press, inviting representatives from the *Daily Sentinel* and the *Gazette* to come upstairs to Wilde's room for a chat. The *Daily Sentinel* correspondent, taking pity on Wilde, postponed his interview until the next day, but the *Gazette*'s representative forged ahead after allowing Wilde one hour to get situated and unwind.[14]

As always, the poet presented an artful tableau for the visiting pressman, reclining on a sofa draped with a huge bearskin rug, smoking a Turkish cigarette, and ostentatiously reading a volume of Joaquin Miller's verse. He was wearing, the interviewer noted carefully, gray trousers, mouse-colored velvet smoking jacket, and matching magenta neckerchief and slippers embossed with golden sunflowers surrounded by silver sprays of lilies. Wilde greeted the newsman warmly, shaking hands with a practiced smile before sitting down to a long-delayed dinner of steak smothered in mushrooms, a dozen raw oysters with sliced lemons, chipped potatoes, and Piper Heidsieck champagne—"extra dry." It was, said the reporter, "a meal much more substantial than the odor of the lily or the bloom of the sunflower, the supposed aesthetical diet."[15]

The talk turned to the various arts—literature, acting, and architecture. Wilde confessed that he found train travel "very tiresome, and if it were not for Howells' novels, I could not endure it. He is your best novel writer." He said he regretted missing actress Genevieve Ward's Fort Wayne performance in *Forget-Me-Not* earlier that night, noting that he was a friend of the play's author, Herman Merrivale. Clara Morris, he said, was the only true American artiste. "She is beyond criticism." As for rising young star Mary Anderson, whom Wilde would later attempt to interest in his languishing drama, *Vera; or, the Nihilists,* he had a few arch comments. "Well, she may be a rising star, sir," Wilde said, "but it will take her a long time to rise. I saw her as Juliet [in New York] and I regret it very much." American hotels, though, were much nicer than their English counterparts. "England has no hotels worthy of the name," said Wilde. "They are so grand and gloomy that visitors once inside of them will submit to any extortion to get out of them." Asked about his tumultuous visit to Chicago, Wilde observed that "commercially it is a wonderful city, but knowing the millions of dollars that have been poured into the city to rebuild it, I was surprised by its poor architecture. There are no artistically beautiful buildings in the city."[16]

Even tired and hungry, Wilde managed to make a positive impression on the interviewer, who found him "an exceedingly clever and intelligent Englishman with a knowledge of art and literature excelled by few men of the present day, and whoever misses him this evening will miss the event of the season." The next morning Wilde was at it again, hosting the *Daily Sentinel*'s reporter while sitting down to a late breakfast at eleven A.M. Never a morning person, Wilde did not make as good an impression as he had the night before. Stifling "a very slight and artificially controlled yawn," he came across to his visitor as sullen, "St. Oscar, patron of the decorative arts." He did have, allowed the reporter (a man), "very kissable lips." Wilde turned on the charm, admitting that he had sat for innumerable press interviews, but "I do not begrudge the time. You American newspapermen are wonderful fellows. I talk a moment to you and you go off and create two-column interviews." Again the subject turned to Chicago, and Wilde insisted that he had been treated "very handsomely" there. "Chicago is a very wonderful city," he said. "I had occasion to say something about some of their architectural eyesores, and I presume my remarks were not appreciated." Still, he found—to the interviewer's open skepticism—that Chicago was more cultured than Boston. "I mean to say, my dear fellow, that I found more cultured people in Chicago," Wilde insisted. On that note the interview ended, and the reporter summed up his subject as "the languishing young Englishman who is just now coining money from the invariable desire of the American people to run after novelty of any sort."[17]

Bad weather kept Wilde inside his hotel until it was time for his lecture at the Fort Wayne Academy of Music on February 16. Fort Wayne, with its large Irish, German, and Polish immigrant population, was an island of Democratic Party sentiment in a solidly Republican state, and Wilde, in an unusual political concession, allowed himself to be introduced that evening by a Democratic gubernatorial candidate. Judging from his reception, he might just as well not have bothered. The now-standard contingent of young men aping Harvard's lead by sporting Aesthetic costumes and carrying lilies and sunflowers waltzed down the aisle before his speech, which, said the *Fort Wayne News,* was a "languid, monotonous stream of mechanically arranged words. He spoke for fully twenty-five minutes before he came to a full stop." His personality was judged to be "unprepossessing as a guide-board," and the lecture itself was "scholarly but pointless; as instructive as a tax list to a pauper, and scarcely as interesting." It was a tough crowd.[18]

Wilde's next two appearances, in Detroit and Cleveland, were uneventful, although a new song, "The Oscar Wilde Galop," appeared as sheet music in the former city. Other songs, including "The Flippity Flop Young Man," "Oscar Dear!" and "The Oscar Wilde Forget-Me-Not Waltz," also came out about this time, and young women in the cities he visited were wont to sing out "Twenty lovesick maidens we" as he went by on the street. In Cleveland he lunched with John Hay, the former amanuensis for Abraham Lincoln during the Civil War, and sat for the obligatory stage-managed interview with the press, this time the *Cleveland Leader,* exact down to the bearskin rug, velvet suit, matching handkerchief, and ever-present cigarette. He ventured the opinion that "America is not a country; it is a world," and summed up his impressions of the various worlds he had visited: "I find New York brilliant and cosmopolitan; Philadelphia, literary; Baltimore, pleasant; Washington, intellectual; Boston, more like Oxford than any city you have. The people in Chicago I found simple and strong, and without any foolish prejudices that have influenced East America"—not that, strictly speaking, there was such a place on the map.[19]

Wilde was a little annoyed that the Cleveland newspaper had chosen to publicize his speaking fee, $500, for the event at Case Hall. It brought to mind the recent flap in Baltimore about his supposed demands for more money. He reminded one reporter that American lecturers were paid comparably, adding sardonically: "I am extremely impressed by the entire disregard of Americans for moneymaking, as shown by the remarks made by many of the western journals. They think it a strange and awful thing that I should make a few dollars by lecturing. Why, money-making is necessary for art. Money builds cities and makes them healthful. Money buys art and furnishes it an incentive. Is it strange that I should want to make money? And yet these newspapers cry out that I am making money." Still, he attempted to take a more elevated view of his situation. "What possible difference can it make to me what the *New York Herald* says?" he wondered. "You go and look at the statue of the Venus de Milo and you know that is an exquisitely beautiful creation. Would it change your opinion in the least if all the newspapers in the land should pronounce it a wretched caricature? Not at all."[20]

From Cleveland, Wilde and his two-man traveling party took the train south to Cincinnati, where he would spend a couple of days before going on to Louisville and Indianapolis for his next appearances. He arrived in Cincinnati in the midst of a deluge. Heavy rains were soaking the lower Midwest; the Ohio River was said to be rising at the rate of two inches an hour, a serious threat for a riverfront town such as Cincinnati. Homes and farms, sawmills and distilleries along the river were being evacuated. Coal yards and slaughterhouses were under water, and Rat Row, Cincinnati's notorious criminal district, was swamped, sending its rodent population—human and animal alike—scurrying to higher ground. Wilde checked into Room 62 at the patrician Burnet House, feeling a little under the weather himself. He called down for a bellhop to bring him the entire stock of sunflowers from the hotel florist shop. Told that they were all sold out of sunflowers, he settled for three dollars' worth of pink and red roses. The flowers, he told a visiting journalist from the *Cincinnati Gazette,* were "a rest and comfort to his soul after the horrors of a railway journey."[21]

Despite the weather, Wilde allowed himself to be talked into a tour of the Queen City. Thanks to its traditional status as a railroad center and river port, Cincinnati was the principal trading gateway to the South, making it in some ways more of a southern city than a northern one. Its enormous German population, crowded atop the hillside district known as "Over the Rhine" in the northeastern section of town, gave it a distinctly European tone. Throwing on his famous green overcoat, accessorized with a rosebud in his lapel, tan gloves, brown felt hat, and ivory walking stick, Wilde persuaded the *Gazette* reporter to accompany him on a tour of the city. "This kind of weather," he sighed, "always gives me a sense of failure."[22]

Wilde and his companion rode by carriage through rainy Cincinnati, while he unburdened himself of his newly formed impressions of America. "I am pleased with it," said Wilde. "It has great possibilities. I am especially delighted with the West, it is so new and fresh, and the people are so generous and free from prejudice. In the older cities in the East, the people are enveloped in a perfect mist of prejudice, quite unlimited; they have imported so many Old World ideas, absurdities, and affectations, that they have lost all sincerity and naturalness." Wilde went into the Robert Clarke & Company bookstore, where he purchased several books by W. D. Howells, Henry James, and Cincinnati's own Mary Louise McLaughlin, a ceramist of some note. From there, he was escorted to the Rookwood Pottery Company, the Cincinnati School of Design, and the Cincinnati Art Museum, whose doors, noted the reporter, "were inhospitably closed." At the School of Design, Wilde's gaze lit on the "No Smoking" sign painted on a window. "Great heaven," he said, "they speak of smoking as if it were a crime. I wonder they do not caution the students not to murder each other on the landings. Such a place is enough to incite a man to the commission of any crime." In the unkindest cut of all, as the *Gazette* recorded, Wilde added, "I wonder no criminal has ever pleaded the ugliness of your city as an excuse for his crimes!"[23]

Back in his room at the Burnet House, still sporting his rosebud boutonnière, Wilde hosted a reporter from the rival *Cincinnati Enquirer.* The hotel staff had managed to locate four calla lilies to go with the basket of roses on the room table, providing a fitting olfactory complement for the interview, which touched entirely on the subject of art. Wilde described his visit to Rookwood Pottery and its owner-operator, Cincinnati heiress Maria Longworth Nichols, a daughter of the city's richest family. Mrs. Nichols's father, Nicholas Longworth, was known as the father of the American wine industry, profitably marketing a German Riesling to the immigrant families of Over the Rhine. One of her brothers, also named Nicholas, was Speaker of the U.S. House of Representatives and later gave his name to the Longworth House Office

Building in Washington. Among his many accomplishments was wooing and winning the formidable Alice Roosevelt, daughter of Theodore
Roosevelt, to be his wife.

Wilde, on his visit to Rookwood, "inspected its work very closely.
Some of it was very good, and much of it indifferent. On the whole
I was very pleased." One artist at the shop, a young man named Arthur
Bowen Davies, was singled out by Wilde for particular praise as one
"who I am sure has true poetic art and fervor." Once again, Wilde displayed a good eye. Davies, as a founding member of the so-called Ash-
can School, would go on to become president of the Association of
American Painters and Sculptors, which mounted the notorious 1913
Armory Show in New York—the exhibition that introduced modern art
to the United States, most notably Marcel Duchamp's revolutionary
cubist painting *Nude Descending a Staircase,* which caused Theodore
Roosevelt to bark, "That's not art!" and the *New York Evening Sun* to
rename the painting *Rude Descending a Staircase.* Told by his interviewer
that a local Cincinnati artist had won a gold medal at the Vienna Exposition for his painting of a hog killing, Wilde remained unflappable.
"Well, I don't know but even that could be treated in an artistic manner," he said. "The lowliest subject, treated with loving earnestness and
sincerity, will, if the artist is competent, give the best results, just as the
plainest words are the most effective in the mouth of an actor." Arthur
Bowen Davies couldn't have put it better himself.[24]

Despite reports that 1,200 families in Louisville had been displaced
or driven to the upper stories of their homes by raging flood waters,
Wilde was able to make it to his next lecture appearance at Louisville's
Masonic Hall on February 21 without undue delay. It turned out to be a
memorable evening, for Wilde in particular. A Mason himself while at
Oxford (before he was expelled for not paying his dues), Wilde appeared
before a cultured crowd that included Henry Watterson, the fabled editor of the *Louisville Courier-Journal* and one of the driving forces in the
"New South" movement to improve relations between North and South

after the Civil War. Perhaps because he had been recently ridiculed himself as a Bunthornian character by unregenerate Republican cartoonist Thomas Nast in the pages of *Harper's Weekly*, Watterson took it easy on Wilde, characterizing him as "a young Englishman of respectable family, of showy, if not, great, talents, and excellent scholarship, who has come to America to travel, see the country, and, if he can, pick up a few Yankee dollars to pay his expenses and take him home." There was nothing wrong with that, said Watterson, allowing that the poet "might shorten his hair and lengthen his breeches," but suggesting also that Wilde's personal idiosyncrasies "ought to be left to his own choosing and the favor of those who favor them, seeing that those who do not are not obliged to be annoyed by them."[25]

One Louisville native in attendance that evening thrilled Wilde with her kindness. Mrs. Philip Speed was the niece of Wilde's great idol, John Keats, "the real Adonis of our age." Her father, George Keats, the younger brother of the Romantic poet, had immigrated to America in 1818, two years before John's lingering death, of tuberculosis, in Rome. Emma Keats Speed herself had attained both the middle age and the happy marriage denied by fate to her genius uncle, and after hearing Wilde in his lecture refer favorably to Keats's use of color, she came backstage afterwards to introduce herself. Touched and flattered, Wilde spent the better part of the next day with Mrs. Speed, who kindly showed him several letters, on yellowing scraps of paper, written by Keats to her father. A few weeks later, she forwarded to Wilde the original manuscript of her uncle's poem "Answer to a Sonnet by J. H. Reynolds," sometimes referred to as "Sonnet on Blue," which begins: "Blue! This the life of heaven—the domain / Of Cynthia—the wide palace of the sun." It is not one of Keats's better poems, but Wilde framed it and kept it in a place of honor in his various homes for the rest of his life. He later told Mrs. Speed: "What you have given me is more golden than gold, more precious than any treasure this great country could yield me." In turn, he sent her a copy of his sonnet "The Grave of Keats," and expressed the hope that she would keep it alongside Keats's own papers so that "it may keep some green of youth caught from those withered leaves in whose faded lines eternal summer dwells."[26]

From Louisville, Wilde zigzagged north again to Indianapolis for an appearance at English's Opera House the next night. Built two years earlier, the performance hall was the brainchild of First National Bank mogul William Hayden English, the Democratic Party nominee for vice president in 1880. English, with scant political experience, had been chosen to run on the national ticket with Union war hero Winfield Scott Hancock of Gettysburg fame, on the premise that he would help to bankroll the campaign. This, English adamantly refused to do, causing Democrats to wring their hands and Republicans to self-righteously castigate English as a miser who, in yet another Thomas Nast cartoon, offered "praise but no money" to his running mate. In the end, the genuine war hero Hancock lost the closest popular-vote election in American history to the bogus war hero James A. Garfield, about whose much-exaggerated ride back to the battlefield at Chickamauga his fellow battle survivor Ambrose Bierce said: "There was no great heroism in it; that is what every man should have done, including the commander of the army. I did so myself, and have never felt that it ought to make me president."[27]

English had gone back to Indianapolis and used some of his carefully husbanded wealth to build the Opera House, upon whose walls full-color posters now promised that Wilde's visit would be "The Fashionable Event of the Season." American soprano Emma Abbott had performed there the previous month in a road company version of *Patience,* further fanning the flames for Wilde's arrival. Miss Abbott, a Chicago native, headlined Abbott's English Opera Company, whose name signified not a link to local impresario William H. English, but rather the fact that the company performed all its operas in English—no particular achievement when dealing with Gilbert and Sullivan musicals. Charles Dennis, editor of the *Indianapolis Saturday Review,* a weekly newspaper, had further prepared the ground for Wilde with a series of humorous reports in which he alleged, entirely falsely, that several of the city's most prominent citizens had started up a homegrown Aesthetic Movement of their own "to counteract the barbaric influence of pork and railroads"—pork and railroads being the twin spines of Indianapolis industry.[28]

Indianapolis was jumping when Wilde arrived. Three separate groups were holding conventions in the city: the Veterans of the Mexican War, who were by then getting a little long in the tooth; the Grand Army of the Republic (GAR); and the Greenback Party, which had held its first national convention in Indianapolis six years earlier. Wilde attracted about five hundred people for his performance—not a bad turnout, all things considered. He gave his standard seventy-five-minute speech ("The Decorative Arts") to an indifferent response. The critic for the *Indianapolis News* seemed more entranced by Wilde's long hair than by his words, which he found monotonous and carelessly delivered. "There was an evident willingness to applaud at times," the critic wrote, "but he made no pauses and the audience could not find an opportunity to break in." Charles Dennis of the *Saturday Review* took note of Wilde's English pronunciations—"handicrawftsmen," "vawse," and "teel-e-phone"—and found Wilde's stocking-clad legs rather disappointing: "They actually had no more symmetry than the same length of garden hose," he complained. The *Indianapolis Journal* summed up the crowd's overall reaction as "tumultuous silence."[29]

As it happened, Wilde would have an unexpected encore. He had already gone back to his room at the New Denison Hotel and retired for the evening when his manager, Vale, turned up shortly before midnight with an aide to Indiana governor Albert Gallatin Porter. The governor, a Republican, was hosting a reception at the chief executive's mansion for the boys in the GAR and the Greenback Party. (The venerable veterans of the Mexican War, presumably, had already gone to bed.) The aide, an industrious young man named Billy Roberts, had suggested that the governor enliven the dull proceedings by inviting Oscar Wilde to come over and throw around some of his patented witticisms. After determining that the governor's mansion was about a mile away from the hotel, Wilde obligingly climbed back into his stage costume and joined Vale and Roberts for the carriage ride. Along the way, Wilde questioned Roberts about the American custom of shaking hands. "I notice," he said, "that the men shake hands a great deal here. Do the ladies shake hands too?" Told that they did, Wilde said he would like to practice the custom on some of the Greenbackers—he called them "peasants"—who were standing in front of the governor's mansion. "Peasants" was perhaps a poor choice of word for American farmers, particularly those enlightened political activists in the Greenback Movement, but the subtle nuance escaped Wilde at the time.[30]

Once inside the mansion, Wilde was introduced to Governor Porter and his family. Porter, a law partner of future president Benjamin Harrison, was in the first of two terms as governor, after earlier stints of public service as a congressman during the Civil War and as Comptroller of the United States Treasury under Rutherford B. Hayes. Porter enjoyed Washington life and had not necessarily wanted to return to his Indiana roots—he had already refused once before to run for governor—but the state's Republican Party had nominated him in 1880 without his knowledge and had presented him with something of a fait accompli, including already printed campaign posters. Porter embraced the role with a vengeance, trading his well-tailored suits and vests for a pair of farmer's blue jeans and a bucolic straw hat. Apparently his tastes carried over to the architecture of his official residence, which evoked Wilde's curiosity: Had the people of Indiana given it to him? Told that Porter had designed the house himself, Wilde shook his head and pronounced the mansion "no better than the Atlantic, if as good." He consented to break bread with the Porters, however, and even tried the new American craze, ice cream, which Charles Dennis of the *Saturday Review* reported that Wilde "spooned in with the languor of a debilitated duck." The poet left hurriedly after finishing his bowl. "Perhaps ice cream disagrees with him," said Dennis, who was still nursing a grudge over the asymmetry of Wilde's pantaloons.[31]

From late-night ice cream with the governor of Indiana, Wilde went back to Cincinnati for his long-awaited speech at the Opera House. As always, the local newspapers were full of ads seeking to take advantage of Wilde's notoriety. One, for B. Frank Hart's clothing store on West 4th Street, touted: "Gents! Have you seen the Oscar Wilde shoes? (They are too utterly too-too.)" Another claimed boldly that "Oscar Wilde says the Opera Puffs Cigarettes are a luxurious luxury and just too-too!" and promised that the celebrated soprano Adelina Patti, whom Wilde had visited backstage during her recent performance at the Music Hall, would benefit from similarly smoking Wilde's brand of tobacco.[32]

Since his appearance in Cincinnati was a matinée, Wilde forswore his usual evening wear of knee breeches and stockings for a modest gray afternoon coat. The crowd, he said, was "dreadfully disappointed" by the wardrobe change, but otherwise received him well, even after he threw in some biting remarks on the local art scene. "At a certain school of design," said Wilde, "I saw moonlight and sunset scenes depicted on dinner plates. This is not the thing to do. Canvas or paper should be the materials for that sort of work, not clay objects that would be sent down to the kitchen to be washed by a maid." One prairie scene of a rabbit staring at the moon seemed to Wilde to be "a mere smudge with a couple of ears." Another scene on a "vawse" put him in mind of "someone who, I should say, had only five minutes to catch a train." At the end of his lecture, Wilde held out a figurative olive branch. "Wars and the clashing of arms and the meeting of men in battles must be always, but I think that art, creating a common intellectual atmosphere between all countries, might, if it could not overshadow the world with the silvery wings of peace, at least make men such brothers that they would not go out to slay one another as they do in Europe"—or America, for that matter. "Art is the only empire that may not yield to conquest."[33]

Wilde's appeal to the better angels of their nature was a hit with Cincinnatians, who swarmed the stage afterwards to shake his hand and invite him to come back in June to speak to the workmen of the city. After a visit to the home of local tycoon and art collector Henry Probasco, a tree-shrouded suburban estate called "the Oaks," and a second stop at Mrs. Nichols's Rookwood, Wilde caught the night train to St. Louis. He was getting out of town just in time. P. T. Barnum's celebrated midget, General Tom Thumb, was due to arrive the next week, followed by the even more militaristic Archibald Forbes the week after. Meanwhile, the city's annual religious festival was under way, and as Wilde departed he could hear strains of the faithful's earthly chorus: "Oh wondrous bliss, oh joy sublime, / I've Jesus with me all the time!"[34]

Wilde reached St. Louis late the next morning. The flood-swollen Mississippi River, turned yellowish-brown by the mud, was foaming and surging over its banks. "No well-behaved river ought to act this way," Wilde remarked from the train. Inside the New Southern Hotel on Walnut Street, a curious crowd of onlookers waited for the famous Aesthete's arrival, craning their necks each time a long-haired guest entered the lobby. It did them no good; Wilde, Vale, and valet John, alighting from their carriage at 10:30, were ushered through the ladies' entrance to the elevator and went directly to Room 70. The usual gang of local reporters, from the *Post-Dispatch,* the *Globe-Democrat,* and the *Republican,* soon paid court.[35]

For some reason, perhaps the weather, the exchanges between Wilde and the reporters were sharper than usual. The correspondent for the *Globe-Democrat,* calling Wilde "the Prince of Languor" and "the Lord of the Lah-de-dah," described him as "uncertain-mouthed" and having "the general appearance of an overtasked medical student," with "a large, soft, rather fat hand." Wilde, always quick on the uptake, parried words with the reporter. Told that the city had no art schools except for a Sketch Club that gathered once a month to drink beer, eat sandwiches, and swap drawings, Wilde smirked, "How truly Bohemian!" The reporter observed that Wilde had "not seen our streets at their best," but that it might rain during the night and "you will see them as we know them best tomorrow." Wilde replied, "I shall await the morrow with supreme interest."[36]

Asked about his general impression of newspaper reporters, Wilde said, "I expected ill-treatment at the hands of the American press. I was warned of it by friends before I left. . . . At first I was greatly annoyed, and with difficulty restrained my feelings, but latterly I have schooled myself not to notice them. My critics have for the most part been mere boys, who knew nothing of the subjects which I treat. Why should I annoy myself by paying attention to their utterances?" He added that he had generally had a pleasant experience with western reporters, prompting the journalist to drolly "return thanks upon behalf of the western press."[37]

The reporter for the *St. Louis Republican,* arriving next, admitted with some disappointment that Wilde was "not the grotesque being that has been described." His subject, fortified by "very weak" sherry punch, assumed an attitude "at once resigned and quizzical." Wilde grew heated again when the reporter asked him if he thought his Aesthetic opinions were practical. "Do you think that we, the young men of England, would give our youth, our energy and whatever of intellect we may possess to their fulfillment if we had the remotest intention of failing? We have already changed the whole condition of English decorative art." Rising to the bait, Wilde continued: "The ordinary critic belongs to the criminal classes, and . . . in many cases the newspapers of America would employ people to write on art whom in England we would not consider qualified to report any case of petty larceny above the value of five shillings." The interview was diplomatically cut short by Wilde's road manager, Vale, and the reporter left, conceding to his readers the next day that "the young gentleman with the Sapphic speech and the mane of Absalom" had some "horse sense" hiding beneath the sunflowers and lilies.[38]

Wilde's reception at Mercantile Library Hall was not much better. There was the usual imitator sitting in the front row with a large calla lily in his lapel, and half a dozen young women wearing artificial sunflowers they had bought from some urchins outside the building. Whispers and giggles greeted his arrival, and the loud cries of the sunflower hawkers on the sidewalk carried through to the hall. When Wilde ventured a polite compliment to "your beautiful streets," it was met with ironically prolonged applause from a group of young toughs in the back row. An exhortation to "adopt a bright and simple dress" brought more shouts and laughter, and Wilde left the platform, rattled and angry. It was the worst treatment he had received thus far on his tour, he said backstage; it had been "villainous." Perhaps, he suggested, "the acoustics weren't very good." Before departing the next night for Springfield, Illinois, Wilde was told by several St. Louis citizens that the city had not been at its best. "I should have thought so," said Wilde, "even though the information was lacking." When a bellboy at the hotel asked him for his autograph, Wilde inscribed a lugubrious bit of verse: "The sea is flecked with bars of gold / The dull dead wind is out of tune." That was very much his sense of St. Louis itself.[39]

CHAPTER 6

A Very Italy, Without Its Art

❧

THE END OF FEBRUARY found Wilde facing a half-empty house in Springfield, Illinois, the adopted hometown and final resting place of Abraham Lincoln. The martyred president was not resting very easily these days: six years earlier a crackpot group of grave robbers had attempted to steal the president's body and hold it for $200,000 ransom. They had failed (the 500-pound wood-and-lead coffin was too heavy for the thieves to move more than a few inches from its marble sarcophagus at Oak Ridge Cemetery), but city fathers had panicked and reburied Lincoln's coffin in an unmarked hole in the basement of the tomb. Only the trio of hastily enlisted gravediggers knew exactly where it was. Nor was Lincoln's widow, Mary, doing too well herself. Having spent the years following her husband's assassination passing in and out of various mental institutions, Mrs. Lincoln was reduced to living in the back room of her sister Elizabeth's house in Springfield. Increasingly frail and nearly blind—she would die five months later—Mrs. Lincoln was in no condition to attend Wilde's lecture at the Springfield Opera House.

It was too bad, in a way, for both of them. Mad Mary Lincoln, with her well-documented love of fine clothes, expensive jewelry, and lavish home decorations, might well have made a better audience for Wilde's words than her more prosaic neighbors did. The *Springfield Republican,* Lincoln's former political mouthpiece, had announced Wilde's appearance with unconcealed distaste: "Oscar Wilde is a secondhand fool. He has written some concupiscent verse which he will be ashamed of when he gets older." Displaying what the rival *Springfield State-Register* termed "a melancholy cast of countenance," Wilde cut his speech in half, but even at forty-five minutes it ran too long for the taste of the *State Journal* reporter, who in a rather fine turn of phrase called Wilde "an exaggerated boy of two or three years who has suddenly expanded to the size of a man, small clothes, flowing locks and all. Our art must, indeed, be in its infancy."[1]

Beginning with Springfield, tour manager J. S. Vale had scheduled Wilde for an exhausting twelve appearances over the next thirteen days, culminating with his second lecture in Chicago in less than a month. With the exception of a March 5 date in Milwaukee, Wilde found himself traveling the back roads and boondocks of the upper Midwest: Dubuque, Rockford, Aurora, Racine, Joliet, Jacksonville, Decatur, Peoria, and Bloomington. The halls were small and the crowds disappointing. In Dubuque, the turnout was so light that Vale had made an announcement from the stage urging the audience to "come up forward." Event promoter A. Kitson pronounced the revenue from ticket sales "exceedingly limpid"; Wilde received $180 for his night's work.

Understandably, the poet was a little depressed. In Racine, on March 4, before a snickering crowd of seventy onlookers, he broke down in the middle of his lecture and left the stage. He explained later that he had been too exhausted to read his manuscript. "I have been to many incipient little places of late," he told a newsman, "and I am almost worn out with hunger. I love my cigarettes and do not know what I should have done without them. I have not been able to obtain a morsel of food that I liked, and have lived on cigarettes." He dashed off a letter to Colonel Morse complaining about the "fiasco" of the previous ten days and urging him to schedule more lectures in big cities such as Boston, New York, and Philadelphia, "where I am sure I would draw large audiences, instead of wearing my voice and body to death over the wretched houses here. It's so depressing and useless lecturing for a few shillings."[2]

Back in Chicago, Wilde checked into his old quarters at the Grand Pacific Hotel to work on a new lecture. "The House Beautiful," as it was eventually titled, was geared more toward practical homemakers than his earlier lectures had been. "I shall begin with the door-knocker and go to the attic," he told a reporter for the *Chicago Tribune*. "Beyond that is Heaven, and I shall leave that to the Church." Wilde may have been willing to leave churchly matters alone, but at least one prominent Chicago church man did not leave him alone. David Swing, a Presbyterian minister known as "the Beecher of the Windy City," had seen fit to denounce Wilde in the pages of his religious publication, the *Alliance*. In an article entitled "Oscar the Small," Swing called Wilde "a perfect specimen of man, the little," charging in a barely disguised attack on Wilde's ambiguous sexuality that "a woman kissing a poodle comes nearer expressing the unmanliness of this peacockism. He is a peddler of childish jimcracks and his domain is not the world, but the showcase of some notion store." To Swing, Wilde was an enigma, "an intellectual and emotional abyss whose intellectual height and depth are best expressed by the tailor and the laundress." What really seemed to offend the reverend was Wilde's alleged boast of earning $1,000 a night while other "great men"—Swing modestly refrained from naming names—were receiving only $300. Finally, "We confess that the water-tower of Chicago has as much right to its 'pepper boxes' as Oscar has to his shoe-buckles and tights."[3]

Wilde responded witheringly in an interview in the *Tribune* on March 5.

There is nothing more depressing than to be attacked by a fool, as one cannot answer and does not fight with the same weapons. If a man attacks one for the clothes that one likes to wear he should go for his answer to one's tailor, and if a man assails one for the flowers that one admires he should discuss the matter with one's gardener; and, as regards the learned professor's sneer at me for receiving a fee for lecturing, he is not the first clergyman that has visited me with such a bitter reproach, which derives all its sting from the fact it comes from a body of men most of whom receive large salaries for preaching.

Confessing his surprise "that anyone with the name of David should be fighting for the Philistines," Wilde said the minister would have been better served "taking a pebble from the river brook and hurling it at that monstrous Goliath of Chicago architecture, the water tower, instead of praising it as being, as he calls it, calm and rational—two most unfortunate epithets."[4]

Wilde's new lecture, as promised, was a top-to-bottom survey of modern houses and, most particularly, their furnishings. On the subject of home decoration, he was blunt, bemoaning "ill-looking rooms in ill-built houses, furnished with blood-curdling evidences of barbarism in the shape of machine rosewood furniture and black-leaded stoves." Houses should be made of naturally colored stone, with wrought-iron railings out front and tiled flooring in the entryways. Red brick or wood were acceptable as a substitute, although he cautioned that wood houses should be better painted. "You must have warmer colors; there is far too much white and that cold grey color." There should be no cast-iron ornaments or railings, "which boys are always knocking down, and very rightly too, for they always look cheap and shabby." He suggested wrought iron, instead. Most houses were too large, their carpets were too loud, and their pictures were hung too high on the walls—although, upon closer inspection, he thought "the demerits of composition" generally showed the height of the paintings to have been "wise and humane." Hat racks, on the other hand, were instruments of torture "as hideous as the rack of the Middle Ages."[5]

Wilde called for wainscoting instead of wallpaper, red brick tiles instead of rugs, and exposed ceilings. "Don't paper it," he advised; "that gives one the sensation of living in a paper box, which is not pleasant." He favored indirect lighting, preferably lamps and wax candles rather than gas lights, and smaller windows—"most modern windows are much too large . . . and are made as if you only wanted them to look out of." As for furniture, Wilde recommended the Queen Anne style, with polished brass and mahogany borders. "One must have a piano I suppose," he wrote, "but it is a melancholy thing, and most like a dreadful, funereal packing-case in form than anything else." Flowers, blown glass, Greek statuary, old china, and traditionally bound books completed his vision of household furnishings. Above all, Wilde advised, "Have nothing in your house that has not given pleasure to the man who made it and is not a pleasure to those who use it. Have nothing in your houses that is not useful or beautiful."[6]

Between lecture writing and verbal donnybrooks, Wilde managed to catch up on his correspondence in Chicago. He first had to chaff James McNeill Whistler a little for being the ringleader behind a mocking letter to the *London Times* in which the painter advised: "Oscar! We of Tite Street and Beaufort Gardens joy in your triumphs, and delight in your success, but—we think that, with the exception of your epigrams, you talk like Sidney Colvin in the Provinces, and that, with the exception of your knee-breeches, you dress like 'Arry Quilter." Colvin was Slade Professor of Fine Arts at Cambridge and a noted biographer of Keats, neither of which achievements much impressed Wilde. The dislike was returned in spades. Colvin later wrote that "Oscar Wilde–ism is the most pestilent and hateful disease of our time." Wilde wrote again to Whistler: "My dear Jimmy, They are considering me seriously. Isn't it dreadful? What would you do if it happened to you?"[7]

Another old friend chimed in with a more negative and mean-

spirited response to Wilde's American trip. J. E. Courtenay Bodley, the
son of a wealthy Irish pottery maker, had known Wilde since their days
in Dublin and Oxford, where they had been close friends—at least
Wilde thought so at the time. Bodley sent a long anonymous article to
the *New York Times* painting Wilde as a somewhat ridiculous figure at
Oxford, a Johnny-come-lately to the Aesthetic Movement who spoke
with a lisp in a heavy Irish accent and was considered by some to be
"epicene." "He has considerable ability, and he has seen fit to use it in
obtaining a cheap notoriety," Bodley wrote. "He is good-hearted, has
been amusing, and probably retains some sense of humor. Will American society encourage him in the line he has taken, which can only lead
to one end, or will it teach him not unkindly a needed lesson and bid
him return home to ponder it in growing wiser?" Wilde did not respond
to the unprovoked attack except to observe afterwards, "It is always Ju-
das who writes the biography." In Paris, years later, Wilde would pre-
tend not to recognize Bodley when they passed on the street.[8]

Wilde was also back in touch with impresario D'Oyly Carte, who
had worked out a lucrative deal for an expanded tour of California—$5,000 for three weeks. The poet would leave from Omaha on the
Union Pacific Railroad on March 24 and ride for a hundred hours
straight through to Sacramento. Or almost straight—the "express"
stopped every thirty minutes or so for fuel, water, and more passengers.
With 230 stops along the way, it would take Wilde's train the better part
of five days to reach the Pacific coast, more than enough time for him to
form a lifelong sense of awe for the sheer size of the American continent.

In the meantime, the poet completed his last four scheduled lectures in the upper Midwest, going first to Minneapolis and St. Paul for a
pair of appearances at the Minneapolis Academy of Music and the
St. Paul Opera House. The hardy Scandinavian settlers of Minnesota
were ready for him, having already been treated to a road show performance of *Patience* by Emma Abbott's ubiquitous English Opera Company a couple months earlier. Local newspapers trumpeted the immi-

nent arrival of "the Distinguished Lily-Consumer," "the Apostle of the Utter," and "the boss [chief] English sunflower." Despite all the pretour publicity, only about 250 people attended the Minneapolis lecture on March 15, including a reporter from the *Minneapolis Journal* who came away, after listening to Wilde's remarks, persuaded "that most things in America are so confoundedly, gorgeously vulgar, from cast-iron gateposts all the way up to soup tureens." Wilde, he said, seemed to be a capable man, "so much the more folly for him to so act and dress and loll and espouse a 'yum yum' style that sensible people now turn away." The *Pioneer Press* adjudged the lecture "a series of artistic platitudes without the slightest trace of artistic revolution." The *Minneapolis Tribune* was even less kind, finding Wilde's English accent hard to understand and his manner of delivery "flat and insipid. From the time the speaker commenced to his closing sentence, he kept up the same unvarying endless drawl, without modulating his voice or making a single gesture, giving the impression that he was a prize monkey wound up and warranted to talk for an hour and a half without stopping."[9]

Across the Mississippi River, in St. Paul, Wilde had a somewhat better reception the next evening at the Opera House. He had changed costumes, from black-velvet to purple-velvet coat, and added a lace handkerchief that he flourished freely as he spoke. According to the *St. Paul Globe,* Wilde "was shocked by our buildings, by the mud in the streets, and especially by the rooms and furniture in the hotels." The *Pioneer Press* observed that city residents were "used to that sort of thing," adding that "the only time he really trod on St. Paul toes was when he asserted that our streets were dirty. This is a sensitive point with all St. Paul people, except the city authorities, whose business it is to keep the streets clean." The next evening, Wilde attended a St. Patrick's Day celebration at the same theater and was called onstage by the event emcee, local Catholic priest Father Shanley, to say a few words as "a son of one of Ireland's noblest daughters." He responded with brief remarks castigating the British—a surefire target—for destroying seven hundred years of Irish culture, but predicting that Ireland would rise again to "regain the proud position she once held among the nations of Europe." He received a warm round of applause. Wilde's impact extended as far south as Dodge Center, where that Christmas a young man with the perfect Wildean name of Cordy Severance won first prize at the annual holiday masquerade for his spot-on knee breeches, shoe buckles, sunflower, and "aesthetic, languid air of the champion of lahdadahism."[10]

Two days later Wilde was in the border town of Sioux City, Iowa, at the navigable headwaters of the Missouri River, east of Nebraska. There, he excitedly reported to Betty Lewis in London, he had seen his first Indians, who he joked were very similar to Sidney Colvin in their appearance, particularly when Colvin was wearing his professorial robes. "Their conversation was most interesting as long as it was unintelligible," wrote Wilde, "but when interpreted to me reminded me strangely and vividly of the conversation of Mr. Commissioner [Robert M.] Kerr," a London judge. At the time, less than six years after Custer's Last Stand, eight hundred miles northwest of Iowa in Montana, the Sioux were peaceable again. Sitting Bull had surrendered with the last of the fugitives from the Custer massacre a few months earlier at nearby Fort Randall, South Dakota. There was no telling which Native American tribesmen Wilde had encountered; despite its name, Sioux City was as likely to have Omaha and Winnebago Indians in its environs as Yankton Sioux. Wilde, of course, was no expert. He reported frankly to Mrs. Lewis, "I don't know where I am: somewhere in the middle of coyotes and cañons: one is a 'ravine' and the other a 'fox,' I don't know which, but I think they change about." He had also seen some miners, "big-booted, red-shirted, yellow-bearded and delightful ruffians" who, he suspected, secretly read Bret Harte in their free time. "They were certainly almost as real as his miners, and quite as pleasant."[11]

Following his speech at Sioux City's three-story Academy of Music—the local *Journal* thought him "a spiritless namby-pamby nondescript"—Wilde traveled due south to Omaha, also on the banks of the Missouri, where he found lodging at the Withnell House, a converted army barracks, prior to his appearance at Boyd's Opera House on March 20. Omaha was a new city, only a couple of decades old in 1882 but already renowned as the "Gateway to the West" owing to its prime position as hub of the Union Pacific Railroad. It had first entered the national consciousness in 1804 as the site of the only death suffered by any member of the Lewis and Clark expedition, one Charles Floyd, who expired from a ruptured appendix on the bluffs overlooking the river.[12]

The Omaha Social Arts Club was sponsoring Wilde's visit, and both local newspapers, the *Herald* and the *Bee,* gave him a respectful hearing, perhaps as a welcome break from a nasty railroad strike that had been put down by armed state militia a few days earlier at the unfortunately named Camp Dump. Omaha, being simultaneously a cattle town, a railroad town, and a river town, was used to eccentric, longhaired travelers. At the opera house, built two years earlier by the Irishborn mayor, James W. Boyd, at the intersection of 15th and Farnham streets, Wilde was introduced by Judge James W. Savage, who had been a groomsman at President Chester A. Arthur's wedding in New York City in 1859. Wilde went over well, with the *Herald* describing his lecture as "a blistering rebuke to the materialism of the age" and giving its own hot denunciation of the "many men and women [who] sneer at Oscar Wilde," saying the poet's "peculiar personal manner and attire have really nothing to do with the simple and salutary thought underlying his strangeness." The *Daily Republican* did not find the need to champion Wilde, but it did observe cryptically that "Oscar Wilde loves Nebraska canned corn"—a statement the poet let stand without contradiction.[13]

Buoyed by his reception in Omaha, Wilde gave a high-spirited answer to a reporter's valedictory question about his future plans. Laughing as he lit a cigarette, Wilde responded: "Well, I'm a very ambitious young man. I want to do everything in the world. I cannot conceive of anything that I do not want to do. I want to write a great deal more poetry. I want to study painting more than I've been able to. I want to write a great many more plays, and I want to make this artistic movement the basis for a new civilization." In the meantime, he steeled himself for the long train ride to California, asking the *Bee* reporter if he would be able to see any wild animals from the train. Told that he could expect to see herds of jack rabbits, antelopes, grizzly bears, buffalo, and mountain lions, Wilde brightened. "How unutterably lovely," he exclaimed.[14]

Ahead lay nearly two thousand miles of variably lovely countryside stretching across the American prairies and through the Rocky Mountains from Omaha to Salt Lake City and then down through the Sierra Nevada Mountains to Sacramento. Wilde traveled first class, which was decidedly better than second class, but the trip was still exhausting. Passengers in first class sat in reclining plush velvet seats and slept in pull-out sleeping berths, compliments of railroad inventor George Mortimer Pullman. Those in second class had to share space with crowds of short-haul "way" passengers—cowboys, farmers, miners, trappers, Indians, and other assorted drifters—who clambered on and off the train at destination way stations located every few miles at tank towns and whistle stops. Hundreds of gamblers, cardsharps, and pickpockets worked the trains, as well as traveling prostitutes colloquially known as "Toodle-oos" who were particularly adept at quick fumbling encounters between compartments.

The transcontinental railroad had been completed less than thirteen years earlier with the sinking of the "golden spike" at Promontory Point (in Utah, fifty-six miles west of Ogden), where the Union Pacific linked up with the Central Pacific. Thousands of railroad builders, mostly Irish for the Union Pacific and Chinese for the Central Pacific, had died during the six years it had taken to complete construction. More thousands would die or be injured operating the trains on their route (in 1888 alone, the first year in which comprehensive statistics were kept, some 2,070 workers were killed on the job and another 20,148 were injured). Blizzards, rock slides, brake failures, car derailments, and bridge collapses imperiled workers and passengers alike, as did the occasional daylight holdup by train robbers like the notorious James Gang and, later, Butch Cassidy's Wild Bunch.

Wilde managed to evade the direst dangers on his trip. The worst indignity he suffered was the lack of a formal dining car, which necessitated his having to climb off and on the train to bolt down the gruesome fare at communal lunch counters along the way. Otherwise, he was content to read, nap, or take in the sights, which he described to his friend Norman Forbes-Robertson in appropriately vivid terms:

> Grey, gaunt, desolate plains, as colourless as waste land by the sea, with now and then scampering herds of bright red antelopes, and heavy shambling buffaloes and screaming vultures like gnats high up in the air, then up the Sierra Nevadas, the snow-capped mountains shining like shields of polished silver in that vault of blue flames we call the sky, and deep cañons full of pine trees and at last from the chill winter of the mountains down into eternal summer here, groves of orange trees in fruit and flower, green fields, and purple hills, a very Italy, without its art.

He was thinly amused to see urchins stumbling down the aisles, selling pirated copies of his book of poems for ten cents apiece. He pulled one boy aside and identified himself as the author. The information did not produce the desired effect; the budding young entrepreneur said he didn't care who the author was, as long as he, the vendor, made a profit from it. Perhaps recalling the encounter later, Wilde would observe that "in America there is no opening for a fool. They expect brains, even from a bootblack, and get them. Stupidity is not one of the national vices."[15]

Curious onlookers regularly turned up on train platforms along the way to catch a glimpse of Oscar Wilde as he passed. They were sometimes greeted with a warm smile and a wave from a tall fellow in knee breeches at the rear of the train. It wasn't Wilde, however, but rather an actor named John Howson, whose Conley-Barton Opera Troupe, like

Emma Abbott's English Opera Company, was putting on *Patience* for the rubes out West. Howson, of course, was playing Bunthorne. Wilde, meanwhile, was wearing much simpler traveling garb: black suit, brown pants, plain scarf, no jewelry, and a broad-brimmed white sombrero. A reporter from the *Sacramento Daily Record-Union* boarded the train on March 25, handed Wilde a handful of flowers the reporter said were from a female admirer in the city, and asked if he could accompany the poet down to San Francisco. Wilde, as usual, was agreeable, treating the reporter to a mini-lecture on art and the common man. "I hope the masses will come to be the creators in art," said Wilde, "that art will soon cease to be simply the accomplishment and luxury of the rich. We must teach the people to use their hands in art." It was very doable, said Wilde. Why, not so long ago, he had actually had an intelligent conversation with an eastern "railroad-repairer" about Alexander Pope.[16]

More reporters climbed aboard the train as it neared San Francisco. Wilde, brushing his long hair back behind his ears, fielded questions about his trip. It had been, he said, "excessively long and tedious," but perhaps he had seen it "at an unfavorable time" of the year. "I fancy that I shall be greatly pleased with California." At Oakland, he took the ferry across the bay, donning his green overcoat for the trip. He carried the now-withering bouquet of daisies and roses. He asked someone where the Chinese lived in San Francisco, volunteering the sweeping if unsought opinion that "Chinese art possesses no elements of beauty; the horrible and grotesque appearing to be standards of perfection. I have seen much that is admirable in Japanese but nothing of excellence in Chinese art." As a boy, he said, he had heard a Chinese fiddler at the Paris Exposition, and "I could discern no music in it."[17]

Charles E. Locke, D'Oyly Carte's California theatrical representative, drove Wilde from the waterfront to the seven-story Palace Hotel at the corner of New Montgomery and Market streets, which he would make his headquarters in San Francisco. The Palace, built by local financier William C. Ralston in 1875 at a cost of $5 million, was reputed to be the most luxurious hotel in the world, with bay windows in every room and reinforced steel bands to make it earthquake proof—always a consideration in wobbly San Francisco. The bands would work as advertised and the hotel would survive the great earthquake of 1906, only to burn down the next day in the fire that followed the initial quake. (Enrico Caruso, staying in the hotel at the time of the disaster, wandered through the rubble of the city carrying an autographed photograph of Theodore Roosevelt and swearing by all that was holy that he would never return to San Francisco again. He never did.) By then, Ralston himself was long since dead. Having gone broke building the hotel, he swam out into the bay near Fisherman's Wharf a few days after the grand opening and did not swim back. No one was sure if it was an accident or a suicide, although a sympathetic coroner ruled the drowning an accident so that the family could collect the life insurance. Fifty thousand mourners attended Ralston's funeral, or one for every hundred dollars he had sunk into his personal money pit.

The Palace, befitting its name, was grandly caparisoned. All of the suites, bathrooms, and closets were supplied with fresh air through a total of 2,042 ventilation tubes. There were separate dining rooms, as well as stores and barbershops; and a new innovation called "lifting rooms"—elevators—ran to each of the seven floors. The hotel claimed more white-clad waiters (156) than any other hotel in the country, with the exception of the Grand Union in Saratoga, New York. Comfortably ensconced in the Palace, Wilde sat for a battery of interviews, San Francisco being a great newspaper town. To the *Examiner,* he denied reports that he was disappointed with America and Americans. "There is very much here to like and admire," said Wilde. "The further West one comes, the more there is to like. The western people are much more social than those of the East, and I fancy that I shall be greatly pleased with California." Still, he expected to return to London soon, "if lecturing does not kill me." To the *Morning Call,* he jokingly threatened to write a book about his American experiences, noting that "human nature may be hardened to almost any degree of endurance. I may even dare to write a book that mine enemies may read and criticize."[18]

Wilde's book apparently would not contain a chapter about Griggs-ville, Illinois, a whistle-stop town whose city fathers had recently asked him to enlighten them aesthetically. "Begin by changing the name of your town," Wilde had telegraphed back. The name, he shuddered to the *Morning Call* reporter, was "the ultimate of vulgarity. Why not Grig-gtown, or Griggs? But Griggsville!" At least California place names like Murder's Bar, Bloody Gulch, and Hangtown "convey an idea, an asso-ciation." The *Chronicle* reporter, with professional skepticism, marveled that "this strange being, who looked as if he had no part in the everyday affairs of our prosy life, could not only talk of the matter-of-fact when he pleased like a man of education and refinement, but like a man who was capable of deep thought and vigorous conclusions." The only flaw, said the reporter, was that Wilde looked so much like Charles Warren Stoddard, a notoriously effeminate Bay Area poet, that fellow members of the Bohemian Club could scarcely believe that it was not Stoddard himself, come back in disguise "to greet them with a poetic and tender embrace."[19]

San Francisco as a whole was ready to embrace Wilde. The city had a long tradition of embracing eccentrics of all stripes and caliber. In the three decades prior to the poet's arrival, a zany procession of more or less harmless lunatics had paraded up and down the city's seven hills. On any given day, residents might encounter such daffy individualists as the Great Unknown, a mysterious, elegantly dressed old gentleman who marched in funereal silence down Montgomery Street every afternoon, the victim, some said, of a tragic love affair. Joining him were Old Rosie, who always wore a trademark flower in the lapel of his threadbare suit; Money King, who lived up to his name by making personal loans out of the pocket of his green, dollar-sign-encrusted coat; and Professor Fred-erick Coombs, an alleged expert in phrenology who capitalized on his vague physical resemblance to George Washington by strolling about town in a powdered wig and full colonial finery, carrying a banner that proclaimed him, perhaps unnecessarily, "Washington the Second." At any time, these solitaries might find themselves eclipsed by a parade of

FIGURE 1. Wilde in his soon-to-be-famous green coat and hat.

Photo by Napoleon Sarony. Corbis Images.

FIGURE 2. Wilde theatrically
reclining with book. Photo by
Napoleon Sarony. Library of Congress.

FIGURE 3. Another Sarony view
of Wilde, seated with cane.
Library of Congress.

FIGURE 4. In his cape and hat, Wilde looks like a benevolent vampire. Photo by Napoleon Sarony. Corbis Images.

FIGURE 5. Hat in hand, Wilde prepares to set forth across America. Photo by Napoleon Sarony. Library of Congress.

FIGURE 6. *Puck* artist F. Opper pictures Wilde's multifarious dreams of an Aesthetic America. Library of Congress.

FIGURE 7. Wilde's first American lecture, at New York's Chickering Hall, January 21, 1882.
Frank Leslie's Illustrated Newspaper.
Library of Congress.

FIGURE 8. Woodcut of Wilde on the lecture platform at Chickering Hall.
Corbis Images.

FIGURE 9. Noted showman P. T. Barnum attended Wilde's second New York City lecture.
Library of Congress.

FIGURE 10. Wilde attending a reception following his debut performance at Chickering Hall.
Frank Leslie's Illustrated Newspaper.
Library of Congress.

HARPER'S WEEKLY.

JOURNAL OF CIVILIZATION.

Vol. XXVI.—No. 1310.   NEW YORK, SATURDAY, JANUARY 28, 1882.   TEN CENTS A COPY
$4.00 PER YEAR, IN ADVANCE.

THE ÆSTHETIC MONKEY.—Engraved, by Permission, from the Picture by W. H. Beard, in the Possession of Mr. Hugh Auchincloss.

FIGURE 11. *Harper's Weekly* brutally sketched Wilde as an "aesthetic monkey," complete with sunflower and lily. Library of Congress.

FIGURE 12. Thanks to Wilde's arrival, lilies have doubled in price. Corbis Images.

FIGURE 13. A less humorous sketch imagines Wilde meeting with presidential assassin Charles Guiteau. British Library.

FIGURE 14. Walt Whitman, the Good Gray Poet, shared a convivial afternoon with Wilde. Library of Congress.

FIGURE 15. The *Washington Post* unfavorably compared Wilde to the Wild Man of Borneo. Library of Congress.

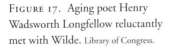

FIGURE 16. Novelist Henry James considered Wilde "a fatuous fool." Library of Congress.

FIGURE 17. Aging poet Henry Wadsworth Longfellow reluctantly met with Wilde. Library of Congress.

FIGURE 18. Julia Ward Howe hosted Wilde in Boston and Newport. Library of Congress.

FIGURE 19. Thomas Nast's cartoon, published in *Harper's Weekly*, shows Wilde jumping over the sort of cast-iron stove he despised. Library of Congress.

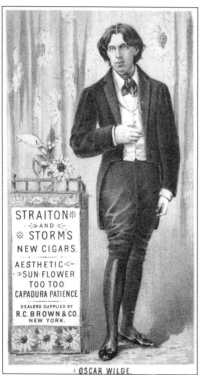

FIGURE 20. Advertisers like Straiton and Storm's Cigars were quick to capitalize on Wilde's visit. British Library.

FIGURE 21. This ad for Schlesinger and Mayer Dry Goods references Gilbert and Sullivan's *Patience*. Harvard Digital Archives.

FIGURE 22. This placard for Clark's Spool Cotton ad combines Wilde and Jumbo.

Harvard Digital Archives.

FIGURE 23. Former Confederate
general P. G. T. Beauregard
guided Wilde around New
Orleans. Library of Congress.

FIGURE 24. Confederate
president Jefferson Davis
was nonplussed by Wilde's
visit. Library of Congress.

FIGURE 25. Actress Mary Anderson declined to appear in Wilde's play *The Duchess of Padua.* Library of Congress.

FIGURE 26. Boldly fashionable Lillie Langtry, in a photo taken about the time of her arrival in America. Library of Congress.

FIGURE 27. A threadbare Wilde, right, prepares to depart from New York, with the manuscript of his unproduced play *Vera* in hand. Bridgeman Art Resources.

members from the tongue-in-cheek social club the Ancient and Honorable Order of E Clampus Vitus, which met in the hall of Comparative Ovations to get their marching orders form the Noble Grand Humbug and serve as "unanimous cochairmen" of the Most Important Committee.

The preeminent local character was an English-born immigrant named Joshua Abraham Norton, the self-proclaimed Emperor Norton I, who ruled over his people with a firm but fond hand for more than two decades after appearing at the city desk of the *San Francisco Bulletin* in 1859 and announcing politely, "Good morning, I am the emperor of the United States." Clad in a colonel's uniform, complete with gold epaulets, cockaded hat, and a ceremonial sword that he had somehow cadged from the garrison commander at the local army post, the Presidio, Norton held court daily at his imperial residence—actually a low-rent rooming house. From his seat of power he issued well-reasoned edicts abolishing the presidency and ordering the army to clear the halls of Congress. He levied taxes of twenty-five cents per business and three dollars for banks, and printed his own imperial bonds in denominations of ten, twenty-five, and fifty cents with his face on the bills. Local shops and restaurants unhesitatingly honored his money at full value.

Each day the emperor made his royal progress down Montgomery Street while his subjects duly bowed and scraped as he passed. He was accompanied on his personal rounds by his two royal mastiffs (actually mongrels), Bummer and Lazarus. The dogs, like their master, ate free at local restaurants and attended the theater in reserved seats, the audience rising respectfully as the shaggy trio made its entrance. When Norton I died, in 1880, thirty thousand mourners filed past his coffin while flags in the city flew at half-mast and the *Chronicle* proclaimed in a streamer headline, "Le Roi Est Mort!" The rival *Bulletin* observed, with some justice, that "the Emperor killed nobody, robbed nobody and deprived nobody of his country, which is more than can be said for most of the fellows in his trade."[20]

Wilde could expect a royal welcome of his own, though not all journalists, even in traditionally live-and-let-live San Francisco, were equally amused. One in particular was clearly unimpressed by Wilde's much-ballyhooed arrival. Ambrose Bierce, the prickly editor of the weekly newspaper the *Wasp*, and perhaps Wilde's closest American counterpart in the daily dispensing of clever aphorisms, pointed witticisms, and lethal retorts, took note of Wilde's arrival in his March 31 column.

> That sovereign of insufferables, Oscar Wilde, has ensued with his opulence of twaddle and penury of sense. He has mounted his hind legs and blown crass vapidities through the bowel of his neck, to the capital edification of circumjacent fools and foolesses. The ineffable dunce has nothing to say and says it with a liberal embellishment of bad delivery, embroidering it with reasonless vulgarities of attitude, gesture and attire. There was never an impostor so hateful, a blockhead so stupid, a crank so variously and offensively daft. He makes me tired.[21]

Bierce's disapproval of Wilde was to be expected. Except for the sharpness of their written and verbal wit, the two men could not have been less alike. Whereas Wilde had grown up in a wealthy if eccentric Dublin household, Bierce had been raised on a dirt-poor farm in northern Indiana. Unlike Wilde, who loved and admired his accomplished parents, Bierce hated his, particularly his mother, considering them little better than "unwashed savages." Anticipating the sort of sunny tripe that fellow Hoosier James Whitcomb Riley would later foist on the American public, Bierce vilified his Indiana roots as "the malarial farm," "the scum-covered duck pond," and "the ditch where the sour-smelling house drainage fell." Unlike Wilde, Bierce had not attended college; his school was the American Civil War, in which, as a member of the 9th Indiana Infantry, he saw more firsthand combat than any other writer of his time. Instead of traversing the graceful quads and shady walks at Oxford, Bierce found himself dodging bullets on various southern battlefields in the front ranks of "hardened and impenitent man-killers, to whom death in its awfulest forms is a fact familiar to their every-day observation; who sleep on hills trembling with the thunder of great guns, dine in the midst of streaming missiles, and play cards among the dead faces of their dearest friends." By the time he fetched up in California, two years after the war, Bierce was well on his way to compiling the material for his best-known work, *The Devil's Dictionary,* and gleefully living up to his reputation as "the wickedest man in San Francisco."[22]

Unsurprisingly, Bierce was not in the audience when Wilde made his San Francisco début at Platt's Hall on Monday, March 27, before a well-turned-out crowd of about five hundred, many of them women wearing brightly flowered hats in honor of the speaker. Wilde gave them a somewhat revised version of his lecture "The English Renaissance," with updates on the inutility of modern appliances. "There is no beauty in cast iron, no poetry in the steam engine," he said. "The value of the telephone is the value of what two people have to say. Give children beauty, not the record of bloody slaughters and barbarous brawls as they call history, or of the latitude and longitude of places nobody cares to visit, as they call geography." San Franciscans, secure in their unrivaled appeal to visitors, responded with laughter and applause.[23]

After an appearance across the bay in Oakland, Wilde returned to Platt's for a second lecture on March 29. This time he spoke on what promoters excitedly pumped as "Art Decoration! Being the Practical Application of the Esthetic Theory to Everyday Home Life and Art Ornamentation!" His reception was more mixed, according to the *San Francisco Chronicle.* Late-arriving attendees drew "a cold, esthetic stare" from Wilde, who created his own disturbance in the crowd by criticizing the "ridiculous bonnets" and "tight, flimsy dresses" made by modern milliners, much to the manifest unhappiness of the modern Minna Street and Sixth Street dressmakers in attendance. As for men's clothing, Wilde recommended looking at old paintings of George Washington to "see how a great and brave man arrayed himself." Finally, in a nod to the widespread anti-Chinese sentiment of the host city, he urged San Franciscans, "Don't borrow any Chinese art, for you have no need of it any more than you have need of Chinese labor." It won him more loud applause.[24]

Despite his anti-oriental pandering, Wilde was eager to visit Chinatown. The next day, at a store on Sacramento Street, below Kearny, he attracted so much attention that police had to clear a return path for him to his carriage. With a local guide on hand to point out the sights, Wilde looked into other Chinese stores, as well as restaurants, theaters, opium dens, and the ominously named Murderers' Alley. He did not venture an opinion on the latter, but in general pronounced himself "delighted in the Chinese quarters. They fascinated me. I wish those people had a quarter in London. I should take pleasure in visiting it often." He was particularly edified to be served a cup of tea on delicate blue-and-white china such as he had used at Oxford. At the Palace Hotel, he complained, "I was obliged to drink my chocolate or coffee out of a cup an inch thick . . . so thick that it suggested the idea that it was intended as a weapon, to be hurled at the heads of those seated at the next table."[25]

Wilde's fluctuating opinion of San Francisco's Chinese population reflected that of the city's long-term residents. Beginning with an influx of 787 immigrants in 1849–1850 to work as houseboys in the newly built mansions of gold-rush millionaires, the Chinese population in San Francisco had grown to 75,000 in 1876, thanks largely to the importation of coolie labor to build the Central Pacific Railroad during the previous decade. Displaced white workers had attacked Chinese immigrants so frequently and savagely that even Ambrose Bierce, no lover of humanity himself, had felt compelled to denounce white-on-Asian violence. As self-appointed "Town Crier," Bierce had noted a few years earlier: "The dead body of a Chinese woman was found last Tuesday morning lying across the sidewalk in a very uncomfortable position. The cause of her death could not be accurately ascertained, but as her head was caved in it was thought by some physicians that she died of galloping Christianity of the malignant California type." The Chinese, for their part, stuck largely to the few blocks of Chinatown, with its dark, mysterious shops selling exotic teas, silks, lacquerware, porcelain, cigars, and, for the more discriminating tastes, opium and child prostitutes, all under the dubious protection of the shadowy Tongs, gangs of hatchet-wielding toughs who camouflaged their true extortionate purposes behind such misleadingly peaceful names as the Chamber of Tranquil Conscientiousness and the Chamber of Far-Reaching Virtue.[26]

Besides his visit to Chinatown, Wilde also paid homage to another San Francisco attraction, the Cliff House, a hotel overlooking Seal Rocks on the oceanfront seven miles outside town. Wilde declared the ocean "grand," but did not comment on the seals—actually sea lions—that gave the rocks their name. He was lucky to see them at all, amid the welter of wooden signs and painted rocks advertising such miracle elixirs as Jackson's Best Plug, Yosemite Bitters, Pacific Stomach Bitters, Harvey's Horse Powder, Tarrant's Seltzer ("Cures Diarrhea"), Wizard Oil, Ax's Scotch Snuff, and Dr. King's New Discovery for Consumption, Colds and Coughs. He hadn't missed much. Fellow writer Helen Hunt Jackson described the lounging sea lions as "gigantic leeches, wallowing in unapproachable clumsiness and all the while making a noise too hideous to be described—a mixture of bray and squeal and snuff and snort."[27]

Another memorable part of Wilde's San Francisco experience involved a dinner invitation to the Bohemian Club at 724 Taylor Street. The club had been founded a decade earlier by wastrel reporters from the *Chronicle,* who expanded its press club atmosphere to include honorary members drawn from the city's artistic community. Charter members included Ambrose Bierce, Mark Twain, Bret Harte, Charles Warren Stoddard, Oliver Wendell Holmes (in absentia), and California's bisexual poet laureate, Ina Coolbrith, a past, present, or future mistress of several fellow Bohemians. Ironically, the club in later years would come to be dominated by Republican politicians and businessmen, including numerous conservative presidents from Theodore Roosevelt to George W. Bush. Wilde, with his uncanny knack for noticing and predicting such things, observed upon entering the club, "I never saw so many well-dressed, well-fed, business-looking Bohemians in my life." According to club legend, some members had intended to drink Wilde under the table and make sport of him afterwards, only to wind up passed out themselves while their guest continued happily drinking and nattering on. In honor of his visit, or at least his unexpected capacity for alcohol, Wilde was persuaded by club member Theodore Wores to sit for a portrait, which henceforth adorned the premises.[28]

Wilde was also the guest of honor at a more informal gathering held one afternoon in a San Francisco studio by a group of young artists. The hosts had gone to great lengths to prepare the room for Wilde's visit, painting roses on the skylight and positioning a mannequin by the door in full hat and veil. Wilde took one look at the skylight and exclaimed: "This is where I belong. This is my atmosphere. I didn't know such a place existed in the whole United States." He accepted a cup of tea from a Chinese waiter specially enlisted for the occasion, then strolled about greeting the other guests. The mannequin was introduced to him as Miss Piffle, and Wilde, without missing a beat, began an animated conversation with her about the joys and consolations of San Francisco. The dummy almost seemed to answer him.[29]

From his base of operations at the Palace Hotel, Wilde ventured outside San Francisco to lecture in Sacramento, Stockton, and San Jose. In Sacramento, then a small town of twenty thousand, several hundred people waited anxiously at the Congregational Church for the famous Aesthete to appear. He was expected to arrive at noon, then at 2:10, then at 7:10, then at 7:30. A pianist played for time onstage. Finally, at exactly 8:20 P.M., Wilde burst through the side door of the auditorium and, without bothering to apologize for the delay, spoke without pause for the next sixty-five minutes. "His thought was exquisite," wrote the drama critic for the *Sacramento Record-Union*, "but his manner and method of delivery were insufferable."[30]

In partial penance for his near no-show, Wilde endured an interminable after-hours reception at the local Bric-à-Brac Club, whose members besieged him with watercolor paintings, embroidered doilies, vocal duets, piano solos, and selected readings from his own book of poems. Wilde escaped by promising to return for a matinée the next week. He kept his word, giving a second lecture in Sacramento and dining afterwards with Mrs. Mary Miller Blakeney, president of the Women's Literary Club, and her family. To Mrs. Blakeney he wrote later, thanking her for sending him a photograph of her ten-year-old daughter, May. The photo, he said gracefully, "will remind me always of the prettiest child I have seen in America. She is like a wonderful little flower, and if flowers could talk so sweetly as she does who would not be a gardener!"[31]

Two more appearances at Platt's Hall concluded Wilde's California tour. The fourth and final lecture was a special address on Irish poetry, which included several long poems of his mother's that Wilde read "with much effect and feeling," according to the *Daily Call*. Throughout the tour, Wilde had been rediscovering, as it were, his Irishness, after years of assiduously ignoring his birthright. "My Irish accent is one of the many things I forgot at Oxford," he observed. He would never be a full-blown nationalist like his parents—he loved English culture, and London, too much for that—but he could glory in Ireland's poets, including his mother. "I do not know anything more wonderful or more characteristic of the Celtic genius, than the quick artistic spirit in which we adapted ourselves to the English tongue," he said in San Francisco. "The Saxon took our lands from us and left them desolate—we took their language and added new beauties to it." He found Irish Americans to have adapted well to their new home. "What captivity was to the Jews," he observed, "exile has been to the Irish. America and American influence has educated them." One can almost hear an echo of James Joyce's self-exiled poet, Stephen Dedalus.[32]

By the time he left San Francisco on April 8 for a two-day train ride to Salt Lake City, even the locomotives were said to have fallen under his sway, whistling "Too-too!" as they left the station. A new catchphrase, "Do you yearn?" swept through the city in honor of Wilde, and sunflower bouquets and boutonnières were in evidence everywhere. Sullivan's clothing shop offered bargain-priced suits guaranteed to be "Too Utterly Utt." Soon, Wilde was telling reporters, "No part of America has struck me so favorably as California. I intend to return to San Francisco and the West Coast next year with a party of friends in the capacity of a private gentleman traveling for his own amusement and not as a public lecturer condemned to go on the platform at every place I stop." It had been, by a wide margin, the most pleasant interlude of Wilde's American tour, which was only to be expected. It was San Francisco, after all; harder hearts than Oscar Wilde's had been left behind by their wistful owners on the fog-draped hills overlooking the bay.[33]

CHAPTER 7

Don't Shoot the Pianist; He's Doing His Best

❧

$\mathcal{I}$F SAN FRANCISCO had proved to be the American city most receptive to the Aesthetic preachments of Oscar Wilde, Salt Lake City figured to be the least. The capital city of Mormon-run Utah Territory, initially named "Deseret" by its founding father, the late prophet Brigham Young, Salt Lake City was a scrupulously clean and carefully laid-out metropolis, filled with equally tidy, squared-off individuals. Following the Civil War, which Mormon leaders had devoutly hoped would finish off both sides and leave them and their coreligionists in control of the country, the city had grown comparatively more welcoming. Wilde's fellow English traveler Sir Richard Burton had judged it "a vast improvement upon its contemporaries in the valleys of the Mississippi and the Missouri." Nevertheless, an ongoing debate over the Mormons' long-time practice of polygamy had led to the passage, three weeks before Wilde's arrival, of an anti-polygamy law that made the practice of polygamy a felony and the presumably lesser crime of bigamy or "unnatural cohabitation" a misdemeanor punishable by fine or imprisonment or both. Utah's lone representative in Congress, George Q. Cannon, had been summarily booted out of Washington for having a relatively modest four Mormon wives (the average was eight). Young himself had left behind a knee-buckling fifty-five wives to mourn his passing in 1877. American newspapers were on fire with lurid reports of "carnal orgies" regularly taking place in Utah. Wilde, who was without religious prejudice himself, would see firsthand what all the uproar was about.[1]

The *Salt Lake Herald*'s San Francisco correspondent had alerted hometown readers of Wilde's imminent approach. "It is too utter to see the silliness exhibited," the journalist wrote. "Oscar's twaddle has realized for him two too-good houses; his third one was thin, but he has raked in enough to make him feel happy as a big sunflower, and as that's his regular business, I suppose is O.K." The competing *Salt Lake Tribune* urged a certain noblesse oblige from the audience. "As a gentleman he is entitled to respect," said the paper. "It is an excellent policy never to laugh at a man who knows more than yourself." The *Herald* agreed: "Those who go expecting to see a person intellectually their inferior will be seriously disappointed." Wilde checked into the Walker Hotel at Second and Main streets at noon on April 10 and announced that he would take lunch in his room, much to the disappointment of the usual crowd of flower-sporting ladies in the dining room who were hoping to catch a glimpse of the famed Aesthete.[2]

A brief, obligatory interview with a reporter from the *Herald* contained no mention of the death of Dante Gabriel Rossetti, which had occurred while Wilde was en route to Salt Lake City. But Henry Wadsworth Longfellow, who had also died recently, received a somewhat backhanded tribute from the English poet, who asserted that "Longfellow was himself a beautiful poem, more beautiful than anything he ever wrote." As for the sort of reception he expected to receive in the Mormon capital, Wilde was optimistic.

I am more and more astonished and pleased every time I lecture at the courtesy with which I am received by my audiences. Everybody, they say, laughs at me and says I am a fraud, yet not only do they fill up any place I choose to lecture in, but they sit out all I have to say with surprising good humor and patience. I am quite conscious that much of what I say may be annoying, but after all I came to America to say it, and so long as audiences with such breeding allow me strut my brief hour upon the stage, I should be singularly stupid not to take advantage of the opportunities given me of trotting out my hobbies.[3]

Wilde's lecture at the Salt Lake Theater the next evening was well attended. He had spent the better part of the day touring the city, where he noted with favor the private gardens and orchards of the residents, with their apricot, peach, and plum trees showing pinkly against the purple-shadowed mountains to the east. He was less impressed with the famous Mormon Tabernacle, which he thought looked like a soup kettle about the size of Covent Garden, with enough room to hold "fourteen Mormon families with ease." The Tabernacle, he said, was "the most purely dreadful building I ever saw," with decorations "suitable to a jail." Undeterred, he paid a visit to the first family of Utah, that of Mormon president John Taylor, who had just moved into the adjacent Amelia Palace, built for and named after one of Brigham Young's favorite wives. Taylor had stood up in the Tabernacle a few months earlier to announce that it had been revealed to him in a vision that he, Taylor, was to have the palace instead of the Widow Young, and that "on this subject there were to be no more revelations of any kind." By then, Taylor had succeeded Young as leader of the Mormons, and his word, if not precisely gospel, nonetheless was good enough for most of his flock.[4]

As the only foreign-born president of the Mormons, Taylor had led a crowded and controversial life. Born in Milnthorpe, England, he had dissented from the Methodist Church, immigrated to Canada, converted to Mormonism, and edited the *Nauvoo Times* and *Nauvoo Neighbor* alongside church founder Joseph Smith in Illinois in the mid-1840s.

He had been imprisoned with Smith and other Mormon leaders and had been shot in the thigh by the same lynch mob that fatally gunned down the prophet in a Carthage, Illinois, jail cell in 1844. Migrating west to Utah, Taylor gained the unofficial title of Poet Laureate of Zion for his geographically challenged ode, "The Upper California, Oh, That's the Land for Me," and had become a valued member of Young's inner circle, undertaking various diplomatic, trade, and missionary duties before advancing to the rather more exalted title of "God's Vice-regent upon the Earth and the Religious Dictator of the Whole World" after Young's death. Wilde pronounced Taylor "a courteous, kindly gentleman" and one of his many daughters "charming"—Taylor had thirty-five children in all, with seven wives, five of whom attended Wilde's lecture with the divine vice-regent that night.[5]

Wilde presented his lecture on house decoration to another gratifyingly large audience. Salt Lake City, with Brigham Young's blessing, had become an avid appreciator of the dramatic arts, perhaps as a way of avoiding other kinds of earthly temptations. The inevitable touring company of *Patience* had preceded Wilde, as well as several circuses, if one can judge by the comments of newspaper reporters in the wake of Wilde's speech. The representative from the *Herald* overheard another spectator say that Wilde's face looked like his pictures in the newspaper: "It is ugly as the devil, but it is very like, very like." The *Herald* reporter thought Wilde had recited his words like a rote-learned schoolboy "without the slightest recollection of what he had to say. He seemed to take no interest whatever in his remarks, for his eyes wandered about and seemed as indifferent as a man could be. He was an enthusiast without enthusiasm." It was a mystery to the *Herald* how a man "so strikingly awkward, so sorry at elocution, so ugly, so straight of hair, so vulgar of front teeth, so painfully dreary in manner of expression should be the best card in the pack of current lecturers, barring female minstrels and leg dramatists." He could only surmise that the answer lay in the fact that "the clown is usually the most intellectual, ablest, and best-paid man about the circus." The *Salt Lake Republican,* the house organ of the

Christian minority, dissented, finding Wilde's lecture every bit as interesting as previous lectures by Henry Ward Beecher, William Tilton, or Tilton's former sister-in-law, Victoria Woodhull—principals in the unholy farrago of greed, adultery, and betrayal that had transfixed the nation a few years earlier.[6]

Wilde, in turn, found Salt Lake City—particularly its female residents—equally homely. The city, he said, interested him mainly as "the first city that ever gave a chance to ugly women," among whose ranks he found the Mormon contingent "commonplace in every sense of the word." Without knowing it, Wilde was echoing the sentiments of fellow writer and humorist Mark Twain, who had visited Salt Lake City two decades earlier en route to Nevada after deserting from the Confederate Army in his home state of Missouri. Mormon women, Twain had observed, were "poor, ungainly and pathetically homely," and "the man that marries one of them has done an act of Christian charity which entitles him to the kindly applause of mankind." Anyone marrying more than one—say, sixty or so—"has done a deed of open-handed generosity so sublime that the nations should stand uncovered in his presence and worship in silence."[7]

Leaving the Mormon capital and its beauty-challenged women behind, Wilde headed east to Denver, the capital of an altogether more terrestrial kingdom: silver-booming Colorado. Having survived a major fire in 1863 and a devastating flood one year later, as well as regular blizzards howling down from the 14,000-foot-high Rockies on the western side of town, Denver had endured to become the richest city between St. Louis and San Francisco. Strike after strike increased the city's net worth, and Denver's population grew threefold between 1870 and 1880. Another urbane visiting writer, Richard Harding Davis, would later compare the burgeoning city favorably to his adopted hometown of New York City.

When the Union Pacific Railroad bypassed Denver altogether in favor of Bridger's Pass, Wyoming, civic leaders quickly raised money for a branch line between Denver and Cheyenne. It was on that line that a reporter from the *Rocky Mountain News* encountered the temporarily marooned Wilde on the night of April 12. Despite worrying that he would keep his audience waiting, Wilde went through his usual verbal paces, reassuring the nervous reporter that "you cannot ask an impertinent question of me." He repeated his long-practiced views on art, architecture, and personal dress, and said that he had seen "any quantity of beautiful young girls whose faces are charming with the blush of youth, whose ideas are radiant, and whose forms are full of beauty. But there are few handsome matrons in this country." He expected to continue touring until June, "if I survive."[8]

Wilde made it to Denver twenty minutes late for his lecture and caught a carriage to the Tabor Grand Opera House in a swirling snowstorm. A reporter for the *Denver Tribune* met him at the station and accompanied him on the ride, which was slowed to a walk by crowds of curious onlookers who blocked the way and peered into the carriage— one man even pressed his nose against the window for closer look and cried out, "Let us see you, Oscar, old boy!" Wilde was blasé about the reception. "It is so everywhere," he said. "This is simply curiosity, you know. It is the evidence of an unfinished civilization. In Europe the people are less curious about public characters, and they are not rude." He might have been more tolerant if he had known about all the trouble Denver's working girls had gotten into recently on his behalf. In the sporting houses along Holladay Street, known locally as the "Street of Love," madams with such obvious aliases as Mattie Silk and Rose Lovejoy decked out their girls in yellow sundresses, knee breeches, and enormous flowered hats. The girls took to crying, "Too too!" and "Utterly utter!" every chance they got, and called out to prospective clients: "We know what makes a cat wild, but what makes Oscar Wilde?" It got so bad that the chief of police, James M. Lowery, had two of the women arrested for the "meretricious" offense of wearing sunflowers and lilies on a public street. The charges were subsequently dismissed, there being no standing city ordinance against wearing flowers in public, and *Denver Tribune* editor Eugene Field called impishly for Wilde to "hurry up and deliver his disciples from the oppression of the tyrant." Meanwhile, said Field, the women would confine themselves to wearing less seductive hollyhocks and dogfennel blossoms.[9]

Field was a bit of a wag, notwithstanding the fact that his greatest fame had come as "the Children's Poet," in which post he had perpetrated two of the more criminally maudlin poems in the English language: "Little Boy Blue" and "Wynken, Blynken, and Nod." In his day job as a journalist, Field was an inveterate joker, signing rival reporters' names to embarrassing bits of doggerel, having them arrested and hauled off to jail on trumped-up charges, and switching hotel guests' shoes outside their doors at night. On crowded trains he would wear fake bandages to ensure himself two undisturbed seats, and he sometimes passed the hat for the relief of orphans (meaning himself). He once reviewed a Shakespearean actor's unsteady performance by observing, "He played the king as though he expected somebody else to play the ace." For an African American politician asked to introduce a visiting orator, Field ghostwrote a doozy of an opening: "Although he has a white skin, his heart is as black as any of ours." And when he heard that Oscar Wilde's idol, Lillie Langtry, was reconsidering her plans to come to America in light of Wilde's boisterous reception in certain American cities, Field assured her that "she need not be alarmed. The people on this side of the pond have better business than that of insulting a woman, no matter how mediocre her talents may be." In advance of Wilde's arrival in Denver, Field got himself up as the poet and was driven through the streets of the city in full Aesthetic garb, complete with a long-haired wig over his own thinning hair, a fur-trimmed overcoat, and a wide-brimmed hat. He rested his head on one languid hand and held an open book in the other, affecting a dreamy-eyed, completely deadpan expression. Told about it later, Wilde said simply, "What a splendid advertisement for a lecture."[10]

Taking into account Denver's newfound wealth, promoter Charles E. Locke had raised ticket prices from $1 to $1.50 for Wilde's appearance. Despite the weather—Denver residents were used to extremes—

another solid turnout greeted Wilde as he stepped through the red curtain at the back of the stage with what a *Denver Times* reporter described as "a languid, dreamy sort of walk such as one would think a lovesick girl would have in wandering through a moonlit garden." He had changed into his speaking garb on the train and, fortified by half a bottle of Piper-Heidsieck champagne in his dressing room, the poet launched immediately into his lecture with no introductory remarks. He had the distinct impression that the audience was watching more than listening to him. The stage had been artfully designed with a single lily blooming from a plain wooden table, beneath which sat a giant basket of flowers. A cut-glass water decanter completed the tableau. Wilde gave his usual remarks on the decorative arts but seemed somewhat distracted, probably owing to his late arrival. He frequently brushed back his hair and smiled "in an ingenuous manner as if realizing something amusing had been said," the *Tribune's* drama critic reported. When it was over, Wilde went backstage and rejoined the *Tribune* writer who had ridden with him from the station, observing a little archly, "Well, this is somewhat jolly, to travel in the close atmosphere of those coaches six hundred miles on a stretch and then give a lecture before resting."[11]

Wilde finished off the champagne with no help from the reporter and then rode by carriage the few blocks between the Opera House and the Windsor Hotel at the corner of 18th and Larimer streets. The five-story Windsor, modeled after its royal namesake, was a veritable English castle improbably nestled in the foothills of the Rockies. Advertising itself as "the largest and most complete hotel between Chicago and San Francisco," the Windsor was also one of the newest, having opened for business less than two years earlier. In keeping with its Anglo-American décor, it flew the Stars and Stripes from the top of the building and Union Jacks from the smaller turrets on the sides. The Windsor had a fully stocked wine cellar, a private farm with its own herd of cows destined for the dining room, and a brace of big-game hunters contracted to provide the hotel with more exotic fare. Three tunnels ran beneath the hotel to Union Station, a carriage barn on Arapahoe Street, and an underground oasis of tile-and-marble baths fed by fresh artesian wells. Once inside the hotel, it was said, no guest ever had reason to go outside again.

The principal owner of the Windsor was no less fabulous than the hotel itself. Horace Austin Warner Tabor, the "Bonanza King of Leadville," was one of the West's richest men and most unlikely success stories. Born in Holland, Vermont, "Haw" Tabor had joined the land rush to Kansas sponsored by the pro-abolitionist Emigrant Aid Company in the mid-1850s. He served for a time in the Free State legislature before returning to New England to get married. He and his rather severe wife, Augusta, then moved to Colorado and spent the next eighteen years prospecting desultorily for gold, running a general store, and renting out rooms to fellow prospectors who were even poorer than they were. Tabor became mayor of Leadville, a ramshackle mining camp just north of Denver, in 1878 and parlayed a small grubstake in the Little Pittsburg mine into a million-dollar bonanza, then bought the Matchless Mine for one-tenth that amount. Soon, he was worth $10 million and pulling down a reputed $2,000 a day in new profits. With his overnight fortune, Tabor bought newspapers, opened banks, and built two showcase performance halls that he named modestly after himself: the Tabor Opera House in Leadville and the Tabor Grand Opera House in Denver.

Elected lieutenant governor of Colorado in 1878, Tabor subsequently began a scandalous liaison with the estranged wife of a Central City, Colorado, saloonkeeper named Harvey Doe. Elizabeth McCourt Doe, nicknamed "Baby Doe" by local miners for her elfin looks, was a mop-topped, curly-haired blonde with enormous soulful eyes and no apparent sense of shame. Leaving the dust of Leadville behind, she became a happily kept woman, with Tabor putting her up in the best suite at the Windsor while he sought a divorce from his distinctly unhappy wife, who was demanding half his fortune for her myriad troubles. Baby Doe was still staying at the hotel when Wilde arrived in Denver, so the management ordered a quick makeover of the second-best suite of rooms. Pink-and-green wallpaper, flocked with lilies, was slapped up in the parlor and bedroom, and a ceiling fresco representing the "Genius of the Renaissance" was installed over a bed imported, for some reason, from Chicago. Statues of Cupid and Venus were placed in the bathroom.

With scarcely a glance at his newly renovated surroundings, Wilde sat down to a waiting supper of fish, potatoes, mutton chops, omelet, relish, bread, butter, and a cup of tea. "Take away this tea and bring me a bottle of this wine, with glasses," he demanded, indicating a white Bordeaux de Graves. He took one bite of the broiled fish before ordering it removed from his sight, then cut into the mutton chop before being interrupted by a series of raps on the door. Tabor walked in to see how his illustrious guest was faring and invited Wilde to visit the Matchless Mine in Leadville. Politely if perhaps drolly, Wilde accepted, observing: "I shall be delighted. Of all things that which I most desire to see is a mine." Tabor went away happy and Wilde returned to his interrupted meal, which the *Tribune* reporter proceeded to interrupt further with questions about Wilde's poems, his unproduced play *Vera,* and his travels out West. It was proving impossible to write poetry while he was traveling, said Wilde, adding that he had time only to take notes of the passing scene. "When I return to Venice," he said, "I will begin to write, and whatever I have seen to impress me in America, whether of the beauties of nature or of men and women, I will write and give America credit for it."[12]

Wilde was feeling less expansive the next morning when he set off for Leadville aboard the narrow-gauge South Park Railroad. He claimed to have received prior warning from some of the camp's toughs that they were going to shoot him or his traveling manager, J. S. Vale, on sight. "I wrote back and told them that nothing they could do to my traveling manager would intimidate me," Wilde observed happily. He informed them that he had been practicing his gun skills with a newly purchased revolver by shooting at sparrows perched on telegraph wires from the train window, and warned glintingly, "My aim is as lethal as lightning." The gun was imaginary, but the danger was real. Two Leadville residents, a gambler and a policeman, had been killed in separate shootings during the previous week. In addition, a couple of prostitutes had gone after each other with razors, and a local madam had taken a horsewhip to Judge A. W. Stone for an unexplained transgression involving her girls.[13]

In general, however, the people of Leadville were rather looking forward to Wilde's visit as a welcome diversion from the soul-deadening labor of silver mining, a time-intensive effort that involved a back-breaking amount of digging, drilling, boring, and blasting in scorching summer heat and Arctic winter cold. Mark Twain had tried silver mining two decades earlier in Nevada, and had quickly put down his pick and shovel. "The trick," he said then, "was not to mine the silver ourselves by the sweat of our brows and the labor of our hands, but to sell the ledges to the dull slaves of toil and let them do the mining." Leadville was one of world's largest working silver camps, with a population of 40,000, most of whom were men. It was located 101 miles southwest of Denver, at an elevation of 10,152 feet, making it the highest incorporated city in the United States. Among its past, present, and future residents were "Texas Jack" Omohundro, Buffalo Bill Cody's hunting and acting partner, who had died in Leadville from pneumonia in 1880; John M. "Doc" Holliday, the murderous dentist who had stood beside the Earp brothers at the Gunfight at the O.K. Corral six months earlier and would briefly make Leadville the site of his last gunfight, when he shot and wounded a former policeman in an argument over a five-dollar bar debt; and the Unsinkable Molly Brown, who called Leadville home before making her famous voyage on the *Titanic* twenty years after Wilde's visit.[14]

Wilde's arrival in Leadville was inauspicious. Drizzle and snow dampened his shoulders, and no official welcoming committee was waiting at the ramshackle railway station. Residents were either working below ground or resting indoors above. Vale commandeered a carriage to take them to the Clarendon Hotel, where the poet immediately took to his bed with a head-spinning case of altitude sickness. A doctor was summoned and diagnosed "a case of light air," writing Wilde a one-dollar prescription. Whatever was in the medicine got him back on his feet in time for the evening's performance at the Opera House. The audience, according to Wilde, was dressed entirely in "red shirts and blonde beards," reminding him of the lead actor in Joaquin Miller's Mormon-based melodrama, *The Danites in the Sierras,* which had made its début in London two years earlier. The poet wore his usual stage outfit, but the absence of sunflowers or lilies disappointed the crowd. After Wilde invoked the name of the Renaissance goldsmith Benvenuto Cellini, the miners wanted to know why Wilde hadn't brought him along. When Wilde said that, regrettably, Cellini was dead, they wanted to know who had shot him.[15]

In a high-spirited letter to London actress Fanny Mary Beere a few days later, Wilde described his lecture: "I spoke to them of the early Florentines, and they slept as though no crime had ever stained the ravines of their mountain home. I described to them the picture of Botticelli, and the name, which seemed to them like a new drink, roused them from their dreams." It was all going very well, Wilde said, until he "unluckily described one of Jimmy Whistler's 'nocturnes in blue and gold.' Then they leaped to their feet and in their grand simple way swore that such things should not be. Some of the younger ones pulled their revolvers out and left hurriedly to see if Jimmy was 'prowling about the saloons' or 'wrestling a hash' at any eating shop. Had he been there I fear he would have been killed, their feeling was so bitter." Whether the local art critics were objecting to Whistler's compositional sense, or merely reacting to the artist's color palette, which unfortunately mirrored that of a Union cavalry officer, Wilde did not say—but on that highly satisfying note, he concluded the lecture.[16]

After going back to the hotel and changing into appropriately rough camp wear, Wilde was taken on a tour of Leadville's booming nightlife. On State Street, he visited in succession the Little Casino, the Silver Thread, the Tudor, the Bon Ton, the Red Light, and the Odeon. Barkers on the sidewalk touted the skills of "female bathers, daring tumblers and other dramatic attractions." In the backrooms of the bars, gamblers pushed around poker chips on green-felted tables beneath swaying kerosene lamps. A row of cribs with full-length picture windows displayed the Cyprian charms of Leadville's legion of prostitutes, some of whom were kept in the so-called French section of town, which boasted of being home to nothing but full-blooded Parisiennes. In Pop Wyman's namesake saloon, Wilde saw a morose piano-player sitting in the corner beneath a sign that read: "Don't Shoot the Pianist; He's Doing His Best." It was, said Wilde, "the only rational method of art criticism I have ever come across."[17]

Leadville mayor David H. Dougan and Haw Tabor's mining superintendent, Charles Pishon, escorted Wilde to the mouth of the Matchless for a dizzying descent by torchlight to the bottom of the mine. In the inky darkness he probably took no notice of the adjacent toolshed into which Baby Doe Tabor would move after her husband's ruinous bankruptcy eleven years later. There the widow would live alone for the next thirty-six years, an object of mingled pity and wonder, before freezing to death on the wooden floor of her unheated shed. (The star-crossed Tabors and their younger daughter, Silver Dollar Tabor, would live on in composer Douglas Moore's 1956 opera, *The Ballad of Baby Doe,* one of only a handful of American operas in the standard performing repertory.) Pishon handed Wilde Tabor's personal underground suit, "a complete dress of India rubber" that fit him surprisingly well except for being too short in the legs. Tucking his long hair inside a miner's cap, Wilde climbed into a bucket and was lowered by rope down the No. 3 shaft. Superintendent Pishon rode along to explain the various gradations of ore they were descending through, which Wilde thought looked oddly commonplace and somber for so great a fortune. Still, he gamely pronounced it "the finest sight in the world."[18]

At the bottom the miners had prepared a banquet table for their guest, and invited Wilde to stay for supper, "the first course being whiskey, the second whiskey, and the third whiskey." When he lit a long cigar, the men "cheered till the silver fell in dust from the roof on our plates; and when I quaffed a cocktail without flinching, they unanimously pronounced me in their grand simple way 'a bully boy with no glass eye.'" Afterwards, Wilde was handed a silver drill and invited to open a new vein of ore. "I brilliantly performed, amidst unanimous applause," Wilde bragged to Fanny Beere. "The silver drill was presented to me and the lode named 'The Oscar.' I had hoped . . . they would have offered me shares in 'The Oscar,' but in their artless untutored fashion they did not. Only the silver drill remains a memory of my night at Leadville."[19]

Leaving Leadville richer in spirit, if not in wealth, Wilde gave a sparsely attended lecture in Colorado Springs, whose *Daily Gazette* defended the poor turnout by charging that Wilde was not Aesthetic enough for the cultured palate of the fashionable spa. The people would have turned out for John Ruskin, said the newspaper, but not for "an advertising dodge" such as Wilde. A second appearance in Denver concluded Wilde's Colorado visit. It was not as well attended as the first, although it included a number of good jabs at modern culture: "The hat rack is one of those beastly inventions that rank with the customs of crime and the terrors of the cross." "Photographs are always libelous; they should be kept in portfolios to show friends whose friendship is not treacherous." "There is nothing more indicative of moral decline than squalor and indifference to dress." "Don't cover your floors with carpets. They collect dust and are very unhealthy." A valedictory ad in the *Denver News* by H. Ornauer, self-proclaimed "aesthetic tailor," made the unchallengeable claim that Wilde had "openly declared Ornauer to be the best tailor in the world and said that hereafter Ornauer only could make his clothes." That would have presented certain logistical hurdles for both tailor and client, but by the time the ad appeared, Wilde was already several hundred miles away, heading east to Kansas on the next leg of his tour.[20]

After his memorable triumph at Leadville, Wilde was due for a letdown, and the flat, invariable countryside of northern Missouri, Kansas, Iowa, and Nebraska in the rainy season was perfectly suited for disappointment. Commercial-minded Kansas City, at the confluence of the Missouri, Kaw, and Blue rivers, came first. The city had grown by more than 100 percent in the past two decades, although its 55,000 human residents were still badly outnumbered by the millions of hogs and cattle waiting to be slaughtered in local packing plants or shipped farther east for breeding. Railroad lines ran through Kansas City in every direction; Wilde pulled into town on the morning of April 17 aboard the Union Pacific express. His advent was announced on page two of the *Kansas City Star,* which reported none too welcomingly that "Oscar Wilde, the long-haired what-is-it, has finally reached Kansas City, and the aesthetic noodles and blue china nincompoops are in the seventh heaven of happiness." A scarcely more hospitable representative of the newspaper located Wilde and his assistants sitting in the club car of the train as it pulled into Union Station. Wilde, said the reporter, was reading a newspaper (no mention of which) while wearing an imitation-Tennyson cloak, pointed shoes, and plaid trousers—the very incarnation of "the regulation English snob." Wilde was surprised to learn that Kansas City was actually in Missouri and wanted to know what the word "Kansas" even meant. The newsman couldn't say, except to note that it was some sort of Indian word. "Topeka," he allowed, meant "small potatoes." Wilde chuckled at the information.[21]

At the Coates House, the poet checked into his room, while a group of women guests and housemaids prowling the halls was heard to whisper as he passed: "Isn't he too utterly beautiful? Too awfully too." Certainly, the unofficial "bard of Kansas City," Colonel George W. Warder thought so. He unburdened himself of a multi-stanza greeting in the *Kansas City Times,* expounding on "the beautiful in beauty" and "the loveliness in love" and hailing his fellow poet for being "true and brave in spirit." Wilde ventured the opinion that two of the stanzas—there were nine in all—"showed deep thought." Another 3,000-line poem by Warder somehow crossed Wilde's desk, this one "a sanguinary lyric" whose most impassioned part, Wilde told a friend, began: "Here Mayor Simpson battled bravely with his Fifteenth Kansas Cavalry." Wilde was somewhat taken aback by Warder's poesy, which was collected in two evocatively titled books, *Eden's Dell; or, Love's Wanderings* and *Utopian Dreams and Lotus Leaves*. In 1903 Warder also published a novel, *The Stairway to the Stars; or, Enola Reverof,* which somehow mixed religion, romance, mysticism, and electricity. But by then, Wilde was safely out of reach.[22]

That night Wilde appeared at the Coates Opera House, where he gave his remarks on art decoration to what the *Times* called "a little cluster of patrons." The paper judged Wilde's lecture "forcible," but noted wryly that the poet was competing for attention with a traveling circus and that a large proportion of local Aesthetes apparently had gone, instead, to see a man shot out of a cannon. The competing *Journal* mongrelized Shakespeare to lambaste Wilde's lecture as "a tale told by an idiot, full of sound and trash signifying nothing. There are some things so infernal bad that they are good and Mr. Wilde's lecture is one of these things."[23]

Saint Joseph, Missouri, still in mourning for the outlaw Jesse James, who had been shot in the back of the head by fellow gang member Robert Ford two weeks earlier while hiding out in the city, gave Wilde an even frostier reception. Announcing his appearance, the *Evening News* predicted: "There will be a big crowd at the opera house tonight, not to hear the lecture, but to see the little fool who has cheek enough to run around among women with breeches coming down only to his knees." Given the civic lamentations for Jesse James—a Confederate guerrilla, bank robber, and murderer—it was not much of a welcome for the more or less law-abiding Englishman. Wilde told Norman Forbes-Robertson that, from his hotel window, he could see crowds of relic hunters pulling apart the bandit's home. "The Americans are certainly great hero-worshippers," said Wilde, "and always take their heroes from the criminal classes." Considering his later observation that "no crime is vulgar, but all vulgarity is crime," it might have been meant as a compliment.[24]

Leaving Jesse to his legion of mourners, Wilde crossed the Missouri River to the tough army post of Leavenworth, Kansas, where a small delegation from the fort turned out for his lecture on decorative arts. The soldiers were practically his only audience. The entire gate, according to a local reporter, was an embarrassing sixty dollars. At Topeka, the state capital, Wilde did a little better, impressing a reporter at the Windsor Hotel with his "lucid manner" and "soulful utterances." He assured the newsman that he was enjoying his tour, despite earlier misgivings. "When I landed in New York and read what newspapers had to say about me, I thought I was about to travel in an extensive lunatic asylum," said Wilde, "but when I went out in society, there I found the most charming cosmopolitan people I ever had the pleasure of meeting." He worried, however, that modern Americans were living their lives without making their lives worth living, by failing to cultivate the beautiful. Sounding a bit like novelist Sloan Wilson in his corrosive indictment of post–World War II conformity, *The Man in the Gray Flannel Suit,* Wilde shuddered: "To me the life of the businessman who eats his breakfast early in the morning, catches a train for the city, stays there in the dingy, dusty atmosphere of the commercial world, and goes back to his house in the evening, and after supper goes to sleep, is worse than the life of the galley slave—his chains are golden instead of iron."[25]

Lawrence, Kansas, which modestly billed itself as "the center of the garden spot of the world," was scarcely more welcoming to Wilde than it had been to William Clarke Quantrill's pro-slavery guerrillas, including Jesse James and his brother Frank, who burned the town to the ground in August 1863 in reprisal for similar attacks on pro-Confederate settlements by Kansas-based abolitionists. The guerrillas' main target, U.S. senator James Lane, managed to avoid the fate of 150 of his fellow townsmen by hiding in a cornfield in his nightshirt. On the day of Wilde's appearance, the audience was "comparatively small," judged the *Lawrence Daily Journal.* Perhaps understandably, in a town that had been forced to rebuild itself from smoky ruins nineteen years earlier, Lawrence residents, while agreeing with Wilde that their homes should be more attractive, wondered plaintively, "If we are to discard all these things, with what will we replace them?" Wilde had no answer. Atchison was worst of all, its streets running with yellow mud in the unrelenting rain. Not even a burro led through the streets with a sunflower pinned between its ears and a wooden placard bearing the words "I lecture at Corinthian Hall tonight" hanging down both flanks could attract a crowd. Only forty-three people waited, half-expecting Wilde to cancel the lecture. Bravely, he went onstage anyway, but failed to move the audience with his lofty descriptions of European architecture. "All the places of variegated marble and the Gothic cathedrals did not prevent the Italians of that time from being treacherous, sensual, revengeful, and generally despicable," scoffed the reviewer from the *Atchison Champion*. "Mankind is not to be raised to the fit companionship of angels by wood-carving nor painting in water colors."[26]

Wilde's overall impression of the upper Midwest was as flat as the countryside. "It seems as though nature had exhausted her resources on the West," he observed from the train, "and had nothing left for those prairies. Oh, it is so dreary, so dissolute with those miles and miles of level plain sweeping across the country with not a tree, not a flower, not even an animal." On his return swing through Nebraska, Wilde headed for Lincoln, the state capital and home of the newly co-ed state university. En route, he was told that legislators had just passed a law directing that all sunflowers, which grew in profusion throughout the Cornhusker State, be cut down. He would have canceled his engagement if he had known about it in advance, said Wilde, adding, "How unaesthetic the Nebraska legislators must be." At Lincoln he made the acquaintance of comparative-literature professor George E. Woodberry, a friend of Harvard scholar Charles Eliot Norton. Wilde and Woodberry had much in common: both were young (Woodberry was twenty-six), wrote poetry, liked wine, and affected a certain skepticism toward organized religion. Woodberry, in fact, was at the end of his leash at the University of Nebraska. He was being dismissed from teaching at the conclusion of the term, after pressure from the local Presbyterian church, for the perceived sins of drinking hard liquor and being an infidel, one of the "anti-God men on the faculty," the complaint alleged. Two other faculty members were also being discharged.[27]

On the morning of Wilde's scheduled lecture on April 24, he and Woodberry rode out from the turbulent groves of academe to visit the locally renowned penitentiary a few miles outside of town. Predictably, both men were horrified by the change of surroundings. In broken sentences, Wilde subsequently described the visit to his friend Nellie Sickert, the sister of painter Walter Sickert: "Poor odd types of humanity in hideous striped dresses making bricks in the sun, and all mean-looking, which consoled me, for I should hate to see a criminal with a noble face. Little whitewashed cells, so tragically tidy, but with books in them." The convicts' reading material he found both good and bad. There were volumes of Shelley and Dante—"Strange and beautiful that the sorrow of a single Florentine in exile should, hundreds of years afterwards, lighten the sorrow of some common prisoner in a modern gaol"—but also the romance novels of Charlotte Mary Yonge. One convicted murderer named Ayers with "melancholy eyes" was spending his last three weeks on earth reading Yonge's Christian romance, *The Heir of Redclyffe*. "If he reads *The Heir of Redclyffe*," said Wilde, "it's perhaps as well to let the law take its course." It was bad preparation, he thought, "for facing either God or Nothing." Fourteen years later, Wilde would find himself inside an English jail likewise reading Dante, if not Yonge, and composing his poignant ode on soul-killing prison life, "The Ballad of Reading Gaol."[28]

Taking leave of Woodberry the next day with an invitation to come see him and "his set" in London, Wilde continued his tour into Iowa, making appearances in Fremont, Des Moines, Iowa City, and Cedar Rapids before concluding with a lecture in Rock Island on the last day of April. By then, the most exhilarating and adventurous leg of his American tour had come to an end. From the Mississippi River to the Pacific Ocean, he had enjoyed, and sometimes suffered, a westward progress that duplicated the grand American pioneer experience. "It was west of Chicago that I found America," Wilde would later say. The jagged vistas of the Rocky Mountains and the Sierra Nevadas left him speechless—an infrequent occurrence in Wilde's life. "The mountains of California are so gigantic that they are not favorable to art or poetry," he told a reporter. "There are good poets in England, but none in Switzerland. There the mountains are too high. Art cannot add to nature." As for the people of the West, he had found them generally gracious and welcoming. They were "ready, but not rough. There were polished and refined compared with the people I met in larger cities farther East. There is no chance for roughness. The revolver is their book of etiquette. This teaches lessons that are not forgotten."[29]

Wilde's lessons, too, were unforgotten. Years later, when he was living in self-imposed exile in Paris after serving a two-year jail sentence in England for "gross indecency," meaning homosexual acts between consenting adults, he would tell a café companion that he was thinking of moving to the American West. It was a place, he said, "where a man is a man today, and yesterdays don't count—that a desperado can make a reputation for piety on his current performance. What a country to live in!" Unfortunately for him, by then it was too late to make the move.[30]

CHAPTER 8

You Should Have Seen It Before the War

❧

AFTER ALL THE COLOR and drama of the West, the East was more than a little dull. Worse than that, it was repetitive. Wilde had already been to Ohio, New Jersey, Pennsylvania, and New York, the next stops on his return itinerary. In Dayton, Ohio, on May 2, he stopped over at the Beckel House, where he broke lances with a reporter from the *Dayton Daily Democrat*. Something of the poet's irritation at being back in overly familiar surroundings seeped into the interview. Asked the typical opening question about how he found America and her people, Wilde broke character for once as the genial host. "Oh, what is the use of generalities?" he groused. "This country is much like other countries; we do not find much difference." The West, still fresh in his mind, was grand, but "the East is much more like the countries of Europe." As for the bulk of the citizens, "either they are now ignorant and insensible to these outrages to taste or else they are existing in utter misery."[1]

Wilde pointed to the furnishings in his hotel room. The chair in his room was badly made, and the coffee cup used in the restaurant was so thick and clumsy that "it disgusts me to drink from it." At least there was no cast-iron stove in the room. "This is the first hotel that I have been in for two or three weeks where my room did not have that horrid thing in it," he said. "If we must have them in our houses with their black iron bodies and ugly coiling pipe, let us have them plain and un-ornamented. But no, they insist upon decorating them, and so they put a garland of roses around them at the bottom—black, grimy horrid machine-made cast-iron roses. What a desecration! And then on top they put a something that so much resembles a funeral urn that we think we are living in a cemetery or sepulchre all the time."[2]

By now, the Dayton reporter must have been edging toward the door, but he made another stab at conversation. "Mr. Wilde, do you think that this present so-called 'aesthetic craze' . . ." Wilde interrupted. "O, *do* not call it a craze," he said. "It is no craze. You Americans have such a way of treating serious things as a joke. And yet you are not a joyous people. In society there is all brilliancy and apparent joyousness, but on the railway trains I do not see happy men and women. Everybody has a troubled anxious look, and everybody is pushing forward in some business project. But the people do not appreciate art and so they call it a craze." The reporter tried to leave graciously. "Well, I must express my thanks to you, Mr. Wilde, for this interview," he said. "I presume you have found us newspapermen a great annoyance since you have been in America." "Oh, no, not at all," said Wilde. "I never allow anything to annoy me. If I don't want to see anybody I tell them so."[3]

Wilde continued to be a little out of sorts during a carriage tour of Dayton with Professor Isaac Broome, the award-winning ceramics artist who had relocated to Dayton after many years with the Ott and Lange Ceramics Company in Trenton, New Jersey. Broome had won medals at the Centennial Exhibition in Philadelphia in 1876, and at the World's Fair in Paris two years later. His "Baseball Vase," depicting three baseball players in the act of pitching, catching, or swinging a bat, was the first American ceramics piece to be officially certified a work of art. Broome had pioneered a new glazing and underglazing process that gave his pieces a characteristic mottled effect; he called his productions "Jupiter-ware" and signed them with the scientific symbol for the gigantic planet. In Dayton he had opened a plant to produce Jupiter-ware and had helped to found the Ladies' Decoration Arts Society; he also taught at the Free Night Industrial School. His daughter, May, lived with him and worked at the pottery plant.

Broome took Wilde to see the new Presbyterian church on Third Street, an odd enough tour stop for the Aesthete. On the whole, said Wilde, the church was "really quite excellent. I am surprised." But he disliked the stained-glass windows, wondering aloud, "Why were they made with so transparent a design and such flaring colors?" Even the great English artist Sir Joshua Reynolds had not been able to pull it off, he said. Broome, a little deflated, allowed that the art of stained glass had perhaps not advanced quite far enough in America. Next, they toured the Montgomery County jail and the pottery plant on Summit Street. There, Miss Broome gave Wilde a piece she had made, which he accepted with a bow and pronounced better in some ways than those he had seen at the Rookwood Pottery Company in Cincinnati. At a local home for old soldiers, he was given a tour fit for a visiting general. The blue-coated veterans of Gettysburg, Antietam, Cold Harbor, and Chickamauga watched with varying degrees of interest as the tall English stranger strolled about, muttering "Good" and "Very nice" as he viewed the home's conservatory, dining hall, theater, and library. Crossing Dayton's Miami River, Wilde spoke approvingly of Indian place names, then gave the city fathers a piece of advice that might have carried over, with profit, for the entire industrialized East: "You should never let your manufacturers pollute the air with smoke."[4]

After his lecture that night at Dayton's Victory Theater, where he spoke about home decoration, Wilde proceeded by train to the Ohio state capital of Columbus. Wilde found "Panhandle Route" an odd name for a rail line, and said that in going from Dayton to Xenia, he felt as though he were "jumping from the pan into the fire." In Columbus he checked into the Neil House and was immediately taken in hand by local art lovers for yet another tour and reception, this one at the home of Mr. and Mrs. Alfred Kelley (Mrs. Kelley was president of the Columbus Arts Association). Wilde then toured the Long Street Academy of Design and the Columbus Art School, which he thought would have been improved "with gardens about it, walks and fountains, instead of plows, reapers and the ding dong of shops." The crowd attending his lecture that night at the Comstock Opera House was large and appreciative, with the exception of the critic for the *Columbus Daily Times,* who thought Wilde a "languid yokel" and the lecture itself "a vain imagining of a morbid brain striving for an Arcadian existence. Mr. Wilde will not probably revisit America, which can well spare him." The Reverend Frank W. Gunsaulus, who was pastor of the Read Street Congregational Church and who introduced the poet, apparently agreed, fleeing the stage after a truncated welcome that managed to contain not one word of praise for its subject. Gunsaulus, like many ministers, fancied himself something of a poet and in the course of his writing career published numerous poems, including an elegy in 1895 for Wilde's old Denver tormenter, Eugene Field, and a poem on "the recession of the falls at Niagara." Gunsaulus was in favor of it.[5]

Keeping his promise to Walt Whitman, Wilde paid the Good Gray Poet a return visit on May 10. This time the public took little notice of it, which was perhaps just as well if one believes the testimony of George Ives, founder of the Order of Chaeronea, a pioneering gay-rights organization in London (and, like Wilde, a later lover of Lord Alfred Douglas). According to Ives, Wilde had confided in him that "I have the kiss of Walt Whitman's still on my lips." Apparently Whitman's kiss lingered in Wilde's mind as well for quite some time, since he later signed John Boyle O'Reilly's autograph book in Boston, beneath an inscription from Whitman, with a quote from Wilde's poem "Humanitad": "The spirit who living blamelessly but dared to kiss the smitten mouth of his own century." According to another Wilde acquaintance, American author

Charles Godfrey Leland, a costumed Wilde had gone to see Whitman "got up as a far-away imitation of a cowboy, whom [Wilde] thought the most picturesque product of America."[6]

Leland, an authority on the language of gypsies, may have been on to something. It was rumored that Whitman had been displeased by the visit, or at least by the outfit, and had called Wilde "a damned fool." That was unlikely, given Whitman's usual courtesy and good manners, but he may have been more than usually out of sorts. The older poet was in the midst of a nasty censorship fight with the district attorney of Boston, Oliver Stevens, who had threatened to ban *Leaves of Grass* unless Whitman removed the offending—and ironically heterosexual— poems "A Woman Waits for Me" and "To a Common Prostitute." Whitman refused, a principled stand that cost him his publisher but won him the support of a variety of human-rights organizations, including the New England Free Love League. The *Springfield Republican* backhandedly editorialized that *Leaves of Grass* was "nothing compared to the dirty poems of Swinburne or such productions as that long poem ['Humanitad'] the modern aesthete Wilde has put in his book."[7]

During his return visit to Philadelphia, Wilde renewed acquaintance with an Irish-born cousin, the Anglican priest Basil W. Maturin. Like Wilde, Father Maturin had been raised in Dublin and attended Trinity College before immigrating to America. He offered to put up his kinsman for the night at his parish church, St. Clement's, but Wilde demurred after taking one look at "the austere and somewhat meager furnishings of an Anglican dormitory." Maturin eventually left the Anglican Church, converted to Catholicism, and became the Catholic chaplain at his famous cousin's alma mater, Oxford. In May 1915, returning to England after a speaking engagement in the United States, Maturin died along with 1,483 of his fellow passengers aboard the *Lusitania* when the ship was torpedoed by a German U-boat in the waters off Ireland.[8]

Arriving in New York on May 11, Wilde stepped into the middle of a controversy. Five days earlier, in Dublin, republican rebels belonging to the Irish National Invincibles had assassinated newly installed Chief Secretary Lord Frederick Cavendish and Under Secretary Thomas Henry Burke. Nine rebels had lain in wait for Burke in Phoenix Park, where they set upon him and the unfortunate Cavendish with razor-sharp surgical knives. Cavendish, a kinsman and long-time protégé of Prime Minister William E. Gladstone, had just arrived in Ireland and taken his oath of office that very morning. The rebels didn't even know he was in the country; it was Burke they were after. Asked as an Irishman to comment on the brutal murders when he arrived in New York, Wilde took a middle-of-the-road stance. "When liberty comes with hands dabbled in blood it is hard to shake hands with her," he told reporters. "But we forget how much England is to blame. She is reaping the fruit of seven centuries of injustice." That comparatively mild criticism predictably outraged more militant Irishmen at home and abroad, but brought Wilde favorable reaction as well. Said the *Philadelphia Press:* "After all the silly twaddle we have heard from Oscar Wilde, it is both surprising and refreshing to hear him utter these sensible words."[9]

Wilde made his New York return appearance at Wallack's Theatre on 31st Street. Although it was a matinée, Wilde violated his own dress code by appearing in full evening wear. The turnout was gratifying—there was "not an empty seat," he bragged to Norman Forbes-Robertson—and included P. T. Barnum, who sat on the front row but presumably did not make Wilde an offer to ride down Broadway atop Jumbo the Elephant. Wilde also deviated from custom by speaking without notes, feeling himself "greatly improved in speaking and in gesture." He spoke on art and architecture, taking the time to particularly praise Charles Leland's school for budding child craftsmen in Philadelphia. Displaying two brass disks and a wood carving done by children of ages nine to thirteen, Wilde said, "In such work as this children learn to abhor the liar in art. It is a practical school of morals. No better way is there to learn to love Nature than to understand Art. And a boy who sees the thing of beauty which a bird on the wing becomes when transferred to wood or canvas, will probably not throw the customary stone."

That was claiming a lot for a nine-year-old boy, but it seemed to go over well with the audience. When Wilde left the stage, a woman in a box seat threw him a lily and another followed with a cascade of roses.[10]

Wilde's second New York lecture had been intended to be his valedictory North American performance, but D'Oyly Carte and his managers noted the strong box office returns, more than $900, and quickly scheduled Wilde for a two-week tour of Canada, commencing on May 15. "I have already civilized America," Wilde bragged to James McNeill Whistler, *"il reste seulement le ciel!"*—i.e., "all that remains is heaven!" Wilde crossed the border at Niagara Falls and journeyed to Montreal for his first lecture, on May 15. After checking into the Windsor Hotel (was every other hotel in North America named the Windsor?), he proudly included in a letter to his friend Norman Forbes-Robertson a pencil sketch of a nearby billboard with Wilde's name on it in six-foot-high letters—"true in those primary colours against which I pass my life protesting, but still it is fame, and anything is better than virtuous obscurity, even one's own name in alternate colours of Albert blue and magenta." He welcomed his friend's planned visit to America and promised to drink "boy" (champagne) with him when Forbes-Robertson got to Boston.[11]

The English- and French-language newspapers in Montreal offered conflicting images of Wilde upon his arrival. *La Patrie* warned its readers that Wilde would attract "all the people of disordered brains, the hysterical women, the coxcombs, the beggared population"—a wide range of admirers, indeed—and *Le Monde* described the newly arrived visitor as looking the part of "a comic-opera brigand" and "a quack doctor." Reporters for the *Daily Star* and the *Montreal Witness,* on the other hand, interviewed Wilde at his hotel and found him not at all the arch-Aesthete they had been led to expect, but a well-spoken member of "an enviable social status" who was "quite consummately" dressed. Wilde bragged of having spoken to 200,000 people in the United States, where "I have found the people very willing and ready to listen and appreciate." Asked for his working definition of "beauty," the poet said he was "quite content to put that off for my old age, if lovers of art have an old age." Did such lovers die young, the reporter for the *Star* wanted to know. "No," said Wilde, "but art is always youthful."[12]

Owing perhaps to the generous if divergent publicity, Wilde's audience at Queen's Hall that night was packed. He was introduced by a prominent Montreal physician, Dr. F. W. Campbell, who had trained with Wilde's father in Dublin and who remembered visiting their home on Merrion Square when Wilde was four. Despite the welcoming introduction, Wilde's performance evoked a lukewarm response. The *Star* reported that there was "only a little splutter of cheering" before Wilde "solemnly receded"; people "would have applauded," said the newspaper, "but feared it would be a desecration." The *Witness* editorialized anthropomorphically that the new English Renaissance in the arts, "ransacking the ages of objects beautified by the bloom of time, might do good, but there is danger of art losing her virginity when she seeks to charm by her own blandishments, and to become herself a queen instead of keeping her modest place as the unconscious handmaid of nature." A matinée appearance brought a better response, as Wilde presented his standby second lecture, "Exterior and Interior House Decoration," in which he observed wittily that "two pictures, hung side by side, kill each other, or rather both commit artistic suicide," and "the modern bonnet keeps off neither sun in summer nor rain in winter. Nothing is more graceful in the world than the broad-brimmed hat of the Rocky Mountain miners."[13]

Before he left, Wilde was given a guided tour of Montreal by leading socialite Sheldon Stephens, a wealthy raconteur who had trained as a pianist in Germany with Franz Liszt. Stephens took Wilde to see the Sacred Heart Convent, a bilingual boarding school for girls, on the Prairies River; Mount Royal, a 763-foot prominence with a panoramic view of the city to which it gave its name; the art gallery in Phillip's Square; and the venerable Notre Dame Church in Old Montreal. The church, a Gothic-style building with stained-glass windows depicting various signal events in Montreal history, left Wilde unmoved; he merely pronounced its windows and gaily colored frescoes "healthy." He inadvertently ruffled local feathers by reporting that he "went up the hill behind your lovely city"—a downgrading of the locals' pride and joy that provoked the *Montreal Star* to grumble, "It was not nice to hear our cherished mountain reduced to a hill."[14]

In Ottawa, the Canadian capital, Wilde continued his criticism of local flora, looking askance at the lumber mills releasing black smoke into the sky and sawdust into the Ottawa River. "The things of nature do not really belong to us," he observed. "We should leave them to our children as we have received them." Checking into the Russell House, a five-minute walk from Parliament Hill on the Rideau Canal, Wilde lectured on the decorative arts at the Grand Opera House on the evening of May 16. The turnout was lackluster, with a number of citizens choosing instead to attend either the University of Ottawa's annual sports banquet or the closing session of Parliament. Wilde went to Parliament himself after his lecture; he spent two hours touring the government buildings and library, ate a late-night snack in the dining room, and occupied the seat of honor beside the Speaker's Chair during the closing debates. Still clad in his customary stage costume of black velvet coat and knee breeches, Wilde so fascinated Vancouver MP Arthur Bunster, reported the *Ottawa Daily Citizen,* that the politician "forgot for a time the burning wrongs of British Columbia."[15]

Unfortunately for Wilde, he did not hold comparable fascination for the nation's leading politician, the Marquis of Lorne, Canada's governor general and the husband of Queen Victoria's art-loving fourth daughter, Louise. The princess, who disliked living in Canada, was back home in England during Wilde's visit, and Lorne, who was widely suspected of homosexual tendencies himself, pointedly declined to attend Wilde's lecture or meet with him privately at Government House. Not wanting to be seen in public with so louche a personality as Wilde, Lorne busied himself with his official speechmaking duties—he had to close Parliament the next day with an address from the throne—although he still found time to go horseback riding and play two full rounds of golf with his aides. Meanwhile, reported the *Kingston Daily News*, "Oscar stayed at a hotel and drank out of a thick tea cup."[16]

Perhaps reacting to the snub, Wilde told an interviewer from the *Toronto Globe* that he was surprised "the Princess Louise, who was such an admirer of art, had not accomplished greater results" in promoting homegrown Canadian artists. As for Wilde, he made time to meet with local artist Frances Richards and recommended her to James McNeill Whistler as someone who was "quite worthy of your blue and white china. I know you will be charming to her." Miss Richards, the thirty-year-old daughter of Albert Norton Richards, the lieutenant governor of British Columbia, was a rather pretty if formidable-looking maiden. She would later study art in Paris, marry an English gentleman named William Edward Rowley, and make her home in Cheyne Walk, London. Five years later, Wilde would sit for a portrait by Richards in South Kensington, joking at the time that it was tragic that although his portrait would never grow older, he himself would. "If only it was the other way," he sighed. That chance remark, said Wilde, was the genesis of *The Picture of Dorian Gray*.[17]

From Ottawa, Wilde double-backed east to Quebec, arriving at daybreak on May 18 after an all-night train ride on the Quebec, Montreal, Ottawa & Occidental Railway. His arrival coincided with the annual assembly of the Eighth Royal Rifles militia on the historic Plains of Abraham, where English general James Wolfe had defeated French general Louis de Montcalm at the Battle of Quebec in September 1759, effectively ending the French and Indian War and ensuring that Canada and the future United States would be primarily English-speaking colonies. Wilde had comparatively little interest in military history, English or Canadian, but he allowed himself to be escorted to the plains that afternoon to witness the regiment's training exercises, which culminated in a full-scale reenactment of the pivotal charge up Citadel Hill 123 years earlier.

Wilde's visit continued its martial theme that night when he was hosted by officers at the Garrison Club prior to his lecture on decorative arts at the Quebec Music Hall. His speech, sponsored by local book-store owner C. E. Holiwell, was attended by a "large and fashionable" audience, but its reception apparently did not satisfy Wilde, who observed afterwards that "Quebec especially has a noble situation, but I was sorry to see that there was so little life or spirit in it." He enjoyed a better experience the next day at a garden party held at the home of the Right Reverend James W. Williams, Lord Anglican Bishop of Quebec. Williams was a fellow graduate of Oxford, and the party reminded Wilde strongly of his bygone college life. *La Vérité* editor J. P. Tardivel reported that the partygoers included "a young lady sagging under the weight of an enormous sunflower" and two young girls who "were seen posturing languidly and looking up at the heavens in such a way that only the whites of their eyes showed."[18]

After stopping to deliver a second lecture in Montreal on May 20, Wilde headed west to Kingston, on the extreme northeastern shore of Lake Ontario. His appearance at the Opera House was sparsely attended, owing to bad weather and heavy rains. Wilde did his best for the "aesthetically thin" crowd, telling a newspaperman afterwards that American lecturer Wendell Phillips had once advised him that "any man could speak well to a crowd, but it required a mighty effort to thrill empty benches." The next morning Wilde endured another tour of local government buildings, inside one of which he met City Clerk Michael Flannigan, who had gone to school in Castlereagh, Ireland, the hometown of Wilde's father. The pair discovered that they shared many of the same acquaintances, and Flannigan pronounced Wilde "a jolly good fellow." At Fort Henry, the poet lunched with a group of army officers before spending the afternoon with another churchman, the Very Reverend James Lyster, Dean of Ontario. Lyster, too, was a fellow Irishman, and Wilde enjoyed his visit so much that he uncharacteristically missed the afternoon train to Belleville and had to wait for the morning express.[19]

Wilde pulled into Belleville on the night of May 23 and was an hour late for his lecture before a mostly female crowd at City Hall Auditorium. He made no apologies and firmly if gently elbowed his way through the post-lecture crowd backstage. A reporter for the *Kingston Daily News* accompanied him back to the Dafoe House, where Wilde "dissect[ed] the elements of beauty which he found in chops and Bass's ale." To the reporter's eye, "Oscar Wilde is getting unaesthetically fat." The Belleville appearance earned sponsors a scant $16, which barely covered the cost of Wilde's table bill.[20]

In Toronto, on the morning of May 24, Wilde was met at the railroad station by an official delegation and escorted to Lieutenant Governor John Beverly Robinson's private box at City Stadium for a lacrosse match between Toronto's home team and the St. Regis Indians from nearby Cornwall Reservation. It was Victoria Day, the queen's birthday, and the stadium was full of citizens taking advantage of the national holiday. People in the grandstand craned their necks for a view of Wilde, who was wearing his black western sombrero. Wilde politely followed the match with apparent attention, laughing heartily when one of the players sprawled to the grass and clapping his hands over a particularly good shot. Departing, he told a *Toronto Globe* reporter, "Oh, I was delighted with it. It is a charming game." He was particularly taken with the "tall, finely built defense man. I admired his playing very much." The athlete in question was Ross Mackenzie, the leading lacrosse player in Canada, who once set a world record by casting a ball 422 feet.[21]

Wilde was careful to give equal time to the ladies at the match, noting that "some of them are very nice and dress exceedingly well" and singling out one little girl who had sat in front of him wearing a dress of a fetching rose-pink, "a beautiful blending of color that corresponded so nicely with her rosy cheeks." He was a little disappointed, he said, that the players on the Indians' team had not dressed in war paint, tomahawks, and feathered headdresses. One could not have everything. All in all, Toronto, judged strictly from the grandstand of a lacrosse match, struck him as "a bright little town," although he thought it shared with other Canadian cities a dismaying preference for white brick over red, which Wilde pronounced "horrid. White brick is such a shallow color."[22]

As in Montreal, Wilde gave two lectures in Toronto, one at night and one in the afternoon. Both were well attended, with overflow audience members sitting on camp stools in the aisles and whistling snatches from *Patience* as they waited for Wilde to make his appearance. He amused everyone by denouncing "very strenuously" the crimson tablecloth that covered his speaking table. It was almost as bad, he said, as the red-and-white checked one he had been forced to endure in Columbus, Ohio. He left the stage to loud applause and laughter, although the *Toronto Telegram* judged him, a little unkindly, to have "a face like a broad-ax" and a smile "like a colicky baby in its sleep." Given a guided tour of the Ontario Society of Artists by founding member Thomas Mower Martin, Wilde gracefully praised the work of homegrown landscape artist Homer Ransford Watson, "the Canadian Constable," but was unmoved by a miniature portrait of Irish beauty Mary Cornwallis West. Miniature painting, he said flatly, was dead. Another painting, of a pell-mell waterfall, evoked a classic Wildean dismissal: "That water is too happy."[23]

Wilde's Canadian swing concluded with lectures in the Ontario Peninsula townships of Brantford, Woodstock, and Hamilton, where he visited in turn the Six Nations Indian reservation, a cabinetmaking factory, and Wesleyan Ladies' College. He returned to Boston on June 2. All in all, the Canadian lectures were a great success, "the most enjoyable part of his tour," in Colonel Morse's view, "more congenial in many ways than the American towns, and with audiences more in sympathy with the man and his subjects." They were, of course, fellow "Pommies"—Prisoners of Mother England.[24]

From the northern expanses of Canada, Wilde dropped down to the American South for the next part of his tour. He had received, as he reported to Morse, "a good offer for two months' light lecturing in the South, which I am anxious to visit." Wilde's southern excursion, much expanded, was being promoted by Memphis-based entrepreneur "General" Peter Tracy. Tracy, a circus man at heart, normally spent his time wrangling with city officials over the Sunday operation of a giant roller-coaster he had built on Chickasaw Bluffs outside Memphis. He offered large box-office guarantees to Wilde, who was eager to visit the cradle of secession.

Less than two decades after the end of the Civil War, the people of the South still dated their lives around that four-year stretch of national insanity. Everything was either "before the war" or "after the war." There was a reason for that. Despite the unregenerate Rebel spirit commemorated by Confederate Memorial Day and the crimson-and-white Stars and Bars flaunted on the official state flags of various Deep South states, it was undeniable to any but the most—or least—forgetful that few causes had ever been more roundly and comprehensively defeated than the one espoused by the American South. Oscar Wilde, as the son of Irish patriots, knew something about lost causes.[25]

Warned about visiting the South at the height of yellow fever season, Wilde joked, "If you survive yellow journalism, you need not be afraid of yellow fever." It was actually more of a threat than he may have realized. Four years earlier, a ferocious yellow fever epidemic had swept the region, carrying off nearly 20,000 victims in a swath of the Mississippi Valley extending from New Orleans to Vicksburg, Memphis, and Chattanooga. The next year the disease broke out again, claiming another 3,000 lives. Among the more celebrated victims was former Confederate general John Bell Hood, who succumbed in New Orleans along with his wife and the eldest of their eleven children; the other ten were later adopted by fellow Southerners. Wilde managed to avoid yellow fever, but at some point in his travels he contracted malaria, which plagued him off and on for the rest of his life.[26]

Wilde commenced his tour in Memphis on June 12, appearing before 600 people at Leubrie's Theatre. One of the attendees, a three-year-old girl, presented him with a large basket of fresh flowers, winning from the Aesthete the encomium that he "was glad to see so early so young and beautiful a disciple." Peter Tracy's advance man, John Gray, had wrongly advertised the title of Wilde's lecture as "The English Renaissance"—it was actually "The Decorative Arts"—and had made the rather sweeping claim that Wilde was speaking to "the largest lecture audiences which have been seen since the days of Charles Dickens." Wilde admonished him, "Do not advertise to catch coarse people, as I only care to speak to audiences that are educated and refined." That didn't stop Gray from draping a white canvas banner over the back of Wilde's Pullman car with the poet's name printed in big black letters on the side—the sort of advertising Tracy used for his circuses.[27]

From Memphis, Wilde dropped down to Vicksburg, site of the pivotal Union victory nineteen years earlier. There, on the Fourth of July 1863, one day after Robert E. Lee's defeat at Gettysburg, Ulysses S. Grant had accepted the surrender of Lieutenant General John C. Pemberton and his beleaguered defenders, effectively marking the end of Confederate control of the Mississippi River. Grant's victory had split the Confederacy in half and given the national forces control over the river, from its headwaters in Minnesota to the bayous below New Orleans. It had also brought an implacable new viciousness to the war, ironically embodied by the least outwardly vicious general on either side. At Vicksburg, whose grass-covered entrenchments Wilde toured on June 14, Grant had not hesitated to bombard southern civilians, including women and children, sheltering in the limestone caves below the river bluffs. The message, replayed by Grant's red-bearded protégé William Tecumseh Sherman at Atlanta, Georgia, a year later, was crystal-clear: there were no civilians anymore. It had helped to win the war for the Union (and the White House for Grant), but it had left a residual bitterness in the South that the ensuing two decades had not effaced.

As Wilde was journeying by rail to New Orleans, fellow writer, lecturer, and wit Samuel L. Clemens, a.k.a. Mark Twain, was passing by river in the opposite direction. For the purposes of a new book, *Life on the Mississippi,* Twain was retracing and imaginatively reliving his halcyon days as a steamboat pilot in the years immediately before the Civil

War. Twain had missed Wilde's appearance in Hartford, Connecticut, in February, and he would also miss his appearance in New Orleans on June 16. Indeed, the next time the two men laid eyes on each other was almost exactly ten years later, in a chance encounter in a hotel dining room in Bad Nauheim, Germany. Wilde was there taking the waters at the spa with his scandalous young friend, Lord Alfred Douglas; Twain was with his family in self-imposed European financial exile, after losing his fortune to bad business investments. The funnymen nodded to each other in passing, but Twain's daughter Clara could not remember what, if anything, had been said by the two most quotable wits of the nineteenth century. All she could recall was the baby sunflower in Wilde's lapel and the brightly colored shoes (presumably yellow) on his feet.

Wilde arrived in New Orleans on the morning of June 16 and checked into the historic St. Charles, two blocks off Canal Street in the heart of the city's American Quarter. The St. Charles, opened in 1837 and rebuilt after a major fire two decades later, was universally acclaimed to be the city's finest hotel. Through the Corinthian columns of its façade had passed Jefferson Davis (at that time a United States senator) and his fellow southern Democrats to plot strategy for the party's ultimately disastrous 1860 nominating convention in Charleston. There, a walkout by many of those same plotters had fatally split the Democratic Party and led to Abraham Lincoln's election as president and, almost immediately, the Civil War. Following the Union capture of New Orleans in 1862, Major General Benjamin "Beast" Butler had commandeered the St. Charles, managed by his wife's kinsman David W. Hildreth, and enacted Draconian measures to occupy and police the city, including the infamous "General Order No. 28," which declared that any woman seen insulting one of his soldiers would be considered a common prostitute.

Unaware, in all likelihood, of the hotel's tumultuous history, Wilde settled in with his cigarettes, scented water, and pile of paperback French novels for the usual round of newspaper interviews. With a reporter for the *Daily Picayune* he started well, saying all the right things about

Southerners being more agreeable and courteous than Northerners, a
behavioral difference he put down to the regions' variable climates. But
Wilde was curiously tone-deaf to his new surroundings. In one of America's most unique and colorful cities, he declared flatly that "one must go
to Asia and Africa for picturesqueness in human costume and habits."
Compounding his error, he maintained to the white reporter that he
had found such colorfulness "only in the Indians and the Negro, and I
am surprised that painters and poets have paid so little attention to
them, particularly to the Negro, as a subject of art." Perhaps because he
was comparatively unprejudiced himself, or at least nonjudgmental,
Wilde failed to realize the depths of racial animosity still existing in the
South and, indeed, throughout the United States.[28]

Wilde was taken around the city by one of its most famous and
revered citizens, former Confederate general Pierre Gustave Toutant
Beauregard, who at Charleston, South Carolina, in April 1861, had given
the command for the first shot of the Civil War. Beauregard was an old
friend of Wilde's late uncle, Dr. J. K. Elgee, who had lived for years in
Rapides Parish and taken a leading interest in southern politics. Besides
their personal connection to Elgee and their innate aristocratic leanings,
the diminutive, goateed general and the tall, clean-shaven Irishman
shared a liking for "the green fairy," absinthe. Called by one modern
scholar "the cocaine of the nineteenth century," the wormwood-based
liqueur was typically served in a special glass topped by a spoon, from
which a sugar cube slowly melted into the beverage below. Catching on
first in France, whose citizens drank an astonishing 36 million liters of
absinthe per year by 1910, the drink had spread to large American cities
such as New Orleans, New York, San Francisco, and Chicago—all visited recently by Wilde. In New Orleans, the Old Absinthe House on
the corner of Bourbon and Bienville streets in the French Quarter served
the house special, Absinthe Frappe. Marketed under such pleasantly in-
nocuous brand names as the Green Opal and the Milky Way, absinthe
was blamed for causing convulsions, hallucinations, birth defects, tuberculosis, insanity, and criminality. That did not deter writers and art-

ists such as Van Gogh, Degas, Rimbaud, Baudelaire, and Toulouse-Lautrec from tasting it and memorializing the pleasures of Paris's "Green Hour," the period between dusk and nightfall. *Harper's Weekly* led a public campaign to outlaw the drink in the United States, calling it "the fast prevailing vice among our gilded youth." By the early twentieth century, The United States and all of Europe except for Spain had banned absinthe from being consumed or distributed.

Following an appearance at the Grand Opera House on June 16, Wilde ventured southwest to Texas for lectures in Fort Worth, Galveston, San Antonio, and Houston. The sun-baked plains were a depressing counterpoint to the shadowy elegance of New Orleans's French Quarter, and the appearances did not go over particularly well. At Galveston's oceanside Pavilion Opera House, where he spoke on decorative art to a crowd described as "mostly ladies," the electricity flickered on and off, and Wilde's talk was largely drowned out by rowdies—presumably males—who stomped their feet in second-floor balcony. "Those who could hear Wilde gave him credit for a thorough familiarity with his subject, Decorative Art," reported the *Galveston Daily News,* "yet the lecture was not a success by any means, and were he to appear tonight he would scarcely rally a corporal's guard." An ad in the newspaper compared Wilde unfavorably to "St. Jacob's Oil, the Great German Remedy for Rheumatism," which supposedly had a more tangible effect on users than the poet's words. Gracious as usual, Wilde praised Galveston for being "set like a jewel in a crystal sea." Six weeks later, the Pavilion burned to the ground in twenty-five minutes while city fire engines floundered helplessly in the deep sand on the beach.[29]

Sometime during the 247-mile train ride from Galveston to San Antonio, Wilde lost his hat to a gust of wind, and the engineer obligingly stopped for him to retrieve it. His reception that night at Turner Hall was less accommodating. Again he was drowned out, apparently without malicious intent, by audience members going back and forth to the bar for drinks. As the *San Antonio Evening Light* reported, "Many of Oscar Wilde's sentences were lost on account of his very poor delivery and the squeaking of the new boots of some of the thirsty ones going out for refreshments. One hour was too long between drinks." The *Evening Light* reporter, at least, was an old acquaintance of Wilde's, a transplanted Englishman from Leicester named Henry Ryder-Taylor, who would later become the business partner of another famous writer, William Sidney Porter, better known by his pen name—one might almost say his alias—O. Henry.[30]

Ryder-Taylor took Wilde around to see the various sights in San Antonio, including the San Jose mission and, inevitably, the Alamo, whose state of neglectful disrepair struck Wilde as "monstrous." The fabled battle site had been used as recently as 1878 by the U.S. Army Quartermaster's Corps to store grain and hay, and an enterprising Frenchman named Honoré Grenet recently had bought the building and remodeled it into a dry-goods store, complete with fake wooden cannons to add a suitably martial touch. Wilde, complaining of a mysterious lassitude that he attributed to the bathwater in Galveston, entrained to Houston, 197 miles away, where he spoke that night at Gray's Opera House to another rowdy Texas crowd. Several particularly raucous theatergoers were removed from the gallery for misbehavior, and Wilde was continually interrupted by the ringing of a large gong in the saloon downstairs. His reception was so bad that the *Houston Post* scolded its citizens the next day for "belittling a man whose ideas of art were sound and much needed in a young community, and who was himself very different from the foolish popular idea of an aesthetic Quixote charging upon American realism with a sunflower."[31]

Resolutely unshaken by his Lone Star experience, Wilde returned to New Orleans and the St. Charles Hotel to prepare for his next scheduled appearances at Spanish Fort and Mobile. A reporter from the *Picayune* found him in buoyant good humor. Galveston and San Antonio, Wilde said, had given him great pleasure to visit, and he had been delighted to see the Texas-bred alligators "sprawl[ing] and yawn[ing] in the sunshine on the trunks of fallen trees and on the muddy banks of the bayous and the great morasses." He encouraged the reporter to address him as "Colonel," saying he had earned the brevet rank in Galveston and intended to write home to England to announce his promotion. In the meantime, he said, he looked forward to calling on the former president of the Confederacy, Jefferson Davis, at his gulfside home in Biloxi, Mississippi. Davis, seventy-four, had just published his massive apologia for treason, the two-volume, 800-page *Rise and Fall of the Confederate Government*. He was living in seclusion with his wife, Varina, and their grown daughter, Winnie, largely forgotten by most of his fellow Southerners, who blamed him mostly for not being as able a war chief as Abraham Lincoln.[32]

Displaying a politically adept if historically shaky understanding of recent events, Wilde declared:

> The case of the South in the Civil War was to my mind much like that of Ireland today. It was a struggle for autonomy, self-government for a people. I do not wish to see the empire dismembered, but only to see the Irish people free, and Ireland still as a willing and integral part of the British Empire. To dismember a great empire in this age of vast armies and overweening ambition on the part of other nations is to consign the peoples of the broken country to weak and insignificant places in the panorama of nations; but people must have freedom and autonomy before they are capable of their greatest result in the cause of progress.

That the Confederacy had been formed precisely to dismember the United States and to break away from any larger shared national purpose, imperial or not, with the North, escaped Wilde's European understanding, and the New Orleans reporter politely (or cannily) let it go.[33]

Wilde was on his way, he said, to observe "the mysterious and curious ceremonies of the devotees of voodoo" who were planning to celebrate St. John's Night in the Old Quarter. The long-reigning voodoo queen of New Orleans, Marie Laveau, had died a few months earlier, but her daughter, Marie Laveau II, had taken her place in dispensing gris-gris, hoodoo, and other witchy charms to the greater glory of

Li Grand Zombi, the snake king. The feast of John the Baptist, patron saint of the voodoo makers, was a mind-blowing mixture of the sacred and the profane, involving Christian—mainly Catholic—ceremonies, the ritual sacrifice of animals, and hours of chanting, dancing, and singing in both known and unknown tongues. Zombies walked the earth. Regrettably, Wilde did not recount for posterity his brief exposure to Caribbean magicks and the dark heart of the New Orleans soul, although it is diverting to imagine him joining the revels, knee breeches and all, on Bourbon Street.

Nor did Wilde describe in any detail his ensuing visit with the equally spectral Jefferson Davis three days later. Gray, rail-thin, and milky-eyed from glaucoma, Davis was literally fading away from the American scene. Having lost all his money in the cauldron of the war and the "raven days" of Republican-enforced reconstruction, Davis had hoped to restore his fortunes by writing the ultimate insider's account of the Confederacy. He had moved into Beauvoir, a vacation cottage on the estate of recently widowed southern novelist Sarah Ann Ellis Dorsey, a former classmate of Davis's wife at Madame Grelaud's French finishing school in Philadelphia. Dorsey had written a best-selling gothic novel, *The House of Bouverie,* before the war, and now she donated her professional—and some said her personal—assistance to the former president. Rumors of an affair between Davis and the much-younger Dorsey had strained the old schoolmates' friendship to the point that Varina Davis refused to set foot on Dorsey's property—a tactical decision she later rethought. All Dorsey's help failed to improve *The Rise and Fall of the Confederate Government,* which most readers, then and later, found as dry and dull as Davis's notoriously arid personality. Dorsey fell ill with breast cancer and died (in the St. Charles Hotel) in 1879. She performed one more service to the South's former president and first lady by willing them the title to Beauvoir, an act of charity that her heirs fought long and fruitlessly to overturn.

Wilde called on the Davises on June 27. He probably mentioned his recent acquaintance with General Beauregard, although that would not have much impressed his host, who had suffered well-documented personal and military differences with the dapper little Creole during the war. Wilde had read—or skimmed—Davis's tome, and he pronounced it "a masterpiece," although he conceded that many of the purely military passages were "a little burdensome." He found Davis's inherited home lovely and the politician himself "a man of the keenest intellect," a born leader of men, with a simple and strong personality. He repeated his debatable linkage of the dead Confederacy with the ongoing struggles between Ireland and England, and concluded sweepingly that "the principles for which Mr. Davis and the South went to war cannot suffer defeat." Again, that would have been news to the comprehensively defeated people of the South, but perhaps Wilde was just being polite. Davis, not knowing what to make of Wilde, retired early, saying later, "I did not like the man," but Varina, Winnie, and their cousin Mary Davis stayed up late discussing art and literature with the visiting poet. Mrs. Davis, it transpired, had known Wilde's uncle in her youth. When he departed, Wilde left behind on Davis's desk one of his presentation photographs from the Sarony session in New York, inscribed: "To Jefferson Davis in all loyal admiration from Oscar Wilde, June '82—Beauvoir." Davis, it was said, resented the gift as presumptuous. He had been, after all, the ruler of a great nation, if only for four disastrous years—not some costumed stage performer.[34]

From Biloxi, Wilde traveled north to appear at Frascati Amusement Park in Mobile. The park, on the western side of Mobile Bay, featured white sand beaches, a pavilion and band shell, and a small zoo with an abundance of screeching monkeys. Before it was destroyed by a hurricane in 1893, Frascati had become the first and most popular outdoor amusement park in the South. In keeping with the park's enterprising nature, a young boy went about hawking sunflowers prior to Wilde's lecture. According to Wilde, the enterprising tyke made twenty-five dollars for his labors. "That boy," he said, "will be a congressman yet."[35]

Wilde followed his open-air appearance in Mobile with a visit to the first Confederate capital, Montgomery. There he was taken in hand by the brothers from the Phi Delta Theta fraternity, who were hosting an annual dance at McDonald's Opera House. The *Montgomery Advertiser,* waxing poetic, described Wilde's reception "in the soft air of the June night, laden with the perfume of flowers." The young ladies, said the newspaper, were charmed by "his splendid figure, polished manners, and pleasing speech," and Wilde in turn was charmed by "the beauty and wit and taste of Montgomery's lovely daughters." One daughter in particular, Miss Alsatia "Lila" Allen, caught Wilde's attention. The reigning belle of the city, Lila Allen had recently appeared in an amateur production of *Patience.* According to the *Selma Times,* in whose adjacent bailiwick she had also performed, Miss Allen "completely captivated" Wilde during his visit to Montgomery. "The utter young Celt pronounced the lady the most beautiful he'd seen in the South, and he sought her society continually," claimed the newspaper.[36]

It may well have been Lila who whispered to Wilde a much-repeated quote that he retold frequently to northern friends. "I was once sitting on the portico of a country house with a young lady admiring the beauty of a limpid stream under the rays of the moon," Wilde recalled. "I said, 'How beautiful is the moonlight falling on the water!' 'It is beautiful indeed,' she replied, 'but, oh, Mr. Wilde, you should have seen it before the war.'" He never attributed the quote, but he did disavow gently his reported admiration for Lila Allen. Shown an article from the *New Orleans Times* in which he was quoted as saying that Miss Allen was "the most beautiful young lady he had seen in the United States," Wilde chuckled: "This is a remark, my dear fellow, I have made of some lady in every city I have visited in this country. It could be appropriately made. American women are very beautiful, and some of the finest types of beauty I have ever seen I found in the South."[37]

Southern belles notwithstanding, by late June Wilde was writing to the long-suffering W. F. Morse to complain about his schedule. "It is very annoying to me to find that my Southern tour extends far beyond the three weeks you spoke of," wrote Wilde. "It is now three weeks since I left New York, and I am informed I have two weeks more. Five weeks for sixteen lectures—nothing could be worse in every way. It is quite stupid and gross and will do me much harm." Wilde was traveling north through Alabama on June 30 when presidential assassin Charles J. Guiteau made his long-awaited rendezvous with the hangman's rope in Washington, D.C. In keeping with everything surrounding the Garfield assassination, it was a seriocomic event from start to finish. Guiteau had already survived two attempts on his life: one by a guard at the jail who had fired at him through a window in his cell—somehow the guard had missed—and the other by an assailant mounted on horseback who fired a round at the prisoner's carriage during the trial. Neither would-be avenger was ever tried for their premature if understandable efforts to permanently silence the absurd assassin.[38]

On the last day of June, Guiteau's luck ran out. After eating a hearty breakfast, taking a bath, and praying for an hour, the condemned man was led out to the courtyard at the Washington jail to be hanged. A light bulb blinked on in his frazzled head. "I'm going to be murdered!" Guiteau cried. "I'm God's man! My murderers will go down to hell! President Arthur is a coward and ingrate!" He had written a special new poem for the occasion, "Simplicity and Religious Baby Talk," which long-suffering officials allowed him to recite in its entirety, it being, in a way, his last will and testament. The poem, which Guiteau read in an affected, high-pitched voice, was intended to represent a young child talking to his parents. It began: "I am going to the Lordy; I am so glad," but veered off into precocious political commentary: "I saved my party and my land, Glory hallelujah! / But they have murdered me for it, / And that is the reason I am going to the Lordy." As a parting gift to the nation, Guiteau suggested that the poem be set to music and taught to schoolchildren. It was not.[39]

Before his southern tour came to an end, Wilde made appearances in Macon, Atlanta, Savannah, Charleston, Norfolk, and Richmond. Interest on both sides seemed to have waned. In Macon, tour manager J. S. Vale had to deny rumors that a counterfeit Aesthete would take the stage. The *Macon Telegraph* editor, who had probably started the rumor in the first place—the same journalist had claimed earlier that the Rankin Hotel in Columbus, Georgia, had been forced to take on an extra porter to carry all of Wilde's flowers and autograph albums—accepted the disavowal at face value. "Now that Guiteau is gone," said the editor, "there is hardly anyone crank enough to impersonate Oscar."[40]

An actual Wilde impersonator, Augustin Smith Clayton, had taken the stage in Atlanta two weeks earlier, although he was not trying to pull the wool over anyone's eyes. Billing himself as "Wild Oscar," Clayton, the editor of the *Drummer,* a weekly newspaper for commercial travelers, had presented a good-natured takeoff on a typical Wilde evening. Appearing at DeGive's Opera House, where the Aesthete would later appear on July 4, Clayton had shared center stage with a giant sunflower and a wheezing collection of wind-up dolls. He wore enormous sunflower-capped slippers, red-and-blue stockings, an orange-and-white waistcoat, a sunflower watch fob, and a long brown wig. Clayton mixed a recitation of Wilde's better-known sayings with his own aestheticized version of Atlanta's history, capped off by a "sunflower dance" performed by six cavorting male and female dancers. Afterwards, Clayton signed pictures of the real Wilde, inscribed "Truly, SC."[41]

After his own appearance at DeGive's, Wilde inadvertently made news upon leaving Atlanta, when his traveling secretary bought three first-class tickets on the overnight train to Savannah. One of the tickets was intended for John the valet. In the Jim Crow–era South, African Americans did not ride first class, and the conductor on the train in question explained as much to Wilde, who, to his credit, refused to accept a refund to downgrade John's ticket. An experienced Pullman porter took John aside and warned him that he was running the risk of being lynched when the train stopped at Jonesboro and white passengers found a black man sleeping in a whites-only berth. Only then did Wilde's valet move to a second-class car for the remainder of the journey.

The rest of the southern swing went off without controversy, although an ad in the Savannah newspapers declared that "Oscar Wilde

could not please the Savannah public, but Jacob Cohen of 152 Brough-
ton Street can." (Cohen was a traveling dry-goods salesman.) The
Charleston News and Courier reporter arrived for an interview whistling
the newest Wilde ditty, "Oscar dear, Oscar dear, How utterly flutterly
utter you are," and described his subject as "two hundred pounds of
aestheticism" and "an enlarged and magnified 'lah-da-dah' young man
[who] speaks with the 'don't-you-know' yawp of the day." Wilde, as
usual, was polite and responsive, although he perhaps betrayed his
eagerness to conclude his southern travels by noting that "upon the
whole I'd rather travel through a country rapidly." When the reporter
observed, a little snidely, that he had seen "a number of colored women
on the Fourth of July parading through the streets with huge sunflowers
in their dresses and hats," Wilde shrugged off the implied jab. "To love
one's life is to love the beautiful," he said.[42]

Rushing through Richmond on July 12, Wilde appeared before a
smallish crowd of 200 people, described slightingly by the *Richmond
State* as "some of our best citizens and a residuum of small potatoes of
the male sex." Despite his earlier professed interest in the southern war
effort, Wilde did not take the time to tour Jefferson Davis's old residence, the White House of the Confederacy, or to view the forest of
monuments to Robert E. Lee, Stonewall Jackson, and other dead Rebel
generals springing up almost daily along First Street. He may not have
seen the South before the war, but he had certainly seen enough of it
after the war. He would not re-cross the Mason-Dixon Line again.[43]

CHAPTER 9

The Oscar of the First Period Is Dead

❧

$\mathcal{B}$EFORE LEAVING THE SOUTH, Wilde already had his next destination in mind. From Augusta, Georgia, he wrote to Julia Ward Howe, who had invited him to visit her summer home in ultra-exclusive Newport, Rhode Island. "I write to you from the beautiful, passionate, ruined South, the land of magnolias and music, of roses and romance," he informed her, where people were "living chiefly on credit, and on the memory of some crushing defeats." He longed for the more civilized society of Newport.[1]

With Howe's brother, Samuel Ward, accompanying him, Wilde arrived at the resort at the height of the social season. The million-dollar "cottages" of the fabulously wealthy adorned the island, whose harbor was jammed with the sails and smokestacks of countless private yachts. The first families of New York were well represented: the Vanderbilts, the Astors, the Belmonts, the Havemeyers, the Van Rensselaers, and

the Bennetts all had summer residences there. Polo matches, both indoors and outdoors, competed with the newest sports craze, lawn tennis. Wilde, the Oxford Aesthete, was favorably reminded of his college
days. It was, he remarked to Charles Eliot Norton of Harvard, "not un-
pleasant to be in this little island where idleness ranks among the vir-
tues." His subsequent lecture at the Newport Casino on July 15 was a
seasonal highlight, attended by "the most fashionable audience that ever
gathered within the walls of the theater," according to the *New York
Sun*. Afterwards, Wilde was invited to dine with naval officers aboard
the gunboat USS *Minnesota*.[2]

Wilde spent a few days with Mrs. Howe and her twenty-seven-year-
old daughter, Maud, prompting rumors that he and Miss Howe were
engaged. Nothing could have been further from the truth, as her mother
hastened to make clear. "If ever there were two people in the world who
had no sympathy in common," she said, "they were the two." Nevertheless, Maud, who much later would share with her sister a Pulitzer Prize
for their joint biography of their mother, found the poet an entertaining
guest. "He talked amazingly well," she said. "In that company all that
was best in the man came to the surface." Some of the worst bubbled
up, as well, with Wilde ostentatiously stretching out his legs on the veranda one night and sighing, "Strange that a pair of silk stockings should
so upset a nation." It wasn't the stockings, said another guest. "It's the
calf that's in the stocking." Wilde was working on a new play, but he
wasn't working all that hard. He told his hosts that he had spent the better part of the morning going over the proofs of one of his poems, and
had taken out a comma. And in the afternoon? "Well, I put it back
again."[3]

Colonel Morse and D'Oyly Carte laid on additional lecture dates
for Wilde throughout the month of August, ranging from the Atlantic
coast to the Catskill Mountains. It was a wandering path, but geography was never Wilde's strong suit. As the *New Orleans Daily Picayune*
reported on July 25, "Mr. Oscar Wilde in the East, says he never could
study geography, the colors on the map were so discordant, and dis-

tressed him so much." In the meantime, he fulfilled an earlier commitment to visit Henry Ward Beecher at the preacher's summer home in
Peekskill, New York. Apparently, the spellbinding minister did not impress the neophyte stage performer during their weekend together.
Months later, at a dinner of the Royal Literary Fund in London, Wilde
was asked to comment on the difficulty of comparing the pulpit skills of
Beecher with those of his Brooklyn rival, Dr. Thomas DeWitt Talmadge. "Indeed, yes," said Wilde, "it would be like comparing the pantaloon with the clown."⁴

Despite a more leisurely travel schedule in keeping with the sleepy
late-summer season, Wilde continued to attract press attention. At Long
Branch, New Jersey, where President Garfield had died eleven months
earlier, Wilde was introduced by Ward to General Ulysses S. Grant, who
had a summer cottage on the shore. What the notoriously taciturn
American general may have discussed with the loquacious Irish poet was
not reported, although the *New York Tribune* advised readers that Wilde
was wearing "a light Scotch suit, carrying an umbrella under his arm
and had on a broad white straw hat and he came strolling through the
crowd with a look of childish pleasure." On Long Beach Island a few
days later, Wilde was sketched by an artist for *Frank Leslie's Magazine;*
the poet was wearing an *au courant* bathing suit and posing, hands on
hips, amid a crowd of beachside frolickers. He was touring the summer
hotels, said the *Tribune* dismissively, "in the wake of the professional
reader, the ventriloquist, the bird-charmer, the trained dogs, and the
tragedian who reads selections from *Othello, Macbeth* and *Lear,* all for a
slight consideration."⁵

During the first week of August, Wilde made appearances in Babylon, New York (on Long Island); Long Beach, New York; and Ballston
Spa, near Saratoga Springs. A highlight of his tour was a gala breakfast
on the east veranda of the Overlook Restaurant atop 900-foot Mount
McGregor, above Saratoga. Traveling by private railcar, Wilde was joined
by fifty other invited guests, including former secretary of state William
M. Evarts, District of Columbia Supreme Court justice Arthur MacAr-

thur (grandfather of World War II general Douglas MacArthur), W. J. Arkell, vice president of the Mount McGregor Railroad, various wives, young couples, and men-about-town. Eli Perkins (real name, Melville Landon), the locally celebrated wit who edited the *Daily Saratogian*, functioned as toastmaster for the event. Perkins had described Wilde in one of his earlier columns as "a new kind of half-breed, a kind of cross between Buffalo Bill and an utterly-utter school girl." The journalist was somewhat less acerbic at the breakfast, which featured a table-buckling menu of salmon and pickerel, beef tenderloin, spring chicken, Spanish omelets, French pancakes, Pommery *sec,* coffee, and cognac. Wilde, said Perkins, was a "lover of the beautiful. He loves America. He loves our eagle. He loves our double-eagles [$20 gold coins]. His name will go thundering down the ages—just about six months longer."[6]

Wilde, who could take kidding as well as he could dish it out, graciously thanked the crowd, all members of the ad hoc Order of the Lily, for "the lovely morning you have given me in this beautiful place. If there is anything more necessary than a good income, it is to have beautiful surroundings, and we have here today just the loveliest that could be: beautiful trees, beautiful landscapes, and above all, beautiful women." Wilde was proving again his contention that "the Englishman abroad is in the main a man of good manners and an agreeable companion." He was both.[7]

While Wilde concluded his late-summer swing, which Morse described—easy for him to say—as "two months of a pleasure trip, for it was really nothing more than a summer outing," the poet turned his attention to his languishing dramatic efforts. Forgetting his earlier-stated aversion to her Juliet, the playwright began wooing twenty-three-year-old California-born actress Mary Anderson to play the lead role of Bianca in his drama *The Duchess of Padua,* which he hoped to put on in partnership with American theatrical producer Steele Mackaye. The tall, slender Anderson, who currently was appearing in Richard Lalor Sheil's play *Evadne* in Boston, was the daughter of an Oxford-educated New Yorker named Charles Henry Anderson. The much-traveled Anderson *père* had moved to Kentucky, transferred his loyalties to the South, and died while serving in the Confederate Army at Mobile in 1863. His daughter's stepfather, Hamilton Griffin, also a Confederate veteran, had pushed Mary into a career on stage. With light-brown hair, hazel eyes, and a long nose, she looked rather like a less-pretty Lillie Langtry. Wilde met with the actress that September at her summer cottage in Long Branch, where he told her sweepingly: "I want you to rank with the great actresses of the earth, and having in you a faith which is as flawless as it is fervent, I doubt not for a moment that I can and will write for you a play which, created for you, and inspired by you, shall give you the glory of a Rachel, and may yield me the fame of a Hugo. I think I have so conceived it that we shall simultaneously become immortal in one night."[8]

Anderson, or at least her stepfather-manager, whom Wilde unfondly dubbed "the Griffin" and described as "a padded horror," had their doubts. They agreed to do the play and to pay Wilde $5,000 for it—$1,000 in advance and the rest when the play was rewritten to their specifications—but they wanted to wait a year before putting it on. Wilde conceded that "the bare, meager outline I have given you is but a faint shadow of what Bianca Duchess of Padua will be." Still, he complained to fellow writer Edgar Saltus, the offer as it stood was "mere starvation wages." And to Steele Mackaye, who was to produce and mount the play, Wilde admitted having difficulty finishing the work. "I cannot write while flying from one railway to another and from the cast-iron stove of one hotel to its twin horror in the next," he said. He eventually finished the play in Paris the next spring, but in the end Anderson declined to take it on, saying of the revised work, "Neither of us can afford failure now, and your Duchess in my hands would not succeed, as the part does not fit me." "This is very tedious," Wilde told a friend. The play, renamed *Guido Ferranti* after its male lead, made a long-deferred début in New York in 1891. It closed three weeks later.[9]

Wilde fulfilled the remaining dates of his tour in late September and early October, going down east to Cape May, Providence, and

Pawtucket, Rhode Island; North Attleboro, Massachusetts; and Bangor, Maine. At Bangor, on October 3, his visit was sponsored by the 271-member Bangor Art Association (116 men), who tastefully decorated the local opera house as a private parlor, augmented with works of art by the members. Wilde gamely pronounced their productions comparable "to that found in the best galleries of Europe." He delivered his usual lecture on decorative arts to a half-full auditorium, diverging from the script to denounce yet again "the present system of education whereby minds too young to grapple with the subjects in the right sense are burdened with long hours of study in the sciences and that calendar of infamy, European history, instead of receiving the practical instruction in ordinary things of today, in the use of their hands, which they ought." Leaving town, he told a reporter for the *Bangor Daily Commercial* that the stately elms along the river were the city's best ornaments and that "the American autumn has suffered at the hands of American artists abroad, who have libeled its gorgeous beauties with unfaithful brush and untruthful colors."[10]

Wilde concluded his eastern tour with a nine-day swing through New Brunswick, Nova Scotia, and Prince Edward Island, in the Canadian Maritimes. His first stop, Fredericton, was located on the Saint John River in New Brunswick. A haven for Tories fleeing the American Revolution, Fredericton was a center of art, government, and education. Twenty-five representatives of the latter, from the University of New Brunswick, interrupted Wilde's lecture at the City Hall, marching in procession, Indian file, down the center aisle with sunflowers in their buttonholes and bouquets of flowers in their hands. Like their predecessors at Harvard, Yale, and various U.S. colleges, the Fredericton students affected languid poses and erupted into loud, mocking applause at the slightest utterance from the speaker. The ringleader was equipped with a large umbrella that he periodically slammed onto the floor with a thump like that of a ten-pound cannon. A woman in the audience was so outraged by the undergraduates' antics that she later offered to sketch mug shots of the students for the police, but Wilde endured the kidding good-naturedly at the time. "They were highly intelligent looking boys, all of them," he said afterwards. "They had their fun and I did not mind them."[11]

The next night's appearance, in the port city of Saint John, went better for Wilde, although it began inauspiciously when the ferryman at the harbor insisted on charging him three cents extra for his bulging travel trunk, hatbox, dressing case, and portmanteau. It was, said Wilde, playing to the crowd at the dock, "a downright crime, a blue-moulded outrage, medieval manslaughter in the ninth degree." But he paid the surcharge, anyway. After checking into the Royal Hotel, he was taken on the obligatory tour of the city, which was still rebuilding from a disastrous fire five years earlier. One new home, a Queen Anne–style residence belonging to the curiously named Mrs. Zebedee Ring, was singled out by Wilde for particular praise. Another leading citizen, wealthy wine merchant Thomas Furlong, hosted a formal luncheon for Wilde at his home on Coburg Street. Furlong, a good Irish immigrant, had turned his mansion into a dormitory for the nuns at Saint Joseph's Hospital, who presumably attended the dinner along with Saint John's mayor, the American consul, and various judges, generals, and newspaper editors.[12]

Also in attendance, although Wilde may not have recognized him, was another Irish immigrant, Dr. Boyle Travers, a legacy of the poet's Dublin youth. Travers, in fact, was the brother of Mary Josephine Travers, a particularly troublesome mistress of Wilde's father. Eighteen years earlier, when Oscar was nine, Miss Travers had alleged publicly that Dr. Wilde had drugged and assaulted her while she was under his care. That was doubtful, given the doctor's proven record of success as a seducer, but Sir William was troubled enough by the accusations to offer to pay the young woman's passage to Australia. Instead, she published her allegations in the local newspapers, then sued Lady Wilde for libel after Oscar's mother accused her of making unfounded accusations. A Dublin court ruled in Miss Travers's favor, but awarded her only a symbolic farthing for her troubles.

Wilde lectured that evening to a full house at the Mechanics' Institute. Inspired perhaps by the large turnout, he spoke for seventy-five minutes—a fourth of an hour longer than usual—and leavened his wisdom with a generous dollop of humor. The sight of a hideous tablecloth, he said, was enough "to start a boy off on a career of crime." He repeated a comment from his Philadelphia lecture on the inadvisability of painted china. "I do not see the wisdom of decorating dinner plates with sunsets and soup plates with moonlight scenes," said Wilde. "We do not want a soup plate whose bottom seems to vanish in the distance. One feels neither safe nor comfortable under such conditions."[13]

His Saint John talk went over so well that he returned eight days later for a second appearance. Local boatmen on Grand Lake renamed one of their vessels the *Oscar Wilde* in his honor, and art-loving citizens made a spirited if ultimately unsuccessful effort to raise money for a combination library, museum, and art school decorated in the approved Aesthetic manner. Proof that Wilde was not universally admired in Saint John came in the form of a letter to the editor of the *Daily Sun,* which branded the distinguished visitor a "fraud, conceited coxcomb, and knight errant of taste." It was, thankfully for Wilde, a minority opinion.[14]

Wilde took the Intercolonial Railway north to Amherst, on the marshy Tantramar River at the far western tip of Nova Scotia. Along the way, he amused himself by leaping on and off station platforms, smoking large cigars, and riding up front in the engine car with the engineer. At Lamy's Hotel he granted an interview to a visiting reporter from the *Halifax Morning Herald.* After some unexceptionable compliments about the overall pleasantness of Canadians and the quality of the nation's timber, the talk turned to newspapers. In general, said Wilde, he considered American journals "in many respects better than the English. I think the American newspaper is the journal of the future. It is filled with news. The reader of the large New York papers knows everything that goes on in the world that is worth knowing, and much more." That said, he found the press coverage of his lectures "incredibly obtuse." Immediately contradicting himself, Wilde maintained that "I think nothing whatever about the criticisms now. It does not interest me as it did at first. I cannot bring myself to care what they say. I cannot possibly do it." He had come to North America, he continued, to talk seriously to people about art, but "they heard me and went away and talked about my necktie and the way I wore my hair. I could not understand how people could do such a thing. I thought it inexpressibly stupid."[15]

Wilde's lecture at the Amherst Academy of Music was well-attended, despite the fact that the town's population (4,500) was the smallest yet on his tour. Truro, his next stop, was even smaller, with only 3,500 residents. The *Truro Guardian* judged Wilde's lecture "a little namby-pamby at times" and suggested that he get a haircut. A fellow traveler at the hotel was surprised to see Wilde throwing back glasses of gin in the bar, assuming that "such a particularly nice young man should probably be in search of rain dropping from a rose leaf, the night dew from lilies and honeysuckles, or some heavenly distillation known only to the fanciful dreamers." Perhaps Wilde was fortifying himself for the complaining letter he would send to Colonel Morse about the local promoter, a Mr. Moore, who Wilde said had paid him only $250 a night, and "no expenses at all." Even worse, "He brought me to wretched villages of 10,000 people where of course they did not come. The business is bad."[16]

Halifax, the last stop on Wilde's Nova Scotia itinerary, was ten times larger and a good deal more welcoming, even though the port city was suffering from the effects of an economic downturn that began a decade earlier. Halifax was home to a large military garrison, serving as the headquarters of the commander of British forces in Canada and hosting the annual summer harboring of the North American Squadron. Wilde was picked up at the dock in a carriage sent by General Sir Patrick L. MacDougall, the current army commander, who was an enthusiastic amateur actor himself. The general hosted Wilde that evening at his Maplewood estate, and the visitor returned the compliment by praising the general for his men's smashing blue-and-red uniforms, which Wilde said stood out in marked contrast to the drab black suits worn by local civilians.

Wilde lectured the next night to a capacity audience of 1,500 at the Academy of Music. The stage props, donated by a local furniture company, included ebony-colored gold-trimmed cabinets, silk tapestries, and a complete tea set. Wilde commended the arrangers for providing him with the best setting this side of Wallack's Theatre in New York, although the effect was undercut somewhat by the life-size statue of a pug dog "gazing in silent astonishment on the beautiful room within." The *Halifax Presbyterian Witness* was underwhelmed—to say the least—by Wilde's performance, declaring him both a mountebank and a baboon and saying that he "ought to have been kicked out of civilized society the moment he published his poems." A local letter-writer signing himself "Aesthete-Hater," castigated Wilde as a false prophet and charlatan and described him as "a narrow-headed, spindle-shanked, shaky, ungraceful specimen of manhood." The citizen had stormed out of Wilde's lecture a mere ten minutes after it began, considering it "the dullest bosh, trash, commonplace talk and uninspired nonsense." Not to be outdone, the Dalhousie University *Gazette* offered readers a helpful recipe for becoming an Aesthete: "One dictionary of art terms, three oil paintings, and a job lot of old crockeryware. Mix—no brains are required."[17]

From Halifax, Wilde made an arduous 150-mile trip by train and steamer to Charlottetown, the capital of rural Prince Edward Island. Known variously as the Garden of the Gulf, the Garden of America, or, more prosaically, Spud Island, the land mass was home to the future best-selling author Lucy Maud Montgomery, of *Anne of Green Gables* fame. It is doubtful that Montgomery, who lived in even more isolated Cavendish and was only eight years old in 1882, attended Wilde's lecture on October 11. In any event, he arrived late to the Market Hall, which doubled as a produce mart and lecture hall. He apologized to the audience—a rarity for Wilde—for not being in proper evening attire and gamely launched into his lecture in a venue that smelled strongly of cabbage. At one point, an irate attendee cried out inexplicably, "Two thirds of the young men of Charlottetown are rogues!" Wilde, who had no frame of reference vis-à-vis the local youths, pretended not to hear the declaration. The columnist for the *Charlottetown Daily Examiner* expressed the wan hope that "those who heard the leader of England's aesthetic party will find consolation in the thought that they may be able to talk about it in their old age."[18]

The final stop on Wilde's nine-day tour of the Maritimes was Moncton, New Brunswick. Both town and visitor would have cause to regret it. Initially, Moncton was not on Wilde's schedule, but popular interest in his comings and goings prompted two boosters in the local Young Men's Christian Association, A. J. Williams and A. M. Hubly, to wire an offer to Wilde's agent, W. S. Husted. Confusion over the date of the appearance induced Husted to accept a different, more lucrative sponsorship offer from a Moncton drug manufacturer. Outraged over the change in plans, the YMCA officials hired a lawyer to serve Wilde with a breach-of-contract suit the moment he arrived in town.

Unaware of the rival claims on his time, Wilde blew off the lawyer, who then sent the local sheriff around to Wilde's hotel room with an arrest warrant. Fortunately, the sheriff declined to detain the distinguished guest, and Wilde spoke as planned at Ruddick's Hall on the night of October 12. A hearing was scheduled to take place in three weeks, and local supporters covered Wilde's $35 appearance bond. He was free to go. Angry and embarrassed by the misunderstanding, Wilde issued a statement to the *Moncton Daily Transcript* accusing the YMCA of "an ill-advised attempt at blackmail" and declaring that "the whole thing illustrated the illegality of most law and the immorality of most moral institutions." In the end, the YMCA dropped its suit and nothing more was said of the incident.[19]

On that less-than-collegial note, Wilde concluded his tour of the Maritimes and returned to New York City to rest and recuperate. To the surprise of his mother and his friends back in England, he did not immediately catch the next boat home. Instead, he flitted restlessly from hotel to hotel for the next ten weeks, staying in turn at the Fifth Avenue, the Brunswick, and the Windsor before taking a private room at 48 West 11th Street in Greenwich Village. "What a long time you are in New York," Lady Wilde wrote wonderingly. Actually, there was a good reason for her son's delay: he was waiting for Lillie Langtry to arrive for her own coast-to-coast tour of America. As Wilde told a reporter for the *Halifax Morning Herald* in Nova Scotia on October 9: "I would rather have discovered Mrs. Langtry than have discovered America. Her beauty is in outline perfectly modeled. She will be a beauty at eighty-five. Yes, it was for such a lady that Troy was destroyed, and well might it be destroyed for such a woman." Wars over women were infinitely preferable to wars over territory, said Wilde, joking that "when I was young I thought the wars of the roses were to decide whether a red or a white rose was the most beautiful. I learned afterwards that it was a vulgar dispute."[20]

In the predawn hours of October 23, one week after his twenty-eighth birthday, Wilde boarded the *Laura M. Starin,* a harbor boat, and steamed out towards the quarantine port off Staten Island. A *New York Times* reporter along for the ride described Wilde as being "dressed as probably no man in the world was ever dressed before. His hat was of brown cloth not less than six inches high; his coat was of black velvet; his overcoat was of green cloth, heavily trimmed with fur; his trousers matched his hair; his tie was gaudy and his shirtfront very open, displaying a large expanse of manly chest." He was also carrying a huge bouquet of lilies, which the reporter somehow neglected to mention. New York theatrical impresario Henry Abbey, who had brought Sarah Bernhardt to America two years earlier and earned a tidy $200,000 for his troubles, was now importing Lillie Langtry, engaging for her the very suite at the Albemarle Hotel that the Divine Sarah had previously occupied. Abbey had laid on a breakfast feast of oysters and champagne for the various reporters, scene makers and stage-door-johnnies on hand to greet Langtry, who was arriving on the S.S. *Arizona,* the same transatlantic ship that had brought Wilde to America ten months earlier. As Wilde restlessly scanned the railing of the large vessel looming on the horizon, the band behind him struck up "God Save the Queen" and "Rule Britannia" for the stage royalty about to descend through the Gotham mist like a modern-day Helen of Troy.[21]

Wilde and the rest of the arrival party climbed aboard and waited amidships for Langtry's appearance. Introduced by her traveling secretary and acting coach, Henrietta Hodson Labouchère, the Jersey Lily entertained questions from the press. What did she think of America? "When the fog lifts, perhaps I can tell you." What about the voyage over? Echoing Wilde, she said she had been a little disappointed in the ocean's performance. "I wanted to see the ocean run mountain high. It ran only hills high." She had taken the time to raise twenty pounds for the seamen's aid fund, she said, although she didn't care about money herself—"Oh, money's pleasant to have, but if you have a great deal, there's no time to spend it all." She was not over her well-known stage fright, she confessed, and could not predict how she would feel once she took the stage in New York. After the reporters left, Langtry renewed her acquaintance with the tall, smiling Irishman in the corner. Wilde handed her the lilies and they spoke briefly before she returned to her stateroom. The brass band back on the *Starin,* with no apparent sense of irony, broke into a spirited rendition of "The Girl I Left Behind Me."[22]

At the Albemarle, Langtry was deluged with flowers, autograph hunters, and would-be suitors, including a ubiquitous Wilde. "Ever since Mrs. Langtry arrived, Wilde has clung to her skirts," reported the Broadway correspondent for the *Chicago Daily News.* Another writer in the same newspaper noted: "As for the love-smitten Oscar Wilde, he is head over heels in love with the much-discussed grass widow, Mrs. Langtry." Whether or not he was actually in love with the actress, Wilde took it upon himself to introduce her into New York society. The day after her arrival, he dashed off a note to Samuel Ward. "My dear Uncle Sam," he wrote. "The Lily is very anxious to see you: suppose that we have *a lunch* on Sunday—*not a dinner*—for her. But of course she will be here five weeks. There is lots of time." A few days later he wrote to Mrs. John Bigelow, his erstwhile hostess at 21 Gramercy Park: "Dear Mrs. Bigelow, Mrs. Langtry is hard at work at rehearsals all day long, will be home at five o'clock, I think, and will be charmed I feel sure to have the pleasure of receiving a visit from you. I hope you will do her the honour of calling—with the accompanying note from me."[23]

Wilde took Langtry downtown to be photographed by Napoleon Sarony, who reportedly paid her $5,000 for the privilege. He shot the actress in dozens of poses, including a number of studies of her as Rosalind in Shakespeare's *As You Like It.* At Wilde's recommendation, she forswore the familiar knee-length boots worn by other actresses in the role, opting instead for jeweled slippers on her less-than-dainty feet. Accustomed to being worshiped, Langtry did not much care for Sarony's abrupt manner or end results. "You have made me pretty," she complained. "I am beautiful." Later, the photographer offered his considered professional opinion of the Jersey Lily. "She has a fine figure, good height, head well balanced, good features and a good expression—when she pleases," said Sarony. A local fashion writer covering a reception the day before her New York début took a more exalted view of Langtry. She was, said the writer, "a symphony, a nocturne, a discourse on earth, space, tuneful birds, rustling streams, the stars." It all sounded very much like something Wilde might have said himself—and perhaps had.[24]

Wilde performed his own act of obeisance to Langtry the next night, when he doubled as guest drama critic for the *New York World.* Dashing from Wallack's Theatre, Wilde commandeered a desk in the newspaper office to review the actress's début as Hester Grazebrook in Tom Taylor's unexceptional old play *An Unequal Match.* (Taylor, who had died two years earlier, was much more renowned, at least in the United States, for writing *Our American Cousin,* the play Abraham Lincoln was attending on the night he was assassinated.) Sporting a new red suit that made him look like "a red squash," in the jaundiced opinion of another theatergoer, Wilde produced a fulsome review that was remarkable for both what it said and what it left unsaid. Langtry, he wrote, was "the ideal representation of marvelous beauty." Hers was a beauty "based on absolute mathematical laws"—he neglected to furnish the formula—a "mingling of classic grace with absolute reality." Her costumes had been "a symphony in silver-gray and pink, a pure melody of color" that triumphed over the "painful" scenery. "That it is a beauty that will be appreciated to the full in America I do not doubt for a moment," wrote Wilde. He pointedly said nothing about her acting ability, perhaps adhering to the adage that the less said the better.[25]

Other critics were not so merciful. The *New York Dramatic Mirror* found Langtry weak-voiced and stiff-limbed, and predicted that "she is not and perhaps never will be an actress of genuine worth." The *New York Times* reviewer judged her performance "weak, vague, and unsatisfactory," as well as "cold, hard, and dull." The same could have been said about Langtry's personality, which would not wear nearly as well on the American public as Wilde's. Her subsequent much-publicized dalliance with twenty-three-year-old New York socialite Freddie Gebhard raised eyebrows from coast to coast, culminating in a blast from the fearsome San Francisco journalist Ambrose Bierce, who dismissed Langtry's acting ability as "the posings of a prostitute recommended by a prince" and described her brutally as having "a brow still reeking of a drunken lecher's royal kisses and the later salutes of a dirty little gambler." As if to prove the adage about life imitating art, Langtry followed her performance in *An Unequal Match* with touring roles in *As You Like It* and *The Honeymoon*. Meanwhile, her husband, Edward Langtry, resolutely undivorced, remained home in England, performing the role of public cuckold.[26]

Back in New York, Wilde was having his own problems. He created a stir at the Park Theater—many thought intentionally—by walking in after the curtain had risen for Act One of a performance of *Othello* by the great Italian actor Tommaso Salvini. In case anyone missed it, he repeated the gesture after each succeeding act. If Wilde was unmoved by Salvini's performance, other notable viewers during his world tour were not. Henry James, catching Salvini's Othello in Boston, wrote the equivalent of a mash note to the actor. In his subsequent review in the *Atlantic Monthly*, James gushed that Salvini had a "powerful, active, manly frame, noble, serious, vividly expressive face, splendid smile, Italian eye. All this descends upon the spectator's mind with a richness which immediately converts attention into faith, and expectation into sympathy. He is a magnificent creature, and you are already on his side." Russian acting coach Constantin Stanislavski, seeing Salvini perform the role of King Lear in Moscow, modeled his entire groundbreaking approach to drama on the Italian's naturalistic style. Salvini himself was not notably modest about his gifts. "I can make an audience weep by reading them a menu," he boasted.[27]

Wilde also ruffled feathers, particularly those of *New York Tribune* editor Whitelaw Reid, by using the bully pulpit of the exclusive Lotos Club on Fifth Avenue to denounce the press's treatment of his just-concluded tour. For once, Wilde was not the guest of honor at the banquet; English actor Charles Wyndham and playwright Bronson Howard shared the laurels. Reid, as club president, doubled as master of ceremonies. He innocently called on Wilde to say a few words, and Wilde "let fall upon his critics most cunningly a finely sifted snow of satire." Among other things, Wilde professed that he was "gratified to have provided a permanent employment to many an ink-stained life." Reid did not appreciate the remarks—the Lotos Club had been founded by a group of newspapermen a dozen years earlier—but club member John Paul urged him to let it go. "Mr. Wilde is but a boy at best," he wrote in a letter to the editor of the *Tribune*, "and not a bad one either, if I guess rightly, though he labors hard in his verse to make one believe to the contrary."[28]

Through no fault of his own, Wilde's visit to the New York Stock Exchange in late September quickly degenerated into a near-riot, with the poet being pursued onto the trading floor by hundreds of NYSE messenger boys. The messengers were part of the substrata of wild boys who patrolled the city's downtown streets twenty-four hours a day, selling newspapers, shining shoes, hawking produce, delivering packages, and doing all sorts of odd jobs to keep themselves alive. Caught up in a state of frenzied excitement, the messengers thronged inside for a glimpse of the distinguished visitor. "The jostling [was] severe," reported *Harper's New Monthly Magazine.* "The sunflower knight [found] it difficult to keep his aesthetic legs." A reporter for the *Washington Post* noted that after Wilde entered the building, "The hoodlums followed. The very bad little boys made the hallways and galleries of the Exchange ring with their enthusiasm. The crowds grew bigger and the cries grew louder. A hundred brokers stood at the floor of the main stairway ready for a concerted rush whereby to get Oscar upon the floor." With some difficulty, Wilde charged down the back stairs and made his escape. An illustration in the *National Police Gazette* depicted a more unruffled Wilde, sunflower in hand, leading a procession of distinctly unsavory urchins past a pair of quaking women.[29]

Wilde got into more trouble one morning in mid-December when he was approached on Fifth Avenue by a thin-faced young man who claimed to be the son of Wall Street banker Anthony J. Drexel and said he had met Wilde in his father's office. Wilde remembered neither the banker nor the son, but he bought the stranger lunch, anyway, then accompanied him to a house on either 15th or 17th Street, between Second and Third avenues, where Drexel wanted to redeem, he said, a winning lottery ticket. (One recent Wilde biographer has suggested that the incident may have been a homosexual tryst—Fifth Avenue being a favorite area at the time for male prostitutes. If so, it was several years before Wilde's first generally acknowledged same-sex encounter, with his friend Robbie Ross, in 1886.) Inside the gaming house, well-dressed gentlemen were throwing dice, and Drexel loaned Wilde his lucky ticket to have a go. In short order, Wilde lost $1,160, for which he wrote three personal checks on his account at Madison Square Bank. He left with Drexel, who complained bitterly that Wilde was "being badly treated" and "I'm going to see about it." After Drexel went back inside the house, Wilde never saw him again, but he had the presence of mind to catch a cab and rush to the bank to stop payment of the checks. Then he went to the 29th Precinct police station on West 30th Street, where he reported the incident to the captain on duty, Alexander S. Williams, admitting ruefully, "I've just made a damned fool of myself."[30]

Williams, nicknamed "Clubber" by his underworld adversaries for his avid and skillful use of the nightstick, showed Wilde some mug shots, and the poet immediately picked out Drexel's face. It was "Hungry Joe" Lewis, said Williams, one of the city's cleverest bunco-steerers, whose scam it was to lure unwary victims to gambling houses where, like Wilde, they would quickly lose their purses, if not their shirts. No arrests were made, but four days later Williams returned Wilde's uncashed checks. It did not seem to strike anyone as suspicious that the policeman had managed so quickly to recover the checks. "I have fallen into a den of thieves," Wilde wrote to John Boyle O'Reilly in Boston. He may have been more perceptive than he realized. Williams, known as "the Czar of the Tenderloin," the notorious crime-ridden section of lower Manhattan whose nickname he had personally bestowed upon it, was later investigated by the Lexow Committee looking into police corruption. Said to be on the payroll of various gambling houses and brothels in his precinct, Williams developed convenient amnesia about the location of any "disorderly houses" and maintained that he had paid for his own vacation home, yacht, and beachfront property in exclusive Cos Cob, Connecticut, by investing wisely in Japanese real estate. At the personal intercession of the current police commissioner, Theodore Roosevelt, who did not want a burgeoning scandal on his watch, Williams was allowed to retire quietly on a pension of $1,750 a year—which no doubt marked a distinct drop in the Clubber's annual earnings.[31]

In the meantime, Wilde went back to his writing pursuits. Having completed his arrangements with Mary Anderson concerning *The Duchess of Padua,* he entered into negotiations with another American actress, Marie Prescott, to star in his other languishing drama, *Vera; or, The Nihilists.* He dined with the twenty-nine-year-old actress and her husband, William Perzel, and discussed certain revisions that Prescott wanted Wilde to make in her part. "Who am I to tamper with a master-piece?" Wilde sighed, but eventually came to terms with the pair, who agreed to pay the playwright $1,000 down and $50 for each performance of the play. They tentatively planned to open *Vera* in the autumn of 1883. A *New York Tribune* reporter, getting wind of the arrangements at the Manhattan Cub, where Wilde had a guest membership through Samuel Ward, went to see the author at his Greenwich Village apartment. "Have you made any arrangements to produce your play?" he inquired. "Why do you ask?" Wilde said. "The public might like to know," said the reporter. "Oh," said Wilde, closing his eyes in thought. "To persons of no reputation, small paragraphs are doubtless an advantage," he said. "But, really, I do not care for them." "But the production of your play might be a matter of a big paragraph," the reporter persisted. "Oh," said Wilde. "Well, I have made no arrangements as yet." Wilde begged off answering any more questions, saying that he was "thoroughly exhausted, you know, and—ah—suffering from severe nervous prostration." He claimed to have no fewer than four physicians on retainer at the moment.[32]

In any event, the doctors would not have Wilde as a patient for much longer. After almost exactly a year in North America, he was putting down his sunflower and going home. Wilde booked passage to London on the Cunard liner *Bothnia,* leaving from New York Harbor on December 27. He climbed the gangplank on his final morning in America "with the languid grace of a Bunthorne," reported the *Tribune,* and was seen off by a skeleton party of two: Polish actress Helen Modjeska and Wilde's old friend Norman Forbes-Robertson. It was a far cry from his much-heralded arrival almost exactly one year earlier. "Oscar Wilde has abandoned us without a line of farewell," the *Tribune* reported with mock regret, "slipped away without giving us a last goodly glance, left without a wave of his chiseled hand or a friendly nod of his classic head. This is the end of the aesthetic movement."[33]

The *Tribune,* in true journalistic fashion, was both right and wrong in its sweeping conclusions. It was right in the sense that the self-conscious posing and questing after Beauty with a capital *B* had ended, at least insofar as Wilde was concerned. As soon as he arrived back in London, Wilde packed away his stage costume of knee breeches, black silk stockings, satin smoking jacket, and Byronic peasant shirt. It was not only passé; it was unnecessary. The pastel moment of Jellaby Postlethwaite and Reginald Bunthorne was over. "All that belonged to the Oscar of the first period," Wilde told his new friend Robert Sherard, the great-grandson of William Wordsworth. "The Oscar of the first period is dead. We are now concerned with the Oscar Wilde of the second period, who has nothing in common with the gentleman who wore long hair and carried a sunflower down Piccadilly." To symbolize his change, Wilde had his famous long hair cut into a severe Romanesque bob. The humor magazine *Punch,* taking note of the dramatic makeover, mockingly advertised for sale "the whole of the Stock-in-Trade, Appliances, and Inventions of a Successful Aesthete, who is retiring from business. This will include a large stock of faded Lilies, dilapidated Sunflowers, and shabby Peacocks' Feathers. No reasonable offer refused."[34]

But the *Tribune* was wrong if it thought that Wilde had abandoned his commitment to art or his devotion to beauty, or that he had forgotten about his host country so quickly. His time in America had taught him—to whatever degree he needed teaching—that he was, in himself, an ongoing work of art. His trademark green overcoat, which he steadfastly kept wearing on the civilized streets of London, reminded him of the great rugged land he had recently crossed, in the same way that his long hair and flamboyant stage presence had reminded American audiences of another hugely successful entertainer, Buffalo Bill Cody, who had also reinvented himself in the popular image. Each was a walking, talking billboard for himself.

Despite reports that he considered his tour a failure, Wilde in truth was proud of his accomplishments in North America—as he deserved to be. The tour had been a remarkable feat of physical and emotional endurance. In all, he had traveled some 15,000 miles, had appeared in

140 cities and towns from Maine to California, from Canada to Texas, and had personally earned, after expenses, at least $5,600—in modern terms, nearly $124,000. If local art schools, crafts centers, and sculpting studios did not spring up everywhere in his wake, as he boasted during his trip, many did indeed spring up, and untold artists, male and female, took personal inspiration from Wilde's message and example. As both a lecturer and a celebrity, he had made an indelible impression wherever he went, alternately shocking, amusing, entertaining, and enlightening thousands of post–Civil-War-era Americans at a time when they were sorely in need of each. It had been a brave, even gallant, endeavor.

As Wilde biographer Richard Ellmann has noted, Wilde's tour constituted "the most sustained attack upon materialistic vulgarity that America had seen." Although readily admitting that he was not a born performer, Wilde had persisted in delivering his message—advocating self-sufficient handicraft and the never-ending quest to create, or at least to enjoy, the beautiful things in life—to audiences varying in size from a handful of people to several hundred. He had endured—and often joined in—the generally good-natured kidding he received from Americans of all ages and walks of life. Along the way, he had virtually invented the now-commonplace practice of celebrity-based self-promotion and the care and feeding of the local press. He might on occasion have complained about the coverage he received, comparing the "yellow press" to yellow fever, but in general he seems to have embraced the notion that bad publicity was better than no publicity. The initial impetus for his visit, to promote the American production of Gilbert and Sullivan's *Patience,* had almost immediately been forgotten. From start to finish, Oscar Wilde had promoted himself.[35]

His American booking agent, W. F. Morse, gave a self-interested but essentially accurate assessment of Wilde's tour. "The effect of this year of hard work upon Mr. Wilde was distinctly and strongly for his good," wrote Morse. "He had, at the end, broadened and deepened, grown stronger, more self-reliant, had seen the unwisdom of the shallow affectations that at first controlled his actions, and come at the last to realize there was something in life better worthwhile than to wear the mask of the poseur and masquerader." True, perhaps, but Wilde would later famously observe: "Man is least himself when he talks in his own person. Give him a mask, and he will tell you the truth." Wilde, in his time, would wear many masks.[36]

After several weeks in Paris recovering from his labors and sampling the joys of the absinthe-flavored "Green Hour" on the Left Bank, Wilde returned to England in the summer of 1883 to give a series of lectures on his American tour. Arranged by Morse, who was opportunely in England for the summer, the series kicked off at Prince's Hall in London on July 11. The lecture was modestly titled "Personal Impressions of America," and Wilde, sporting a heavy watch chain and a large diamond on his shirtfront, gave a briskly paced, mostly affectionate survey of his recent adventures in the New World. He repeated many of his familiar lines about the brides at Niagara Falls, the Mormons in Salt Lake City, the miners in Colorado, the water tower in Chicago, and the Chinese in San Francisco. He evoked the size, the noise, and the speed of America, the national love of gadgets and inventions, the informality of the men, and the beauty of the women. He took pains to debunk the "popular superstition that in America a visitor is invariably addressed as 'Stranger.' I was never once addressed as 'Stranger.' When I went to Texas, I was called 'Captain'; when I got to the center of the country, I was addressed as 'Colonel'; and on arriving at the border of Mexico, as 'General.'" Americans had not treated him as a stranger, and he had not felt like one. His conclusion was both gracious and grateful: "It is well worth one's while to go to a country which can teach us the beauty of the word *freedom* and the value of the thing *liberty*."[37]

Inevitably, Wilde's moment as a national phenomenon in America passed, once he had departed its shores. No visiting celebrity, not even one as memorable as Oscar Wilde, could single-handedly effect lasting change in a country as vast and complex as the United States. In the end, America changed Wilde more than Wilde changed America. A man who could face down both the undergraduates at Harvard and the gold miners in Colorado could certainly meet the challenges of a Belgravia dinner party or a gallery opening in Chelsea. Fortified by renewed self-confidence and toughened, both physically and mentally, by his months in North America, Wilde henceforth would look inward rather than outward for his sense of achievement. It was just as well. The Aesthetic Movement gradually waned, in both England and North America, as the nineteenth century entered its last decade and as dirty little wars in South Africa, Cuba, and the Philippines co-opted the front pages of the newspapers. People caught up in the adventure of empire building no longer had time for lilies and sunflowers.

Wilde returned to America only once: in the late summer of 1883, he came to New York to oversee the début of his play *Vera,* with Marie Prescott in the title role. It was a far briefer and more unsatisfactory visit than his earlier trip. The play closed after only seven performances and a number of bad reviews. "It comes as near failure as an ingenious and able writer can bring it," the *New York Times* judged coolly. Even Wilde was said to dislike it. After a few weeks' respite in Newport and Saratoga, he returned to England, a sadder and perhaps wiser man. His friend and fellow playwright Dion Boucicault gave him a piece of advice that Wilde would follow profitably in the decade to come: he should write plays that depended less on the skill of the actors than on the beauty of their lines. "When I write a play," Boucicault told Wilde, "if the leading man gets sick . . . I call up one of the ushers—and if he repeats my lines, the play will be a success." By the time he came to write the glittering series of drawing-room comedies that culminated in *The Importance of Being Earnest* in 1895, Wilde probably could have summoned the girls from the ticket window onto the stage and still have found a Lady Bracknell or two among them.[38]

The disappointing fate of *Vera* notwithstanding, Wilde thought of America frequently, and usually fondly, in the years to come. He continued to lecture for several years throughout Great Britain on his personal impressions of the younger country, and he wrote three amusing—and amused—essays on American men, American women, and American schoolchildren. A major character in his play *A Woman of No Importance* is the American heiress Hester Worsley, an open-hearted if somewhat puritanical young woman who proves very important, indeed, to the play's hero, Gerald Arbuthnot, who plans to marry her and live happily ever after in America. And while he has the cynical and urbane Lord Wotton remark slightingly in *The Picture of Dorian Gray* that when bad Americans die, "They go to America," Wilde neatly reverses the equation in his rollicking short story "The Canterville Ghost." The Americans in the story, the Otis family of California, are imbued with an unflappable commonsense approach to Old World problems—even those of a centuries-old revenant on their newly purchased English estate. Mysterious bloodstains, phantom footsteps, and rattling chains cannot withstand a good dose of Pinkerton's Champion Stain Remover and Paragon Detergent or Rising Sun Lubricator, and even the shadowy Garden of Death proves no match in the end for the love and sympathy of a sunny-natured American girl.[39]

Youthful, vigorous, and forward-looking himself, Oscar Wilde found similar qualities in Americans. In turn, many Americans, to their credit, saw beyond the superficial image that Wilde presented on stage to hear and heed the essential good sense of his words. It was a mutually enriching experience. "America," he had said during his tour, "is not a country; it is a world." Coming from Wilde, who was himself considerably larger than life, this was perhaps the ultimate compliment.[40]

Notes

Acknowledgments

Index

Notes

Introduction

1. Arthur Ransome, *Oscar Wilde: A Critical Study* (New York: Mitchell Kennerley, 1912), 64.

2. Oscar Wilde, "Phrases and Philosophies for the Use of the Young," in *The Complete Works of Oscar Wilde* (London: HarperCollins, 2003), 1245. Hereafter cited as *Works*.

3. "Oscar Wilde's Arrival," *New York World,* January 3, 1882, 1.

4. James C. Simmons, *Star-Spangled Eden: 19th Century America Through the Eyes of Dickens, Wilde, Frances Trollope, Frank Harris, and Other British Travelers* (New York: Carroll and Graf, 2000), 290. "A Talk with Wilde," *Philadelphia Press,* January 17, 1882, 2. Oscar Wilde, "The American Man," in *The Artist as Critic: Critical Writings of Oscar Wilde,* ed. Richard Ellmann (New York: Random House, 1968), 64. Oscar Wilde, "The Canterville Ghost," *Works,* 185.

5. Oscar Wilde, "The Truth of Masks," *Works,* 1166.

6. Robert Harborough Sherard, *The Real Oscar Wilde* (London: T. Werner Laurie, 1916), 200.

1. Too Too Utterly Utter

1. Richard Ellmann, *Oscar Wilde* (New York: Alfred A. Knopf, 1988), 14.

2. Ibid., 8–9. Louis Kronenberger, *Oscar Wilde* (Boston: Little, Brown, 1976), 7. Oscar Wilde, *The Importance of Being Earnest*, in *The Complete Works of Oscar Wilde* (London: HarperCollins, 2003), 371. Hereafter cited as *Works*.

3. Kronenberger, *Oscar Wilde*, 11–12, 19–20. Ellmann, *Oscar Wilde*, 44–46.

4. Merlin Holland, *The Wilde Album* (New York: Henry Holt, 1997), 50. Ellmann, *Oscar Wilde*, 39. Kronenberger, *Oscar Wilde*, 11.

5. David Hunter Blair, *In Victorian Days and Other Papers* (New York: Books for Libraries Press, 1969), 122. Sir Frank Benson, *My Memoirs* (London: E. Benn, 1930), 139.

6. Oscar Wilde, "The English Renaissance," in *Essays and Lectures by Oscar Wilde* (London: Methuen, 1913), 120.

7. Carolyn McDowell, "Arts & Crafts Movement: William Morris the Art that Is Life," *The Culture Concept Circle,* November 1, 2011. Available at www.thecultureconcept.com/circle/arts-crafts-movement-william-morris-the-art-that-is-life.

8. Oscar Wilde, "The Soul of Man under Socialism," in *Works,* 1192. Vincent O'Sullivan, *Aspects of Wilde* (London: Constable, 1936), 171.

9. Walter Pater, *The Renaissance: Studies in Art and Poetry* (Los Angeles: University of California Press, 1980), 188. Oscar Wilde, *The Complete Letters of Oscar Wilde,* ed. Merlin Holland and Rupert Hart-Davis (New York: Henry Holt, 2000), 349. Hereafter cited as *Letters.* W. B. Yeats, *Autobiographies* (London: Macmillan, 1955), 130.

10. Kronenberger, *Oscar Wilde,* 28. Wilde, "The Soul of Man under Socialism," *Works,* 1186. Quoted in Lionel Lambourne, *The Aesthetic Movement* (Oxford: Phaidon, 1996), 119.

11. *Punch,* July 17, December 25, 1880, January 15, 1881. Ellmann, *Oscar Wilde,* 136.

12. *Punch,* November 12, 1881.

13. Ellmann, *Oscar Wilde,* 111. Lillie Langtry, *The Days I Knew* (London: George H. Doran, 1925), 86–87.

14. *Punch,* July 23, 1881. Oscar Wilde, *A Woman of No Importance,* in *Works,*

493. Josephine M. Guy and Ian Small, *Oscar Wilde's Profession: Writing and the Culture Industry in the Late Nineteenth Century* (New York: Oxford University Press, 2001), 37.

15. Oscar Wilde, "The Grosvenor Gallery," *Dublin University Magazine,* July 1873.

16. John Ruskin, *Fors Clavigera,* July 2, 1877. Ellmann, *Oscar Wilde,* 133. *Letters,* 220, 220n; Kronenberger, *Oscar Wilde,* 37.

17. Ellmann, *Oscar Wilde,* 128.

18. W. S. Gilbert and Arthur Sullivan, *Patience; or, Bunthorne's Bride!* (London: Chappell, 1911), 13. *New York World,* January 8, 1882.

19. W. F. Morse, "American Lectures," in *The Works of Oscar Wilde,* vol. 15 (New York: Brainard, 1909), 73–75.

20. Robert Harborough Sherard, *The Real Oscar Wilde* (London: T. Werner Laurie, 1916), 288. *The World,* November 30, 1881.

21. Lloyd Lewis and Henry Justin Smith, *Oscar Wilde Discovers America* (New York: Harcourt, Brace, 1936), 28. Ellmann, *Oscar Wilde,* 156. James Russell Lowell, *New Letters of James Russell Lowell,* ed. M. de Wolfe Howe (London: Harper Bros., 1932), 262. *Letters,* 132n.

22. Ellmann, *Oscar Wilde,* 158. Lewis and Smith, *Oscar Wilde,* 32–33.

23. Lewis and Smith, *Oscar Wilde,* 32.

24. "Oscar Wilde's Arrival," *New York World,* January 3, 1882, 1.

25. Ellmann, *Oscar Wilde,* 157. *New York World,* January 3, 1882.

26. "Oscar Wilde," *New York Evening Post,* January 4, 1882, 4.

27. Arthur Ransome, *Oscar Wilde: A Critical Study* (New York: Mitchell Kennerley, 1912), 64.

2. More Wonderful Than Dickens

1. On the Grants' English visit, see William S. McFeely, *Grant: A Biography* (New York: W. W. Norton, 1981), 454–459.

2. William Dean Howells, "A Sennight of the Centennial," *Atlantic Monthly* 38 (July 1876), 93. Oscar Wilde, "Literary and Other Notes—III," reprinted in *Reviews* (Hazleton: Pennsylvania State University Press, 2006), 222.

3. *Hampshire Review,* August 19, 1886, September 11, 1890.

4. Oscar Wilde, "The House Beautiful," in *The Complete Works of Oscar Wilde* (London: HarperCollins, 2003), 913; hereafter cited as *Works.* Oscar Wilde, "The American Invasion," in *Works,* 964–966.

5. Mary Warner Blanchard, *Oscar Wilde's America: Counterculture in the Gilded Age* (New Haven: Yale University Press, 1997), 4.

6. Lloyd Lewis and Henry Justin Smith, *Oscar Wilde Discovers America* (New York: Harcourt, Brace, 1936), 57. *Brooklyn Daily Eagle,* January 3, 1882. *Washington Post,* January 22, 1882.

7. On Jumbo, see Susan Wilson, "An Elephant's Tale," *Tufts Online Magazine,* Spring 2002, 1–11. Lewis and Smith, *Oscar Wilde,* 187. *Daily Saratogian,* August 5, 1882.

8. Candice Millard, *Destiny of the Republic: A Tale of Madness, Medicine, and the Murder of a President* (New York: Doubleday, 2011), 186, 235, 239. Kenneth D. Ackerman, *Dark Horse: The Surprise Election and Political Murder of President James A. Garfield* (New York: Carroll and Graf, 2003), 442.

9. Richard Grant White, "A Morning at Sarony's," *Galaxy,* March 1870, 409.

10. Ibid., 410–411.

11. Lewis and Smith, *Oscar Wilde,* 39. Barbara Belford, *Oscar Wilde: A Certain Genius* (New York: Random House, 2000), 95–96.

12. Merlin Holland, *The Wilde Album* (New York: Henry Holt, 1997), 92. Oscar Wilde, *The Woman's World* (London: Cassell, 1888), 40.

13. Oscar Wilde, *The Complete Letters of Oscar Wilde,* ed. Merlin Holland and Rupert Hart-Davis (New York: Henry Holt, 2000), 127. Hereafter cited as *Letters.*

14. Oscar Wilde, "Personal Impressions of America," in *Works,* 938, 941.

15. Lewis and Smith, *Oscar Wilde,* 47.

16. Richard Ellmann, *Oscar Wilde* (New York: Alfred A. Knopf, 1988), 160–161.

17. *Demorest's,* June 15, 1877.

18. For Clara Morris, see Barbara Wallace Grossman, *A Spectacle of Suffering: Clara Morris on the American Stage* (Carbondale: Southern Illinois University Press, 2009). Ellmann, *Oscar Wilde,* 163. "Oscar Wilde," *Chicago Tribune,* March 1, 1882, 7.

19. Wayne S. Turney, "Clara Morris," n.d.; available at www.wayneturney.20m.com/claramorris.htm. *Letters,* 150.

20. On Samuel Ward, see Kathryn Allamong Jacob, *King of the Lobby: The Life and Times of Sam Ward* (Baltimore: Johns Hopkins University Press, 2009). Lewis and Smith, *Oscar Wilde,* 49, 85.

21. Ellmann, *Oscar Wilde,* 161–162.

22. Mrs. Thomas Bailey Aldrich, *Crowding Memories* (Boston: Houghton Mifflin, 1921), 246. Jerome Loving, *Walt Whitman: The Song of Himself* (Berkeley: University of California Press, 1999), 407.

23. *Letters,* 124. "The Science of the Beautiful," *New York World,* January 8, 1882, 2. "The Theories of a Poet," *New York Tribune,* January 8, 1882, 7.

24. *New York Times,* January 10, 1882. Lewis and Smith, *Oscar Wilde,* 57.

25. *New York Times,* January 10, 1882.

26. Helen Potter, *Impersonations* (New York: Edgar S. Werner, 1891), 195–197. *New York Times,* January 10, 1882.

27. *New York Times,* January 10, 1882.

28. Ibid.

29. Ibid. Ellmann, *Oscar Wilde,* 166. Lewis and Smith, *Oscar Wilde,* 60–61.

30. *Letters,* 126.

3. Those Who Dawnce Don't Dine

1. "A Talk with Wilde," *Philadelphia Press,* January 17, 1882, 2.

2. Ibid. Oscar Wilde, *The Complete Letters of Oscar Wilde,* ed. Merlin Holland and Rupert Hart-Davis (New York: Henry Holt, 2000), 127. Richard Ellmann, *Oscar Wilde* (New York: Alfred A. Knopf, 1988), 185. Lloyd Lewis and Henry Justin Smith, *Oscar Wilde Discovers America* (New York: Harcourt, Brace, 1936), 204.

3. *Philadelphia Press,* January 17, 1882.

4. Ibid.

5. Ibid.

6. Ibid.

7. Ibid.

8. Ibid.

9. Lillie Langtry, *The Days I Knew* (London: George H. Doran, 1925), 86. "The Aesthetic Bard," *Philadelphia Inquirer,* January 17, 1882, 2.

10. "The Aesthetic Bard," 2.

11. Ibid.

12. Ibid.

13. Ellmann, *Oscar Wilde,* 199. *Letters,* 205.

14. Ellmann, *Oscar Wilde,* 167.

15. For Whitman's Civil War career, see Roy Morris, Jr., *The Better Angel: Walt Whitman in the Civil War* (New York: Oxford University Press, 2000).

16. Walt Whitman, *Memoranda During the War* (Old Saybrook, CT: Globe Pequot Press, reprinted 1993), 4. Floyd Stovall, ed., *Walt Whitman: Prose Works 1892*, 2 vols. (New York: New York University Press, 1963–1964), 2:384–385, 369–370. Walt Whitman, *Leaves of Grass* (New York: W. W. Norton, 1973), 591–592.

17. Ellmann, *Oscar Wilde*, 167–168. *Philadelphia Press*, January 19, 1882.

18. *Philadelphia Press*, January 19, 1882.

19. Ibid. *Letters*, 145n.

20. Ellmann, *Oscar Wilde*, 169.

21. Ibid., 170.

22. Ibid. Horace Traubel, *With Walt Whitman in Camden* (New York: D. Appleton, 1908), 11.

23. *Philadelphia Press*, January 18, 1882. *Philadelphia Record*, January 18, 1882. Lewis and Smith, *Oscar Wilde*, 73. Oscar Wilde, "Aristotle at Afternoon Tea," *Pall Mall Gazette*, February 28, 1885.

24. Ellmann, *Oscar Wilde*, 174. *New York Tribune*, January 19, 1882. *Letters*, 130.

25. *Letters*, 129n.

26. *Washington Post*, January 21, 1882. *Letters*, 129.

27. Ellmann, *Oscar Wilde*, 175. *Letters*, 134–135.

28. *Baltimore American*, January 22, 1882. *Letters*, 130.

29. *Letters*, 131. *Washington Post*, January 22, 1882.

30. *Washington Post*, January 24, 1882. *Washington Star*, January 24, 1882. *Harper's Weekly*, January 28, 1882.

31. *Letters*, 131.

32. "Wilde and Forbes," *New York Herald*, January 21, 1882, 3. *St. Louis Globe-Democrat*, February 26, 1882.

33. *Washington Post*, January 21, 1882. Quoted in Louis Kronenberger, *Oscar Wilde* (Boston: Little, Brown, 1976), 43.

34. Lewis and Smith, *Oscar Wilde*, 89.

35. Leon Edel, *Henry James: A Life* (New York: Harper and Row, 1985), 273. Ward Thoron, ed., *The Letters of Mrs. Henry Adams, 1865–1883* (Boston: Little, Brown, 1936), 338, 342.

36. Ellmann, *Oscar Wilde*, 178, 178n. Oscar Wilde, "The Decay of Lying," in *The Complete Works of Oscar Wilde* (London: HarperCollins, 2003), 1074. *Philadelphia Press*, June 13, 1882. Quoted in Roy Morris, Jr., *Ambrose Bierce: Alone in Bad Company* (New York: Crown, 1996), 4.

37. Ellmann, *Oscar Wilde,* 178–179. Henry James, *The Tragic Muse* (London: Macmillan, 1921), 23.

38. Lewis and Smith, *Oscar Wilde,* 89–90.

4. What Would Thoreau Have Said to My Hat-Box!

1. "An Interview with the Poet," *Albany Argus,* January 28, 1882, 8.

2. Oscar Wilde, *The Complete Letters of Oscar Wilde,* ed. Merlin Holland and Rupert Hart-Davis (New York: Henry Holt, 2000), 29. Hereafter cited as *Letters.*

3. Richard Ellmann, *Oscar Wilde* (New York: Alfred A. Knopf, 1988), 103–104. *Letters,* 107.

4. Barbara Belford, *Oscar Wilde: A Certain Genius* (New York: Random House, 2000), 77–79. Ellmann, *Oscar Wilde,* 234.

5. *Boston Evening Transcript,* January 28, 1882.

6. "Oscar Wilde," *Boston Herald,* January 29, 1882, 7.

7. Ibid.

8. Ibid.

9. William Dean Howells, *My Mark Twain: Reminiscences and Criticisms* (New York: Harper and Brothers, 1910), 63. William Dean Howells, "Criticism and Fiction," in *Anthology of American Fiction,* vol. 2 (New York: Macmillan, 1980), 596, 599.

10. *New York Daily Graphic,* January 19, 1882. "With Mr. Oscar Wilde," *Cincinnati Gazette,* February 21, 1882, 10.

11. "The Aesthetic Apostle," *Boston Globe,* January 29, 1882, 5.

12. "They Will Show Him," *Chicago Inter-Ocean,* February 10, 1882, 2.

13. Ibid.

14. "With Mr. Oscar Wilde," *Cincinnati Gazette,* February 21, 1882, 10. *Boston Evening Traveller,* January 30, 1882.

15. Chris Healy, *Confessions of a Journalist* (London: Chatto and Windus, 1904), 130. Ellmann, *Oscar Wilde,* 181.

16. Lloyd Lewis and Henry Justin Smith, *Oscar Wilde Discovers America* (New York: Harcourt, Brace, 1936), 122–126.

17. Ibid., 127. Ellmann, *Oscar Wilde,* 182–183.

18. *Boston Evening Transcript,* February 2, 1882. *New York Sun,* February 4, 1882.

19. For Higginson, see Christopher Benfey, *A Summer of Hummingbirds:*

Love, Art, and Scandal in the Intersecting Worlds of Emily Dickinson, Mark Twain, Harriet Beecher Stowe, and Martin Johnson Heade (New York: Penguin, 2008), 13–37.

20. Thomas Wentworth Higginson, "Unmanly Manhood," *Woman's Journal* 13, February 4, 1882. Oscar Wilde, "Charmides," in *The Complete Works of Oscar Wilde* (London: HarperCollins, 2003), 797–813. Hereafter cited as *Works*.

21. Higginson, "Unmanly Manhood."

22. *Boston Evening Transcript*, February 16, 1882.

23. *Letters*, 142–143, 175, 175n.

24. Lewis and Smith, *Oscar Wilde*, 119–131.

25. *Letters*, 138, 141. *New York World*, May 4, 1882.

26. *Utica Weekly Herald*, February 6, 1882. *Alta California*, March 30, 1867.

27. Lewis and Smith, *Oscar Wilde*, 155. "A Man of Culture Rare," *Rochester Democrat and Chronicle*, February 8, 1882, 4.

28. Lewis and Smith, *Oscar Wilde*, 156.

29. Ibid., 156–158. *Rochester Union and Advertiser*, February 8, 1882.

30. Kathi Morrison-Taylor, "The Poet's Cabin: Joaquin Miller in Washington," *Beltway Poetry Quarterly* 9, no. 3 (Summer 2008). Available at washingtonart.com/beltway/jmiller.html. Carey McWilliams, *Ambrose Bierce: A Biography* (New York: A. and C. Boni, 1929), 100.

31. *Letters*, 142n.

32. Ibid., 141–143.

33. Lewis and Smith, *Oscar Wilde*, 160–161. *Buffalo Courier*, February 8, 1882.

34. Lewis and Smith, *Oscar Wilde*, 161–162. *Buffalo Courier*, February 8, 1882.

35. Oscar Wilde, "Personal Impressions of America," in *Works*, 939.

36. Lewis and Smith, *Oscar Wilde*, 163. "Wilde Sees the Falls," *Buffalo Express*, February 9, 1882.

37. Lewis and Smith, *Oscar Wilde*, 164. "A Man of Culture Rare," *Rochester Democrat and Chronicle*, February 8, 1882, 4.

5. No Well-Behaved River Ought to Act This Way

1. *Chicago Daily News*, February 10, 1882.

2. Page Smith, *The Rise of Industrial America: A People's History of the Post-Reconstruction Era* (New York: Penguin, 1984), 371.

3. Ibid., 370.

4. Lloyd Lewis and Henry Justin Smith, *Oscar Wilde Discovers America* (New York: Harcourt, Brace, 1936), 166.

5. "The Apostle of Art," *Chicago Inter-Ocean,* February 11, 1882, 4.

6. Lewis and Smith, *Oscar Wilde,* 172. "A Man of Culture Rare," *Rochester Democrat and Chronicle,* February 8, 1882, 4.

7. Lewis and Smith, *Oscar Wilde,* 157, 172.

8. Ibid., 177.

9. Ibid., 178.

10. Ibid.

11. Ibid.

12. Ibid., 179. *Chicago Daily News,* February 14, 1882.

13. Oscar Wilde, *The Complete Letters of Oscar Wilde,* ed. Merlin Holland and Rupert Hart-Davis (New York: Henry Holt, 2000), 176, 177n. Hereafter cited as *Letters.* Quoted in Rupert Croft-Crooke, *The Unrecorded Life of Oscar Wilde* (New York: David McKay, 1972), 90. *New York Times,* July 7, 1903.

14. *Chicago Daily News,* February 14, 1882.

15. *Fort Wayne Gazette,* February 15, 1882.

16. Ibid.

17. Ibid.; *Fort Wayne Daily Sentinel,* February 16, 1882.

18. *Fort Wayne News,* February 17, 1882.

19. "Wilde," *Cleveland Leader,* February 20, 1882, 6.

20. "Truly Aesthetic," *Chicago Inter-Ocean,* February 13, 1882, 2. "A Man of Culture Rare," *Rochester Democrat and Chronicle,* February 8, 1882, 4.

21. "With Mr. Oscar Wilde," *Cincinnati Gazette,* February 21, 1882, 10.

22. Ibid.

23. Ibid.

24. "Oscar Wilde," *Cincinnati Enquirer,* February 21, 1882, 4.

25. *Louisville Courier-Journal,* February 22, 1882.

26. *Letters,* 157–158. See also Denise Gigante, *The Keats Brothers: The Life of John and George* (Cambridge, MA: Harvard University Press, 2011), 410–413.

27. Ambrose Bierce, "A Little of Chickamauga," in *The Collected Works of Ambrose Bierce,* 12 vols. (New York: Neale Publishing Company, 1909–1912), 1:274–275.

28. Lewis and Smith, *Oscar Wilde,* 195–196.

29. *Indianapolis News,* February 23, 1882. *Indianapolis Saturday Review,* February 23, 1882.

30. Lewis and Smith, *Oscar Wilde,* 197–198.

31. Ibid.; *Indianapolis Saturday Review,* February 23, 1882.

32. Lewis and Smith, *Oscar Wilde,* 191.

33. Ibid., 200.

34. Ibid., 201.

35. Ibid., 202.

36. "Speranza's Gifted Son," *St. Louis Globe-Democrat,* February 26, 1882, 3.

37. Ibid.

38. "Oscar As He Is," *St. Louis Republican,* February 26, 1882, 13.

39. Lewis and Smith, *Oscar Wilde,* 208–211.

6. A Very Italy, Without Its Art

1. Lloyd Lewis and Henry Justin Smith, *Oscar Wilde Discovers America* (New York: Harcourt, Brace, 1936), 196, 211.

2. Ibid., 211–215. Oscar Wilde, *The Complete Letters of Oscar Wilde,* ed. Merlin Holland and Rupert Hart-Davis (New York: Henry Holt, 2000), 146. Hereafter cited as *Letters.*

3. "Oscar Wilde," *Chicago Tribune,* March 1, 1882, 7. Lewis and Smith, *Oscar Wilde,* 213–214.

4. "David and Oscar," *Chicago Tribune,* March 5, 1882, 5.

5. Oscar Wilde, "The House Beautiful," in *The Complete Works of Oscar Wilde* (London: HarperCollins, 2003), 913–925.

6. Ibid.

7. *Letters,* 139, 142. Richard Ellmann, *Oscar Wilde* (New York: Alfred A. Knopf, 1988), 177n.

8. *New York Times,* January 20, 1882.

9. *St. Paul and Minneapolis Pioneer Press,* January 3, March 16, 1882. *Minneapolis Journal,* March 16, 1882. *Minneapolis Tribune,* March 14, 1882.

10. *St. Paul Globe,* March 17, 1882. *St. Paul and Minneapolis Pioneer Press,* March 17, 1882; Lewis and Smith, *Oscar Wilde,* 224–226. *Dodge Center Index,* December 30, 1882. See also John T. Flanagan, "Oscar Wilde's Twin City Appearances," *Minnesota History* 17 (March 1936), 38–48.

11. *Letters,* 153–154.

12. *Sioux City Journal,* March 21, 1882.

13. *Omaha Weekly Herald,* March 24, 1882. *Omaha Daily Republican,* March 25, 1882. See also Carl Uhlarik, "Oscar Wilde in Omaha," *Prairie Schooner* 14 (Spring 1940), 45–53.

14. "Oscar Wilde in Omaha," *Omaha Weekly Herald,* March 24, 1882. *Sacramento Bee,* March 26, 1882.

15. *Letters,* 158. Oscar Wilde, "The American Man," in *The Artist as Critic: Critical Writings of Oscar Wilde,* ed. Richard Ellmann (New York: Random House, 1968), 62.

16. "Oscar Arrives," *Sacramento Record-Union,* March 27, 1882, 3.

17. "Oscar Wilde: An Interview with the Apostle of Aestheticism," *San Francisco Examiner,* March 27, 1882, 2.

18. Ibid. "Oscar Wilde's Views," *San Francisco Morning Call,* March 27, 1882, 4.

19. Ibid. "Lo! The Aesthete," *San Francisco Chronicle,* March 27, 1882, 3.

20. Roy Morris, Jr., *Ambrose Bierce: Alone in Bad Company* (New York: Crown, 1996), 113.

21. *San Francisco Wasp,* March 31, 1882.

22. Ambrose Bierce, "On a Mountain," in *The Collected Works of Ambrose Bierce,* 12 vols. (New York: Neale Publishing Company, 1909–1912), 1:233. *San Francisco Wasp,* November 3, 1883.

23. *San Francisco Examiner,* March 28, 1882.

24. Ibid., March 30, 1882. *San Francisco Daily Chronicle,* March 30, 1882.

25. Lewis and Smith, *Oscar Wilde,* 248–249.

26. *San Francisco News Letter,* October 8, 1870.

27. Oscar Lewis, *This Was San Francisco* (New York: David McKay, 1962), 175–176.

28. *San Francisco Examiner,* April 11, 1882. Lewis and Smith, *Oscar Wilde,* 255–256. See also Lois Foster Rodecape, "Gilding the Sunflower: A Study of Oscar Wilde's Visit to San Francisco," *California Historical Society* 19 (June 1940), 97–112.

29. Ellmann, *Oscar Wilde,* 203.

30. *Sacramento Record-Union,* April 1, 1882.

31. Lewis and Smith, *Oscar Wilde,* 252. *Letters,* 160.

32. *San Francisco Daily Call,* April 6, 1882. Ellmann, *Oscar Wilde,* 38. Quoted in Barbara Belford, *Oscar Wilde: A Certain Genius* (New York: Random House, 2000), 100.

33. Rodecape, "Gilding the Sunflower," 98. "Oscar Wilde," *Salt Lake Herald*, April 12, 1882.

7. Don't Shoot the Pianist; He's Doing His Best

1. Richard F. Burton, *The City of the Saints and Across the Rocky Mountains to California* (New York: Knopf, 1963), 221. Lloyd Lewis and Henry Justin Smith, *Oscar Wilde Discovers America* (New York: Harcourt, Brace, 1936), 271–273.

2. *Salt Lake Herald*, April 10, 1882. *Salt Lake Tribune*, April 9, 1882. Lewis and Smith, *Oscar Wilde*, 275.

3. "Oscar Wilde," *Salt Lake Herald*, April 12, 1882.

4. "Art and Aesthetics," *Denver Tribune*, April 13, 1882, 8. Oscar Wilde, "Personal Impressions of America," in *The Complete Works of Oscar Wilde* (London: HarperCollins, 2003), 140. Hereafter cited as *Works*.

5. Wilde, "Personal Impressions of America," in *Works*, 140.

6. Lewis and Smith, *Oscar Wilde*, 279–280. *Salt Lake Herald*, April 12, 1882. *Salt Lake Republican*, April 12, 1882.

7. *Denver Tribune*, April 13, 1882. Mark Twain, *Roughing It* (Berkeley: University of California Press, 1993), 97–98.

8. "Oscar Wilde," *Rocky Mountain News*, April 13, 1882, 8.

9. Martin Fido, *Oscar Wilde* (New York: Viking, 1973), 56. Lewis and Smith, *Oscar Wilde*, 286.

10. Lewis and Smith, *Oscar Wilde*, 289–290. Richard Ellmann, *Oscar Wilde* (New York: Alfred A. Knopf, 1988), 191.

11. *Denver Times*, April 13, 1882. *Denver Tribune*, April 13, 1882.

12. "Art and Aesthetics," *Denver Tribune*, April 13, 1882, 8. Lewis and Smith, *Oscar Wilde*, 306.

13. Wilde, "Personal Impressions of America," in *Works*, 940.

14. Twain, *Roughing It*, 195.

15. Lewis and Smith, *Oscar Wilde*, 312. Oscar Wilde, *The Complete Letters of Oscar Wilde*, ed. Merlin Holland and Rupert Hart-Davis (New York: Henry Holt, 2000), 161. Hereafter cited as *Letters*. Wilde, "Personal Impressions of America," in *Works*, 940.

16. *Letters*, 161–162.

17. Lewis and Smith, *Oscar Wilde*, 315. Wilde, "Personal Impressions of America," in *Works*, 940.

18. Lewis and Smith, *Oscar Wilde,* 316–317.

19. Wilde, "Personal Impressions of America," in *Works,* 940. *Letters,* 162.

20. *Colorado Springs Daily Gazette,* April 15, 1882. *Denver Tribune,* April 16, 1882. *Denver News,* April 19, 1882.

21. *Kansas City Star,* April 17, 1882.

22. *Kansas City Times,* April 17, 1882. *Letters,* 165.

23. *Kansas City Times,* April 18, 1882. *Kansas City Journal,* April 18, 1882.

24. *Saint Joseph Evening News,* April 18, 1882. *Letters,* 164.

25. *Topeka Capital,* April 20, 1882.

26. *Lawrence Daily Journal,* April 22, 1882. *Atchinson Champion,* April 23, 1882.

27. "Aesthetic: An Interesting Interview with Oscar Wilde," *Dayton Daily Democrat,* May 3, 1882, 4. Lowry Charles Wimberly, "Oscar Wilde Meets Woodberry," *Prairie Schooner* 21 (Spring 1947), 108–116.

28. *Letters,* 166. Ellmann, *Oscar Wilde,* 166.

29. *New York World,* May 6, 1882. *Denver Tribune,* April 13, 1882. Ellmann, *Oscar Wilde,* 204–205.

30. Bernard West, "Oscar Wilde: A Reminiscence," *Theatre,* June 1918.

8. You Should Have Seen It Before the War

1. "Aesthetic: An Interesting Interview with Oscar Wilde," *Dayton Daily Democrat,* May 3, 1882, 4.

2. Ibid.

3. Ibid.

4. Charlotte Reeve Conover, "Oscar Wilde in Dayton," *Dayton Daily News,* June 13, 1937. Lloyd Lewis and Henry Justin Smith, *Oscar Wilde Discovers America* (New York: Harcourt, Brace, 1936), 341–342.

5. *Ohio State Journal,* May 4, 1882. *Columbus Daily Times,* May 4, 1882.

6. Richard Ellmann, *Oscar Wilde* (New York: Alfred A. Knopf, 1988), 171.

7. Lewis and Smith, *Oscar Wilde,* 344; Jerome Loving, *Walt Whitman: The Song of Himself* (Berkeley: University of California Press, 1999), 415–417. *Springfield Republican,* May 26, 1882.

8. Lewis and Smith, *Oscar Wilde,* 78.

9. *Philadelphia Press,* May 9, 1882.

10. Oscar Wilde, *The Complete Letters of Oscar Wilde,* ed. Merlin Holland

and Rupert Hart-Davis (New York: Henry Holt, 2000), 169. Hereafter cited as *Letters*. Lewis and Smith, *Oscar Wilde*, 344–347.

11. *Letters*, 172, 168.

12. Lewis and Smith, *Oscar Wilde*, 348. Kevin O'Brien, *Oscar Wilde in Canada: An Apostle for the Arts* (Toronto: Personal Library, 1982), 57. "Oscar Wilde in Montreal," *Montreal Daily Witness*, May 15, 1882, 8. "Oscar Wilde: The Arch-Aesthete on Aestheticism," *Montreal Daily Star*, May 15, 1882, 3.

13. *Montreal Star*, May 16, 1882, 2. *Montreal Daily Witness*, May 15, 1882. Lewis and Smith, *Oscar Wilde*, 357.

14. O'Brien, *Oscar Wilde*, 62. *Montreal Daily Star*, May 17, 1882.

15. *Ottawa Daily Citizen*, May 17, 1882. O'Brien, *Oscar Wilde*, 80.

16. O'Brien, *Oscar Wilde*, 73–77.

17. Ibid., 78–79, 83–86. *Letters*, 171–172. *St. James's Gazette*, September 24, 1891.

18. *Toronto Daily Mail*, May 25, 1882. O'Brien, *Oscar Wilde*, 88–89.

19. O'Brien, *Oscar Wilde*, 92. "Oscar Wilde Interviewed," *Kingston Daily News*, May 23, 1882, 3.

20. O'Brien, *Oscar Wilde*, 93–94.

21. "Oscar Wilde," *Toronto Globe*, May 25, 1882, 3.

22. Ibid.

23. Lewis and Smith, *Oscar Wilde*, 353. O'Brien, *Oscar Wilde*, 102–103.

24. W. F. Morse, "American Lectures," in *The Works of Oscar Wilde*, vol. 15 (New York: Brainard, 1909), 84.

25. *Letters*, 163.

26. *New York Times*, July 23, 1883.

27. Lewis and Smith, *Oscar Wilde*, 355, 358.

28. *News Orleans Daily Picayune*, June 16, 1882.

29. *Galveston Daily News*, June 20, 1882.

30. *San Antonio Evening Post*, June 22, 1882.

31. Dorothy McLeod MacInerney, William Warren Rogers, and Robert David Ward, "Oscar Wilde Lectures in Texas, 1882," *Southwestern Historical Society* 106 (July 2002–April 2003), 551–572. *San Antonio Evening Post*, June 27, 1882. *Houston Daily Post*, June 23, 1882.

32. "Oscar Wilde Talks of Texas," *New Orleans Picayune*, June 25, 1882, 11.

33. Ibid.

34. "Oscar Wilde: Arrival of the Great Aesthete," *Atlanta Constitution*, July 5, 1882, 8. Hudson Strode, *Jefferson Davis: Tragic Hero: The Last Twenty-*

Five Years 1864–1889 (New York: Harcourt, Brace, 1964), 459–461. Mary Louise Ellis, "Improbable Visitor: Oscar Wilde in Alabama, 1882," *Alabama Review* (October 1986), 250–251.

35. Ellis, "Improbable Visitor," 252–253. "Oscar Dear, Oscar Dear!" *Charleston News and Courier,* July 8, 1882, 4.

36. Ellis, "Improbable Visitor," 258. *Montgomery Advertiser,* June 30, 1882. Lewis and Smith, *Oscar Wilde,* 369.

37. Lewis and Smith, *Oscar Wilde,* 396. "Loveliness and Politeness," *New York Sun,* August 20, 1882, 5.

38. *Letters,* 174.

39. Kenneth D. Ackerman, *Dark Horse: The Surprise Election and Political Murder of President James A. Garfield* (New York: Carroll and Graf, 2003), 444–445.

40. *Macon Telegraph,* July 2, 1882.

41. *Atlanta Constitution,* June 17 and July 6, 1882.

42. "Oscar Dear, Oscar Dear!" *Charleston News and Courier,* July 8, 1882, 4.

43. *Richmond State,* July 13, 1882. Lewis and Smith, *Oscar Wilde,* 376.

9. The Oscar of the First Period Is Dead

1. Oscar Wilde, *The Complete Letters of Oscar Wilde,* ed. Merlin Holland and Rupert Hart-Davis (New York: Henry Holt, 2000), 175. Hereafter cited as *Letters.*

2. *Letters,* 177. *New York Sun,* July 16, 1882.

3. Richard Ellmann, *Oscar Wilde* (New York: Alfred A. Knopf, 1988), 203. Lloyd Lewis and Henry Justin Smith, *Oscar Wilde Discovers America* (New York: Harcourt, Brace, 1936), 382–383.

4. *New Orleans Daily Picayune,* July 25, 1882. Ellmann, *Oscar Wilde,* 192.

5. *New York Tribune,* July 16, 1882. *Frank Leslie's Magazine,* August 12, 1882.

6. Lewis and Smith, *Oscar Wilde,* 385. *New York Daily Saratogian,* August 5, 1882.

7. *New York Daily Saratogian,* August 5, 1882.

8. W. F. Morse, "American Lectures," in *The Works of Oscar Wilde,* vol. 15 (New York: Brainard, 1909), 93. Mary Anderson, *A Few More Memories* (London: Hutchinson, 1936), 20. *Letters,* 179.

9. *Letters,* 184. Ellmann, *Oscar Wilde,* 209. *Letters,* 181, 186, 203n.

10. Rose Snider, "Oscar Wilde's Progress Down East," *New England Quarterly* 13, no. 1 (March 1940), 7–23. *Bangor Daily Commercial,* October 6, 1882.

11. Kevin O'Brien, *Oscar Wilde in Canada: An Apostle for the Arts* (Toronto: Personal Library, 1982), 117–118.

12. Ibid., 121–122. "Arrival of the Renowned Aesthete," *Saint John Evening News,* October 5, 1882, 2.

13. *Saint John Daily Telegraph,* October 6, 1882.

14. O'Brien, *Oscar Wilde,* 123–125. "Oscar Wilde and the Newspapers," *Saint John Daily Sun,* October 18, 1882, 1.

15. O'Brien, *Oscar Wilde,* 127. "The Apostle of Beauty in Nova Scotia," *Halifax Morning Herald,* October 10, 1882, 2.

16. O'Brien, *Oscar Wilde,* 129–130. *Letters,* 183.

17. "Oscar Wilde's Lecture Last Night," *Halifax Morning Chronicle,* October 10, 1882, 3. *Halifax Presbyterian Witness,* September 30, 1882, 308. O'Brien, *Oscar Wilde,* 131–132. *Dalhousie Gazette,* November 11, 1882, 10.

18. O'Brien, *Oscar Wilde,* 136. "Oscar Wilde at the Market Hall," *Charlottetown Daily Examiner,* October 12, 1882, 1.

19. O'Brien, *Oscar Wilde,* 137–139. "Oscar Wilde Explains," *Moncton Daily Transcript,* October 18, 1882, 2.

20. Quoted in Ellmann, *Oscar Wilde,* 206. "The Apostle of Beauty in Nova Scotia," *Halifax Morning Herald,* October 10, 1882.

21. *New York Times,* October 24, 1882. Lewis and Smith, *Oscar Wilde,* 416.

22. *New York Tribune,* October, 24, 1882. *New York Times,* October 24, 1882.

23. *Chicago Daily News,* October 31 and November 23, 1882. *Letters,* 187–188.

24. Lewis and Smith, *Oscar Wilde,* 418–419, 423.

25. Ibid., 426. Oscar Wilde, "Mrs. Langtry as Hester Grazebrook," in *The Complete Works of Oscar Wilde* (London: HarperCollins, 2003), 942–944. Hereafter cited as *Works.*

26. *New York Dramatic Mirror,* November 11, 1882. *New York Times,* November 7, 1882. Franklin Walker, *Ambrose Bierce: The Wickedest Man in San Francisco* (San Francisco: Colt Press, 1941), 38.

27. "Tommaso Salvini," in George Iles, ed., *19th Century Actor Autobiographies.* Available at www.authorama.com/19th-century-actor-autobiographies-10.html.

28. *New York Tribune,* October 29 and November 5, 1882.

29. *Harper's New Monthly Magazine* 71 (November 18, 1882), 844. *Washington Post,* September 20, 1882, 2.

30. *New York Tribune,* December 29, 1882. *New York Times,* December 29, 1882.

31. *Letters,* 192. Nathan Miller, *Theodore Roosevelt: A Life* (New York: William Morrow, 1992), 230.

32. Edgar Saltus, *Oscar Wilde: An Idler's Impressions* (Chicago: Brothers of the Book, 1917), 15. *New York Tribune,* November 27, 1882, 3.

33. *New York Tribune,* December 28, 1882.

34. *Punch,* March 31, 1883.

35. Ellmann, *Oscar Wilde,* 205. *New York Times,* July 23, 1883.

36. Morse, "American Lectures," 94. Wilde, "The Critic as Artist," in *Works,* 1142.

37. Wilde, "Personal Impressions of America," in *Works,* 939, 941.

38. *New York Times,* August 21, 1882. Barbara Belford, *Oscar Wilde: A Certain Genius* (New York: Random House, 2000), 120.

39. Oscar Wilde, *The Picture of Dorian Gray,* in *Works,* 41.

40. *Cleveland Leader,* February 20, 1882, 6.

Acknowledgments

First and foremost, I would like to thank my long-time agent, Georges Borchardt, for his unflagging efforts to place this book. Without Georges's kind commitment of time and thought, *Declaring His Genius* would never have seen the light of day. I would also like to thank John Kulka, my editor at Harvard University Press, for giving me the benefit of his calm and cogent advice, and senior editor Maria Ascher for adding her much-appreciated insights. Thanks also to Heather Hughes of Harvard for her efficiency, promptness, and organizational skills.

My deepest thanks, as always, go to my wife, Leslie, and our (adult) children, Phil and Lucy, each of whom read the book in manuscript form and provided enthusiasm, advice, and support. In the course of doing so, they were exposed to more Wildean quips than anyone—even a close relative—might reasonably be expected to endure, although I remain convinced that a daily dose of Oscar Wilde does no one any harm.

As I stated in the introduction, I'm particularly grateful to Matthew Hofer and Gary Scharnhorst for collecting Oscar Wilde's newspaper interviews in an easily accessible and skillfully annotated form. Thanks, as well, to the Oscar Wilde Society of America and the Oscholars for providing much useful information on our mutual friend. I would be remiss not to thank the eminent Wilde scholar Kevin O'Brien for his groundbreaking work on Wilde's visit to Canada, which no less an expert than Wilde's tour manager, W. F. Morse, considered the high point of his client's North American trip. Perhaps it was the common language Oscar and the Canadians shared. I wouldn't know—I'm an American myself.

Index